SECOND EDIT

CONFIDENCE
IN
WRITING

A BASIC TEXT

SECOND EDITION

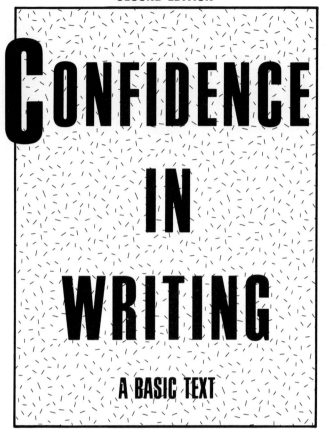

CONFIDENCE IN WRITING

A BASIC TEXT

ED REYNOLDS
Spokane Falls Community College

MARCIA MIXDORF
Everett Community College

Harcourt Brace College Publishers
Fort Worth   Philadelphia   San Diego
New York   Orlando   Austin   San Antonio
Toronto   Montreal   London   Sydney   Tokyo

Requests for permission to make copies of any part of the work should be mailed to: Permissions Department, Harcourt Brace Jovanovich, Inc., 8th Floor, Orlando, Florida 32887.

ISBN: 0-15-512987-2
Library of Congress Catalog Card Number: 90-84208

Printed in the United States of America

For Jennifer, Jeff, and Stacey.
And for Matt, wherever you are.

TO THE INSTRUCTOR

Basic writing students form one of the most diverse groups on a school campus, yet they share two characteristics: they have little writing experience, and they have even less confidence in their writing abilities. In *Confidence in Writing: A Basic Text*, Second Edition, we have attempted to give you a book that addresses both of these characteristics. We address the first by making writing the students' primary activity, and we address the second by teaching a writing process that has discrete steps, each carefully modeled. From the beginning of the first chapter, students put their ideas, observations, and experiences on paper, and because they are shown exactly how to do this, their first writing activity can bring them nothing but success. Subsequent steps and writing activities are similarly described and modeled, so the students' chances for success are always high. This success builds confidence.

This book continually emphasizes writing and offers an approach that has grown out of many years of success in a writing lab in which students work at their own pace and freely consult an instructor. The book's format and design, however, make it equally useful in either a writing lab or a conventional classroom setting.

Although this edition of *Confidence in Writing: A Basic Text* contains many changes, much remains unchanged from the first edition. Most important, we have not changed its basic philosophy that students can gain both confidence and skill by mastering the writing process. To better facilitate that approach we have added professional examples to help students see and appreciate how "real" writers have handled similar tasks. We have worked to clarify sections of the book that students have found confusing. And we have restructured (and retitled) the appendix in order to make it more helpful and more clearly a handbook that students can use to answer questions and solve problems with grammar, punctuation, and sentence structure.

We still rely heavily on the willingness of instructors and students to work together. That, after all, is the single most important factor in learning, regardless of the textbook used.

We gratefully acknowledge the following reviewers for their comments on this book: C. Harry Bruder, University of Southwestern Louisiana; Margi Glazier, Merced College; Christopher Gould, University of North Carolina; Judy Hathcock, Amarillo College; and Marilyn L. Walker, Illinois Central College. We also thank former students Annette L. Clothier, Linda R. Corbett, Daniel Porras, Polly Snow, Victor O. Adams, David A. Knight, Donna Quale, Nickolaos Roussos, and Dannette Walters for permission to reprint their work.

We have enjoyed creating this book. Our hope is that you and your students will enjoy using it.

ED REYNOLDS
MARCIA MIXDORF

TO THE STUDENT

Writing is a skill that, like any other skill, can be learned. You don't need talent, and you don't need to have been "good in English" in school. But you do need to be willing to follow instructions and to work hard.

This book will take you, step by step, through the process of writing a paragraph, and it will give you plenty of opportunity to practice your skills as you learn them. We begin with writing the paragraph because it's short and therefore easy to work with and talk about. Also, writing paragraphs allows you to practice nearly all the skills necessary for any writing assignment. Other sections of this book give you practice in writing essays, responses to college writing assignments, and summaries.

Most of this book talks about school writing assignments, but you will find many other uses for your developing writing skills. Most jobs that graduates take require writing skills, and, in fact, most job applications must be written. Letters to the editor about issues that concern you, letters to friends about important events, and letters to companies or government officials are all examples of the many demands on your writing skills. But you will also write just for yourself. You may keep a journal or diary; most chapters open with excerpts from journals that our students have kept, so you can see some of the kinds of journal entries you might make. You might also write poems or other pieces to express your feelings, or just jot down ideas so you can remember them. As your writing skills improve, you will find that your daily writing becomes not only easier but also more enjoyable.

ED REYNOLDS
MARCIA MIXDORF

CONTENTS

12 READINGS FOR MORE SUMMARY PRACTICE   211

HANDBOOK: THE MECHANICS OF WRITING   239

I PARTS OF THE SENTENCE   240

SECOND EDITION

CONFIDENCE
IN
WRITING

A BASIC TEXT

PREVIEW FOR CHAPTER 1

Each chapter preview will show you excerpts from student papers or journals that might help you think about the writing assignment for that chapter. Here are some excerpts about people.

> She wore massive amounts of jewelry, mostly crosses and small silver chains. She had a mohawk for a while, with a peace sign shaved onto the right side of her head.

> Winto's saxophone playing makes cloudy days bright and sunny days explode with even more sunshine. His music makes the neighborhood spring to life.

> She has an uncanny ability to see through people. I was telling her we needed new tires before we went on any long trips. She said, "Why do you hate visiting my parents?"

> He was such a bully. When I asked him politely to move, he said, "This seat doesn't have your name on it," and he pushed me down in the aisle.

> Her name was Suzanne. She was a friend of a friend of mine. I didn't think she even knew my name. She walked up to me in the cafeteria one day and said, "Do you like what I'm wearing, or not?"

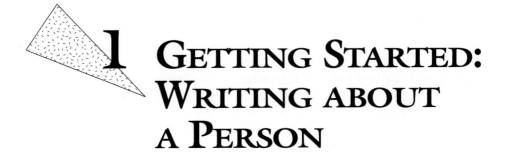

1 GETTING STARTED: WRITING ABOUT A PERSON

SKILLS INTRODUCED

Using a five-step writing process:

1. Brainstorm
2. Write the topic sentence
3. Outline
4. Draft
5. Revise

Understanding how writing is judged

Writing is a way of using language, and you have been using language for most of your life. In fact, you have been writing for much of your life, but you are certainly more skilled as a speaker than you are as a writer, for you have used spoken language much more than you have used written language. A first step in developing your writing skills is to recognize some important differences between speaking and writing.

When you speak, you almost always have a listening audience, someone who can, with a look or a question, ask you to explain when you haven't communicated clearly. In writing, you do not have that advantage. On the other hand, writing offers you a better chance to explore and clarify your ideas before you share them with others, and sharing ideas with others is the most important use of language, whether written or spoken.

Writing can help us in many ways. It helps us in our own personal development, and it helps us to connect with other people. For example, writing can help us to explore and better understand our own experiences and ideas and thus to understand ourselves better. Sometimes writing can lead us to new insights and help us discover things we have to say. It can help us to learn, for as we write about what we know or what we are studying, we begin to see connections that we might not otherwise see. Writing allows us to communicate with and to influence other people—to change their minds, to make them laugh or cry, or to teach them how to do something.

Our aim in this book is to help you develop your skills in communicating through writing. You have much to write about—you are a real person with real ideas, concerns, and experiences. There has never been and will never be anyone exactly like you. As a result, when you study and think about a subject, you may come to an understanding that is somewhat different from anyone else's. Even what you see as common and ordinary may be new to someone else, and your writing may help others to see the world a little bit differently and to understand it a little bit better.

It is important that you write about what you know—your friends and family, your environment, your activities, and your questions about or understanding of new things you see and learn. Writing about what you know will help you to write honestly and in your own *voice*. Just as you have an individual *style* of speaking, you will develop your own style and voice in writing.

As we say in the introduction to this book, writing is a skill. The only way you can learn any skill is by doing it, so let's start writing. Because it is important that you write about familiar subjects, your first writing exercise will be a paragraph about someone you know. A **paragraph** (as we will use the term) is a unit of writing that states and explains a single idea, and we'll take you step by step through the process of paragraph writing. Since writers almost never begin with a complete understanding of what they want to say, we'll start by **brainstorming** to discover what we might say about our subject.

STEP 1:
Brainstorm to Discover What You Know

Think of a person you know or remember well. What does the person look like? What do you do together? What do you like about this person? What don't you like? How does he dress? Where does she live? What is special about this person? There are hundreds of questions you can ask and answer about people you know, and that questioning is the first step in the writing process. We call it brainstorming, but it goes by other names as well: pre-writing, exploring, discovering, and so forth. As you think of details about your subject, write them down in whatever words or phrases come to your mind.

Here is a list of details that Linda, one of our students, made as she thought about her grandmother.

1. 92 years old
2. 4 feet 9 inches tall
3. sparkling blue eyes
4. wrinkled face
5. a little stooped
6. big ears
7. uses a walker
8. thin
9. likes things her way
10. starts arguments
11. is almost deaf
12. wears silk nightgowns as slips
13. wears bobby socks under her nylons
14. safety pins all around her hats
15. always counting her money
16. independent
17. ornery
18. loves orange and purple
19. watches word game shows on tv
20. drinks herb teas
21. never takes medicine
22. putters in her rose garden
23. sometimes absent minded
24. does crossword puzzles "to stay sharp"
25. doesn't put up with nonsense from her grandkids
26. still swats my dad if he does something she doesn't like
27. gets mad if she loses an argument
28. used to embarrass me
29. 12 grandchildren
30. thinks of self as "big, strong woman"
31. ready for any emergency
32. white hair in a bun
33. pins roses on her dresses

Writing Activity 1.1

- Think carefully about the person you've chosen to write about.
- Quickly list as many ideas about that person as you can. Don't worry about spelling, punctuation, or exact wording.
- List at least twenty or thirty things. Include anything that comes to mind about this person, ignoring whether or how one idea relates to another. Your purpose is to list anything and everything that comes to mind about your subject.

STEP 2:
Write the Topic Sentence

As we said earlier, the paragraphs you will study will state and explain a single idea. The **topic sentence** will be the statement of that idea. We also refer to the topic sentence as the **controlling idea** because it controls what goes into the paragraph and what stays out. It focuses the attention of both the writer and the reader on a single aspect of the subject. It is a one-sentence summary of what the paragraph will say. It tells the readers in general what the paragraph will be about, and it leads them to predict what specific details they might find in the paragraph. In other words, the topic sentence appeals to the readers' curiosity and gets them actively involved in the exchange of ideas.

The topic sentence names the subject of the paragraph and says something about that subject. It must be a complete sentence. You have already written a brainstorming list on a specific subject. Now look back through your list to see which details have something in common that will focus your readers' attention on something particular about your subject. To illustrate this process, we'll show you the steps that Linda took as she wrote her topic sentence.

The subject of Linda's paragraph will, of course, be the grandmother, but what will the paragraph say about her? It needs to focus the readers' attention on something specific about the grandmother, and the brainstorming list offers many choices.

As Linda looked back through her list, she saw several items that suggested her grandmother's age:

shrunken to 4 feet 9 inches tall

uses a walker

white hair in a bun

sparkling blue eyes

thin

wrinkled face

shoulders a little stooped

sometimes absent minded

She thought she might write a paragraph about how her grandmother looks to other people, so she wrote this topic sentence that focuses on her grandmother's age:

Grammy looks every one of her 92 years old.

This topic sentence leads the readers to want to know more about how Grammy's looks show her age. They have seen many old people, but they have not seen Grammy, and they expect to see just what it is that makes her look old.

The list also contains many other details, some of which might be even more interesting to both reader and writer, so Linda looked back at it for another set of related items. She found the following items that say something about how Grammy dresses:

wears silk nightgowns as slips

wears bobby socks under her nylons

safety pins all around her hats

loves orange and purple

pins roses on her dresses

Because she had never known anyone else who dressed so unusually, Linda chose to focus on the word "eccentric." Her topic sentence for this group of details is

Grammy is the most eccentric dresser I know.

That sentence leads the reader to expect to see details about how Grammy dresses and to expect those details to be quite unusual.

Other details on the list dealt with Grammy's personality, so Linda grouped them together to see what topic sentence they might suggest:

ornery

doesn't put up with nonsense from her grandkids

still swats my dad if he does something she doesn't like

thinks of self as big, strong woman

starts arguments

likes things her way

independent

gets mad if she loses an argument

These similar items suggested a focus for another topic sentence:

Grammy is a feisty woman.

Finally, Linda grouped items that had to do with her grandmother's daily activities.

always counting her money

watches word game shows on tv

drinks herb teas

does crossword puzzles "to stay sharp"

putters in her rose garden

From this list she produced a topic sentence that focused on her grand-mother's busyness:

Grammy always has something to keep her busy.

From one brainstorming list, then, Linda generated four topic sentences from which she might choose. As she thought about what she most wanted to say about her grandmother and about what might be most interesting to her readers, Linda thought of how often she and her family had laughed together about the way Grammy dressed. She decided to amuse her readers by sharing with them the details of Grammy's eccentric habits of dress.

Writing Activity 1.2

• Look closely at your list from Activity 1.1. Read it through again to get a good "feel" for what you know about this person. Are some ideas more vivid than

- others? Are some items especially significant about this person?

- Next, as Linda did in the examples, choose several related items that interest you and that might interest others. Group these items together so that you can analyze their relationship. What do they say about your subject?

- Now write a complete sentence that names the subject and says something specific about that subject.

- Work with two to four groups of related items, writing a topic sentence for each group.

Look at your list of possible topic sentences. Which do you, as writer, find most interesting? Which do you think a reading audience such as the people in your classroom might find most interesting? How do you want your audience to respond to what you write?

STEP 3:
Outline the Paragraph

Outlining is an excellent way to plan and organize your writing. An outline includes the topic sentence and the most important details that will go into the paragraph. Our method of outlining is very simple. First, turn your topic sentence into a question. Begin your question with one of these words: *who, what, when, where, why, how,* or *in what way*. When you write your topic sentence question, you will use most of the words from your topic sentence.

One of Linda's topic sentences is

Grammy is a feisty woman.

Changed to a question, the sentence becomes

How is Grammy a feisty woman?

Another of her sentences is

Grammy looks every one of her 92 years old.

That sentence becomes the question,

> **In what ways does Grammy look every one of her 92 years old?**

A third topic sentence is

> **Grammy always has something to keep herself busy.**

The question is

> **What things does Grammy have to keep herself busy?**

The fourth sentence is

> **Grammy is the most eccentric dresser I know.**

Turned into a question, it becomes

> **In what ways is Grammy the most eccentric dresser I know?**

Notice that in every case the question is complete (not just a single word) and that it uses most of the words from the topic sentence.

Writing Activity 1.3

• Choose one of the topic sentences you wrote for activity 1.2 and turn it into a single question. Be sure your question begins with *who, what, when, where, why, how,* or *in what way.* Be sure, also, to use most of the words from your topic sentence in your question. When this step is complete, you're ready to finish your outline.

To finish your outline, simply answer the question you have asked. Your answers will become the most important details of your paragraph—the details that *must* be included and discussed if your paragraph is to accomplish its purpose. Be sure that your answers directly answer the question and that each answer is a complete sentence. Here's Linda's outline:

Topic Sentence:

Grammy is the most eccentric dresser I know.

Topic Sentence Question (The question won't appear in your paragraph. It appears in your outline only as an aid in planning the paragraph.):

In what ways is Grammy the most eccentric dresser I know?

Answers:

1. **She wears silk nightgowns as slips.**
2. **She wears bobby socks under her nylons.**
3. **She wears safety pins all around the bands of her hats.**
4. **She loves to wear orange and purple dresses with roses pinned on them.**

Writing Activity 1.4

- Look carefully at your topic sentence question, and then answer that question directly.
- Write at least three answers. Be sure to write complete sentences, and be sure your answers do, in fact, answer the questions you've asked.
- Make your outline as complete as you can. This step of the writing process might seem time-consuming at first, but careful work at this stage can save you from needless headaches, sweat, and tears in the later stages of the process.

STEP 4:
Write the First Draft

The words **first draft** simply mean that it's your first try at writing your full paragraph. It's very rare for any writer to write something perfectly (or even nearly perfectly) the first time, so get used to the idea that you'll need to do two or three or more drafts of just about everything you write. We promise that writing is hard work, but we think you'll be interested and sometimes excited to see what happens to your writing as you take it through various drafts.

We'll use the outline as a guide, but we won't just copy it, for doing that would give us a paragraph that looks like this:

> **Grammy is the most eccentric dresser I know. She wears silk nightgowns as slips. She wears bobby socks under her nylons. She wears safety pins all around the bands of her hats. She loves to wear orange and purple dresses with roses pinned on them.**

That certainly lets us know that Grammy is unusual, but it doesn't give us a clear enough picture. Linda's original purpose was to amuse her reading audience by sharing with them the things she knows about her grandmother, and she knows much more than that bareboned paragraph tells us. The details from the outline need to be developed with information that will answer the questions that readers will probably have. For example, a reader might very well wonder why anyone would wear nightgowns as slips, bobby socks under her nylons, and pins around her hats, so the paragraph should answer at least those questions. Let's look at how Linda's first draft does that.

> **Grammy is the most eccentric dresser I know. She always wears silk nightgowns as slips. That way she is ready for bed when she gets tired. She also wears bobby socks under her nylons so her feet won't slip around in her shoes. Her hats always have safety pins all around the bands, just in case someone might need one. She likes purple dresses, and she also likes orange dresses, but she has a purple and orange dress that she wears a lot of the time. When you see her on the street, her dress is the first thing that catches your eye, but then you see the three large, yellow roses pinned on her right shoulder. She says she doesn't have to buy perfume because the roses smell so good.**

That's Linda's first draft, but before you write your own first draft, let's review the steps Linda took to get this far. First, she explored her subject by listing ideas about her grandmother as they came to mind. She had chosen a subject, but she hadn't decided what to say about that subject yet; she was only exploring some of the possibilities. Second, she reviewed the possibilities by identifying and grouping some details that she and her readers might find interesting. She chose to focus on her grandmother's eccentric habits of dressing to amuse her readers. Third, she outlined the paragraph to be sure that all her major details were clearly related to the topic sentence. Fourth, she wrote a draft of her paragraph in which she stated and explained the major details from her outline.

Writing Activity 1.5

- Write a first draft of your own paragraph. As you write, focus on the controlling idea expressed in your topic sentence.

- Remember that every detail you include in your paragraph must, in some way, explain the controlling idea.

- As you write, think about your audience and your purpose. Who are your readers? How do you want them to respond to what you write? Keep in mind that they are not familiar with your subject and that you must give them all the information necessary for them to understand what you want them to understand.

- Put your rough draft aside and let it sit overnight so you can come to it fresh when we go through the last step of our process.

STEP 5:
Revise the Paragraph

Revising your work means much more than fixing the spelling and punctuation. Such fixing is called **proofreading**, and it is one of the last steps in revising. Revising can mean moving sentences around, taking out sentences, adding new sentences, combining sentences, adding or changing words, or even starting again from scratch. It requires that you look carefully at your paragraph and ask whether it communicates what you want to communicate.

There is a widely agreed upon set of standards for judging writing. The categories below and the questions in each reflect those standards and will aid you as you revise. Read through the categories and the questions right now so that you'll begin to be familiar with them, and plan to refer to them as you revise anything you write.

Standards for Judging Writing

1. Audience—Who are your intended readers? How might you present your ideas so that your readers will best understand them? What words and details will best help you communicate with them? What kinds of things might they expect to see in a paper written by a college student? (Unless you have a specific reading audience in mind, consider your readers to be the people in your classroom—your fellow students and your teacher.)

2. Purpose—How do you want your reading audience to respond to what you write? Do you want them to laugh? To cry? To nod in agreement? To say, "Oh, now I understand"?

3. Controlling Idea—Is your topic sentence clear and complete? Does it contain a word or short phrase that focuses your readers' attention on the idea that will be developed in the paragraph?

4. Unity—Does your paragraph focus on only one central idea? Does it stay with your subject? Does all of your material relate directly to the original topic?

5. Development—Do your details fully develop and support the main idea? Have you provided enough material for the reader to see or feel or understand what you're talking about?

6. Vocabulary—Is your phrasing clear, precise, accurate? Are your words direct and to the point? Are you using the kind of vocabulary your subject requires and your audience expects?

7. Coherence—Does it all make sense? Are relationships among the ideas clear? Is your paper logically sound? Can your reader follow your line of thought without getting confused? Can you add transitional words or phrases to help your reader?

8. Sentence Structure—Have you used complete sentences? Is there some variety in your sentence structures? Are there sentences you could combine to make your ideas flow more smoothly and effectively?

9. Mechanics—Is your writing free of spelling errors? Does it follow standard rules of punctuation? Are capital letters, quotation marks, commas, apostrophes, and other punctuation in the right places?

There may be some terms in this set of standards that you don't understand right now. Don't worry. Your instructor can explain them to you, or you might look for them in the index to this book. Also, in the handbook section of this book, we discuss some of the most common problems students can have in sentence structure and punctuation, and we show you how to correct them. No one expects you to be an expert at this stage of your writing course, but we predict that you'll be very pleased with the way your understanding grows as you study and practice your writing.

Now let's see how using the above questions can help us revise a paragraph. Below is the first draft of Linda's paragraph. Her reading audience, people who don't know Grammy, probably has a clear enough picture of the eccentric old woman. Linda's purpose is to amuse her audience by describing the unusual nature of her grandmother's dress, and that purpose seems to be accomplished. The controlling idea, eccentric, is clearly stated, and the paragraph has unity because it focuses on that one idea. Development is good, but it could be better as we will see in the revision. Her vocabulary could be more precise and accurate. "A lot," for example, tells us very little about how often she wears the dress. Coherence could be improved by grouping some of the details differently and by using some transitional words. Sentence structure and mechanics often improve as one revises, so we won't worry much about them for now.

The original draft is followed by Linda's revision. In this book we will usually show you two drafts of paragraphs, a first draft and a revised draft. In fact, each of the paragraphs goes through more than two drafts, and you will see that your own writing almost always requires several drafts.

Linda's First Draft:

Grammy is the most eccentric dresser I know. She always wears silk nightgowns as slips. That way she is ready for bed when she gets tired. She also wears bobby socks under her nylons so her feet won't slip around in her shoes. Her hats always have safety pins all around the bands, just in case someone might need one. She likes purple dresses, and she also likes orange dresses, but she has a purple and orange dress that she wears a lot of the time. When you see her on the street, her dress is the first thing that catches your eye, but then you see the three large, yellow roses pinned on her right shoulder. She says she doesn't have to buy perfume because the roses smell so good.

Linda's Revised Draft:

My 92-year-old grandmother, Grammy, is a most eccentric dresser. For one thing, she dresses to anticipate problems. Safety pins of various sizes decorate the bands of her hats, "in case someone might need one," she claims. In case she gets tired, she wears pretty silk nightgowns as slips under her dresses so she'll be ready for bed. To keep her feet from slipping around in her shoes, she wears bobby socks underneath her nylons. She also favors outlandish colors. Most of her dresses are either deep purple or brilliant orange, but her favorite is a purple and orange striped dress that she wears at least three days a week. All summer long, regardless of what dress she has on, Grammy pins (with one of her biggest safety pins) three bright yellow roses to her right shoulder. "That way I don't have to buy perfume," she says smugly, "because the roses smell so grand."

Linda's topic sentence change does a little more to introduce Grammy to the reader and to lead more smoothly into the paragraph. Changing the order of sentences helped Linda take the readers more logically from one idea to the next. The use of direct quotations from Grammy helps the audience to know her better. Linda dropped "When you see her on the street" because she felt that the change helped keep the picture of Grammy more clearly in the reader's mind. The changes seem to make the paragraph more amusing as well, thus helping the writer accomplish her purpose more fully.

Writing Activity 1.6

- Reread your first draft, asking the questions listed in the "Standards for Judging Writing" section (pages 14–15).

- Write your second draft, making any changes you think will improve it. If you need to, change your topic sentence to make the controlling idea clearer. Add specific details to develop your ideas fully. Re-

move or revise any ideas that stray from your controlling idea.

- Always keep your audience and purpose in mind as
you write, and try to make changes that will help
your readers understand your meaning and respond as you want them to.

- Write additional drafts until you are satisfied with the
paragraph.

- Finally, before you share your paragraph with others,
proofread it carefully. Read it aloud and exaggerate
the pauses after each period or question mark.
These pauses will help you be sure that all of your
sentences are complete. Look carefully at spelling
and punctuation. If you have questions about how a
word is spelled or whether the punctuation is correct make a note of each case so you can ask your
instructor. You work hard at expressing your ideas;
don't let mechanical errors interfere with a reader's
understanding of what you have written.

You have now completed the five steps of the writing process, and the
result is a paragraph you can be proud to have written. First you brainstormed ideas to explore what you might say about your subject. Next you
grouped related ideas together to explore possible topic sentences, and you
decided on a controlling idea for your paragraph. Third, you outlined your
paragraph in order to plan what ideas you might present and the order in
which you would present them. Fourth, you wrote a rough draft developing
those ideas, and you let it sit for a time. Finally, you reviewed your rough draft
by asking a series of questions about it, and then you wrote one or more
revisions of your paragraph, letting the questions guide you as you added,
subtracted, or changed material. These five steps form the writing process
which we will use throughout this book.

Samples from Professional Writers

To end this chapter, we'd like to share with you two examples of how
professional writers have described people. The first of the writers is William
O. Douglas, who served for many years on the United States Supreme Court

and who wrote extensively about the time he spent in the outdoors. This selection from *Of Men and Mountains* is about his friend Roy Schaeffer.

> Roy has a great affection for horses. When this powerful man is near a horse, he is unfailingly gentle. His hand on a horse that is ill or injured has the tenderness of a father's hand at his child's sickbed. His voice is soft. And his gentleness with horses is reciprocated. I have seen a trembling three-year-old, wild and unbroken, become calm as he touched it and talked to it in a low voice.
>
> Roy has never owned a pair of hobbles. His horses never leave him in the hills. This means, of course, that he picks his campgrounds with an eye to the comfort and pleasure of the horse as well as to his own. He looks first for horse feed—not for grass that horses can eat in a pinch, but for sweet and tender grass that is rich in protein, like the alpine bunchgrass that grows as high as 8000 or 9000 feet in the Wallowas. As a result, Roy's horses are never far away in the morning. A handful of oats and his soft whistle will bring them to him. From November to May they run wild in the winter range on the lower reaches of the Big Minam; but when Roy goes to get them in the spring, they come right to him. Then he puts his arm around their necks and pats them, greeting them as one would a friend long absent.

The second selection is from the short story "The Angel of the Bridge" by John Cheever, one of America's best-known story writers.

> You may have seen my mother waltzing on ice skates in Rockefeller Center. She's seventy-eight years old now but very wiry, and she wears a red velvet costume with a short skirt. Her tights are flesh-colored, and she wears spectacles and a red ribbon in her white hair, and she waltzes with one of the rink attendants. I don't know why I should find the fact that she waltzes on ice skates so disconcerting, but I do. I avoid that neighborhood whenever I can during the winter months, and I never lunch in the restaurants on the rink. Once when I was passing that way, a total stranger took me by the arm and, pointing to Mother, said, "Look at that crazy old dame." I was very embarrassed. I suppose I should be

grateful for the fact that she amuses herself and is not a burden to me, but I sincerely wish she had hit on some less conspicuous recreation. Whenever I see gracious old ladies arranging chrysanthemums and pouring tea, I think of my own mother, dressed like a hat-check girl, pushing some paid rink attendant around the ice, in the middle of the third biggest city in the world.

Other Suggestions for Writing

1. Write about your first impression of a person you now know well.

2. Write about a character from a comic strip that you have been following for some time.

3. Write about a person whom you don't know but whom you often see—a fellow student, a bus driver, a store clerk.

4. Write about a person who has been your role model or a person who has been your rival.

5. Write about a person whose first or last name is amazingly appropriate.

6. Write about a person you really dislike—a Marine sergeant, a school principal, a boss, a landlord.

PREVIEW FOR CHAPTER 2

I felt in those days as if I wasn't good enough to even think about being with them. They were all so perfect. Unlike them, I wasn't smart or pretty, athletic or rich. I couldn't dress, walk, or act the right way. I wanted to talk like them but, just my luck, I was given a brassy alto blare.

I had my first hit of pot when I was in the sixth grade. I wanted to play basketball with my brother because none of my friends were around. He was getting stoned when I found him in his room. I asked him to play, and he said he would if I would take a hit off his pipe.

The lounge at the campus Women's Center makes me feel comfortable. Its soft, cushiony couch and always full coffee pot are there to welcome me when I feel overwhelmed by this new experience of being in school.

When I first walked into the Writing Lab, the first thing I saw was the fish tank. Then my eyes moved to the green plants, the posters and cartoons, and the students working quietly or deep in conversation with the tutors. "Well," I thought, "maybe they *can* help me."

We celebrated the Fourth of July in Riverfront Park with blankets spread on the lawn and a giant picnic lunch. We got there early to get a good spot to see the fireworks. The rain didn't start until just before dark.

2 MORE ABOUT BRAINSTORMING FOR IDEAS

SKILLS INTRODUCED

Using three methods of brainstorming:

1. Listing (plus observation chart)
2. Clustering
3. Freewriting

For most of us, there is nothing as terrifying as a blank piece of paper. We know that we eventually want to produce a neatly written paragraph with clearly stated ideas, an interesting approach, and no mechanical errors. But that blank page staring up at us sometimes makes this task seem impossible. Just remember, though, that a piece of writing rarely comes out perfectly the first time, even for professional writers. You simply have to start somewhere and work your way through until you've said what you want to say in the best way you can.

Sometimes when you write you will have a clear idea of what you want to say, but that's not always the case. Much of the time, you'll want to start the writing process with **brainstorming**—getting ideas on paper as fast as possible. When you brainstorm, don't worry about your handwriting, how you say something, whether it's interesting, or whether it's properly punctuated. Just get words on paper. This brainstorming does two things: it gets your ideas flowing, and it starts to fill up that blank page.

You can use brainstorming to explore a very general topic, a very specific topic, or anything in between. If you are not given a specific assignment, you can start by brainstorming for a subject. If you are to write from memory, your first step would be to brainstorm about subjects you know well. What do you know about that other people might want to know? Once you've decided on your subject (or if a more specific subject has been assigned), you can do some **focused brainstorming**. This is brainstorming that focuses on a very specific subject. In this chapter we will show you three methods that you can use for general or focused brainstorming.

Brainstorm by Listing

In Chapter 1 you already made a list of ideas about a person, so you know something about how **listing** is done. There are, however, a few rules to keep in mind when you list ideas to brainstorm a topic.

Rules for Listing

1. Don't worry about spelling, punctuation, sentence structure, or anything else. No one is going to grade or criticize your list. Its only purpose is to help you think about your subject.

2. Don't worry about using phrases or words that other people might not understand. The list is a shorthand note from you to yourself. Its purpose is to help you discover what's in your mind.

3. List as fast as you can. Stopping to think will only give your mind a chance to wander to other things. Also, one idea about a subject can often lead to another idea, and stopping will interrupt that flow.

4. List as much as you can. It doesn't matter how silly or unimportant an idea may seem at the time. Don't evaluate, just write. The more information you get into your list, the more ideas you'll have to choose from when you decide on a subject or a controlling idea.

For the writing assignment in Chapter 1, you had to pick a subject. That is, you had to choose someone to write about. You probably did a mental list of people and were able to choose a subject fairly quickly. Sometimes, though, the choices are harder, and in those cases, writing a list can help you choose your subject. If, for example, you are asked to describe a place on your campus and you can't decide which place to write about, simply begin by listing as many places as you can think of on your campus. Don't stop to ask whether a place is a good subject or not. That comes later. For right now, you're just brainstorming the possible subjects. Here's an example of a brainstorming list we did about places on our campus.

Places on campus

1. student union
2. music auditorium
3. cafeteria
4. football field
5. social science building
6. English building
7. bookstore
8. financial aid office
9. counseling center
10. computer lab
11. parking lot
12. library

In looking over our list, we decided we felt most comfortable with describing the bookstore, so we went there and made a list of things we saw. When we were first brainstorming to find a subject, our list was very general. Our next list of observations about the bookstore was more specific, however, since its purpose was to help us find what's worth writing about in the bookstore. We call this **focused listing** since our attention is focused on a single subject. Your brainstorming in Chapter 1 began with a focused list—a list of details you recalled as you thought about one person. Here's our more detailed brainstorming.

The Bookstore

1. cubbyholes where you must leave your belongings before entering
2. turnstiles
3. T.V. security cameras
4. school stuff for sale—T-shirts, sweatshirts, beer mugs, banners
5. textbook sections—divided by subject
6. many colors of books
7. notebooks, tablets, pencils, writing gear, "pee chee" folders
8. art materials—brushes, frames, canvases, paints, portfolios

9. munchies—candy bars, chips, cookies, Lifesavers

10. checkout counter

11. electronic cash register

12. signs—checks for amount of purchase only, no returns

Several things in this list might call our attention to specific parts of the bookstore. We might, for example, decide to write about how we feel about the security system in the bookstore, or we might choose to write about the food that is available. This focused list helps us explore our subject further and discover what is worth saying about it.

We have seen how listing can help us explore our memories about a person and how it can help us to observe a place, but listing can also help us to explore ideas. In his book *Blue Highways*, William Least Heat Moon includes a list that he made as he observed a place. His purpose in observing was to test the idea that the Texas desert is bare and lifeless.

It was the Texas some people see as barren waste when they cross it, the part they later describe at the motel bar as "nothing." They say, "There's nothing out there."

Driving through the miles of nothing, I decided to test the hypothesis and stopped somewhere in western Crockett County on the top of a broad mesa, just off Texas 29. At a distance, the land looked so rocky and dry, a religious man could believe that the First Hand never got around to the creation in here. Still, somebody had decided to string barbed wire around it.

No plant grew higher than my head. For a while, I heard only miles of wind against the Ghost [his van]; but after the ringing in my ears stopped, I heard myself breathing, then a bird note, an answering call, another kind of birdsong, and another: mockingbird, mourning dove, an enigma. I heard the high zizz of flies the color of gray flannel and the deep buzz of a blue bumblebee. I made a list of nothing in particular:

1. mockingbird

2. mourning dove

3. enigma bird

4. gray flies

5. blue bumblebee

6. two circling buzzards (not yet, boys)

7. orange ants

8. black ants

9. orange-black ants (what's been going on?)

10. three species of spiders

11. opossum skull

12. jackrabbit (chewed on cactus)

13. deer (left scat)

14. coyote (left tracks)

15. small rodent (den full of seed hulls under rock)

16. snake (skin hooked on cactus spine)

17. prickly pear cactus (yellow blossoms)

18. hedgehog cactus (orange blossoms)

19. barrel cactus (red blossoms)

20. devil's pincushion (no blossoms)

21. catclaw (no better name)

22. two species of grass (neither green, both alive)

23. yellow flowers (blossoms smaller than peppercorns)

24. sage (indicates alkali-free soil)

25. mesquite (three-foot plants with eighty-foot roots to reach water that fell as rain two thousand years ago)

26. greasewood (oh, yes)

27. joint fir (steeped stems make Brigham Young tea)

28. earth

29. sky

30. wind (always)

That was all the nothing I could identify then, but had I waited until dark when the desert really comes to life, I could have done better. To say nothing is out here is incorrect; to say the desert is stingy with everything except space and light, stone and earth is closer to the truth.

Having used his list as a tool to help him see, the author concludes that the popular opinion is wrong—that the desert is not a lifeless place.

One special form of a list is the **observation chart** shown in Figure 2-1. Its columns force you to pay attention to all of your senses, so it can help you do a more thorough, specific observation. We are most accustomed to relying on our sight, but smells, tastes, sounds, and touch can sometimes give us

Old Movie Theater			
Sight	*Sound*	*Smell / Taste*	*Touch / Movement*
1. young kids running to get seats in front 2. teens slouching in back row, throwing popcorn 3. families in the middle 4. grimy, chipped beige paint on walls 5. large, shiny white screen 6. tiny, dim lights near floor on aisles 7. overflowing trash cans in back 8. couples arriving late, trying to find seats in the dark	1. familiar old songs playing before movie begins 2. excited voices of children 3. loud bursts of laughter from teens 4. hush that comes over audience as music stops 5. "excuse me" as people squeeze past to go get popcorn 6. swell of music and voices as previews begin	1. munching fresh popcorn 2. drinking Coke and Pepsi 3. eating "Dots" and throwing licorice ones on the floor 4. strong perfume from woman sitting in next row 5. new batch of popcorn popping in lobby	1. rough nylon seat covers 2. jagged rips in fabric 3. gum stuck under arms and seats 4. smooth, cool armrests 5. sticky floor from spilled soda pop 6. rough texture of stucco walls 7. toes stomped on by kids as they push past on way to lobby

Figure 2-1   Observation Chart

more important information about a subject. As a writer, you must become aware of all the information that is available to you, for only then can you make an informed decision about your subject and your controlling idea. Figure 2-1 records a direct observation of the interior of an old movie theater in a small town.

Writing Activity 2.1

- List places on your campus that you might describe.
- Choose one of the places on your list.
- Go to that place and observe it. As you observe, list your observations on plain paper or an observation chart. Follow the Rules for Listing on page 22.

Brainstorm by Clustering

A second useful way of brainstorming is called **clustering**. The best way for us to talk about clustering is to show you what a cluster looks like, then to make some suggestions about how you can use this method. Figure 2-2 is a cluster that one student made as she thought of possible subjects for an assignment to write about a childhood memory.

Looking at this cluster, you can see that this method is quite different from listing. It shows how ideas relate to each other, and it does more to help one idea lead to another. There are four basic rules to follow when you brainstorm by clustering.

Rules for Clustering

1. First, in a circle near the center of a page, write the subject you want to brainstorm. This can be just a word, an idea, or a feeling, like "afraid," or it can be something more specific, such as "my first day in college" or "why I should not get married."

2. Next, show other related ideas in other circles. Draw lines to show how those ideas are related to the main idea or to each other. This step can also help you organize your ideas.

3. Again, work quickly. Don't stop to evaluate your idea; don't worry about spelling; don't worry about whether other people can make sense out of what you are doing.

4. When your cluster is finished, look at it. Is one part more detailed or more interesting to you than the rest? That may be the part you'll want to write about. If you're clustering to explore a subject, choose one part of your cluster and make a second cluster on that part to explore your ideas more thoroughly. This will be a focused cluster, and you might

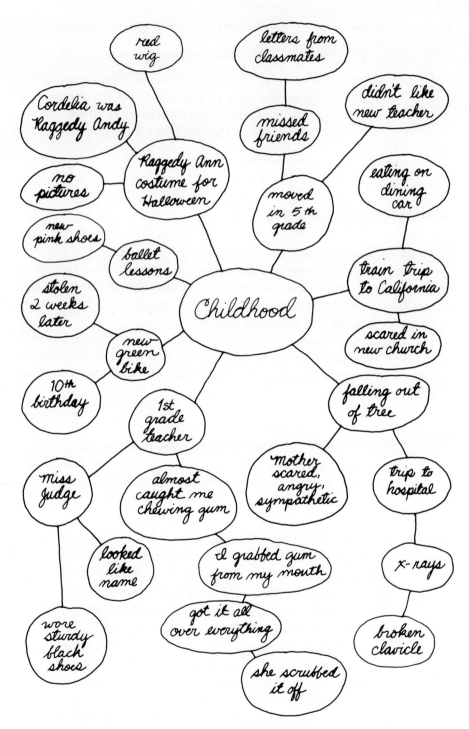

Figure 2-2   Clustering

decide to do a third or fourth cluster, each more sharply focused than the one before.

In our student's cluster on a childhood memory, the part about the first grade teacher is the most detailed, but she found the Raggedy Ann costume section more interesting. It's what she really wanted to write about, so she chose to explore it further by **focused clustering**. Figure 2-3, then, is the second cluster on a childhood memory. It is focused on a specific memory suggested by the Raggedy Ann costume—Halloween in the fourth grade.

As is the case with listing, clustering can be used to explore a variety of topics—ideas, places, memories, and so on. As you continue to use these various brainstorming methods, you will see how useful they can be.

Writing Activity 2.2

- Make a cluster of holiday celebrations you remember.
- Choose one celebration and make a focused cluster on that celebration.
- Follow the Rules for Clustering on page 27.

Brainstorm by Freewriting

The third method of brainstorming we'll discuss is called **freewriting**. The techniques are simple but effective.

Rules for Freewriting

1. Start writing about anything, and don't stop. Try to write for at least ten minutes without picking up your pen from the paper or your fingers from the keyboard of your word processor. If you need to repeat a word, repeat it. If you need to write nonsense, write nonsense. Just don't stop writing. As one of our colleagues says, "Write your heart and guts out."

2. Don't pay attention to spelling, punctuation, proper language, or anything else like that. No one needs to see this but you, and no one will tell you it's wrong.

3. When you're finished, look over what you've written. Have you repeated an idea several times? Is there anything that

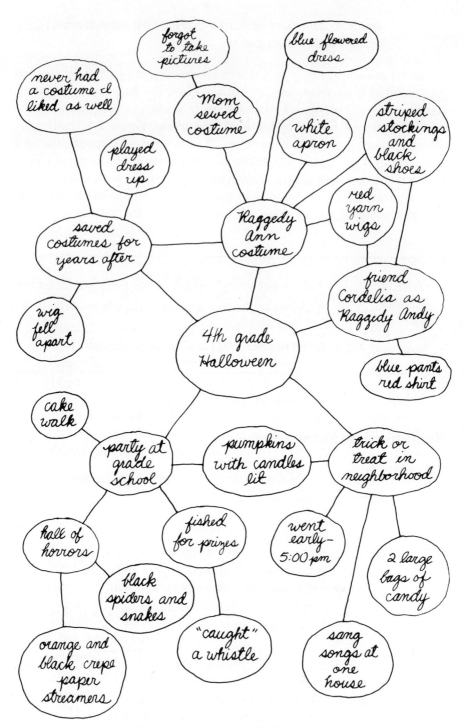

Figure 2-3   Focused Clustering

stands out as especially interesting? These are possible topics for your writing.

4. To explore one of these topics, select an idea, concentrate on it for a few minutes, then freewrite again for at least ten minutes. This is called **focused freewriting**, and, like the other forms of focused brainstorming, it helps you to explore ideas more fully.

Here's an example of freewriting that one of our students did. Like the clusters assignment, it is about a childhood experience.

Freewrite on a Childhood Experience

Riding horses at grandpa's farm . . . riding in the car with my mom and dad, going to the park I liked to lead the ponie . . . riding my bike in the early mornings. My birthday. My surprise birthday party. We were over at a friends housemyfamily and I. It was my birthday that day. I was telling everyone it was my birthday. going to the party—I was excited. I was always the most excited when we visited grandma and grandpa at their farm. that farm. It was in Alberta. Sleeping upstairs, getting up early, puffed wheat in the kitchen. The barn, the cows, milking the cows killing that chicken messy. Granpa let us ride the horse up and down the road. the time I fell off and had to walk home with dad.

As the student reread her freewrite, she quickly realized that she wanted to write about the times she had at her grandpa's farm. She then continued with a focused freewrite on that more specific subject.

Focused Freewrite on Experiences at the Farm

I remember sleeping upstairs on a soft soft bed with a down quilt over me. Getting up at the crow of the roosters and hurriedly eating breakfast, a bowl of puffed wheat. Grandma bought a great big plastic bag of this cereal. I like it to this day. Then I'd hurry outside and run to the barn with uncle Bob and help him milk the cows, he would let me try to squeeze the utter but I couldn't get much milk out. Then he would give me a squirt of milk in my mouth, but I wasn't

too crazy about warm milk. They did have milking ma-
chines and I got to put my finger in one—just a nice gentle
squeeze. Then it was collecting the eggs and feeding the
animals. There were twin calves born just before we got
there and my sister and I got to name them. We called
them Spic and Span. The mama cow was very gentle and
grandpa would let us ride her around the barnyard. She
was bony and very uncomfortable so we didn't ride her very
much. I remember the time grandpa had to kill some
chickens for our dinner. He let one go after its head was
chopped off just so we could see what happened, what a
mess but we laughed and screamed with excitement.
What a morning it was when my sister and I got to ride on
the tractor with my uncle to the cows that were in another
pasture down the road. We could see our breath it was so
cold. An early frost that year. I remember the flighty young
horse, too flighty for young inexperienced children like us.
My dad put us on the back of the horse and lead us down
the road. I was the smallest and I was on the back . . . I
began to slip and held on to my sister and we both ended up
in the ditch. I had the wind knocked out of me so I walked
back home beside my dad.

This focused freewrite provided a wealth of specific detail for the student.
She did not know that she remembered so much about the farm, and she
ended with many possible topics from which to choose.

Like listing and clustering, freewriting can be used to brainstorm any
subject. We have told you about it and shown you how it works; now try it for
yourself.

Writing Activity 2.3

- Freewrite to explore possible subjects for a paragraph
  about a childhood experience.

- Choose an experience and do a focused freewrite on
  that experience.

- In both of these steps, follow the Rules for Freewriting
  on pages 29–31.

As you wrote your paragraph for Chapter 1, you probably added details that were not on your original brainstorming list, for the flow of ideas continued as you drafted and revised. Brainstorming is, above all, a way to get started, but its usefulness doesn't end there. Writing is a process of dealing with ideas, and ideas change as we deal with them. As a result, you may find yourself going back to the brainstorming step as you draft and revise what you write.

If part of a paragraph gives you trouble, do a list, cluster, or freewrite on that part. Every step of the writing process can lead you to new discoveries about your subject, and a new discovery can take you back to an earlier step in the process. This is good. As you progress through this book, you will develop the ability to see when you need to move from one step to another and back, but what's important right now is that you know how to use the techniques of brainstorming—listing, clustering, and freewriting.

You have had some practice in these techniques, and you will use them throughout this book. You will probably find that you prefer one method over the others, but you will also find that different techniques are useful in different writing situations. The more experience you have in using these techniques, the better you'll be able to choose the right one for you in any situation. Refer back to this chapter whenever you need to refresh your memory.

Preview for Chapter 3

When I was a little girl I would pretend it was a pirate's treasure chest with gold doubloons inside. Now the old trunk sits in a dusty corner in my attic. Cracked brown leather straps wrapped around each end hang uselessly over the edges. Two small grayish labels with writing that is no longer readable stick crookedly to the front. There's a rusty metal lock on the lid, but it doesn't lock anymore.

A good word for my baseball bat would be magical. The gold lettering on the black bat reminds me of the eyes of a black cat on the shoulder of a witch.

My insulin bottle looks like a fat squatty man. Its solid lower frame supports a hairless barrel chest which holds a short, chopped-off neck. Its pinkish sunburned head is shoved through a shiny metal helmet.

My motorcycle has its original seat, old rusty metal now because the covering has disintegrated over the years. Some of the parts are rusty, but you can easily mistake the rust for dirt because the bike is so filthy.

My radio is jet black with a high-luster finish similar to Darth Vadar's mask. The red and yellow blinking lights make it more lifelike, and the telescopic antennas give it a robot-like look.

3 WRITING ABOUT AN OBJECT

SKILLS INTRODUCED

Considering audience and purpose
Observing an object
Identifying the dominant impression
Selecting specific nouns and adjectives

Why do we write descriptions of objects? Isn't it easier to take a photograph or draw a picture? Often, of course, a photo or drawing can convey more clearly than words what something looks like. Still, field guides to birds or animals always accompany illustrations with written descriptions, and a magazine article about, say, relics discovered in an old shipwreck will have explanatory captions with the photographs. Pictures may help, but they're seldom enough. A photo or drawing can tell us only part of what something looks like. It can't tell us about its weight or texture or odor, and it often can't tell us as much about the artist's response to it as can a written description.

We describe objects because we respond to them and we want to share our response. We write about an object because we think that someone else should know in detail what the object is like. We might write about an object because we think it's especially well made or poorly made. We might want to describe something we've made because we're proud of our work. We might write about something especially beautiful, ugly, or unusual, or we might describe an object so that someone else will be able to identify it.

And who might be the reading audience for such descriptions? The most natural reading audience is someone who is interested in the object or kind of object being described. But almost any object can be made interesting to nearly anyone. If a writer is intrigued by an object for any reason, he can certainly share his interest with a reader, and a reader who senses the writer's interest will be a willing audience.

STEP 1:
Brainstorm to Discover What You Know

In our experience, the most common problem students encounter when they are asked to write about an object lies in the choice of the object itself. To complete the assignment quickly, students often choose to describe the first thing they see—a pop can or a pen, for example. Such choices almost always lead to paragraphs that simply don't work. The writing doesn't communicate anything because the writer has found nothing to communicate. A writer who doesn't care about the subject can't help but write a paragraph that the reader won't care about. The audience's response is "So what? What is the writer's **purpose** in telling me this?"

Here, for example, is a paragraph written by one of our students about a Pepsi can:

> This Pepsi can is colorful. Around its gold top is a white ring about three eighths of an inch wide with red and blue letters advertising a game. The background of the body is made up of gold stripes separated by thinner white stripes, the gold stripes being only about a sixteenth of an inch wide. Red and blue letters and shapes, each outlined in white, decorate most of the can, telling us that it's caffeine free and that it's Pepsi. A mostly white advertisement tells in blue and red letters about a contest that can get you "a dream vacation anywhere in the world." The bottom of the can is a natural aluminum color. All in all, this red, white, blue and gold can is quite colorful.

Now that paragraph certainly focuses on and develops its controlling idea, colorful, but there's no life to it. It states the most readily observed characteristics of a very common object, but it doesn't show the readers anything they couldn't see for themselves in a quick glance or two.

Does that mean that someone couldn't write an interesting paragraph about a Pepsi can? Of course not. A paragraph telling us what the can might say about American values or a paragraph about how the writer thinks the can was manufactured might be fascinating. Either of those paragraphs could give us some insight into the writer's knowledge or the processes of design, production, and marketing. Either might raise some questions in our own minds and make us want to seek further knowledge. The interest is not necessarily in the object itself but in what the writer chooses to tell us about the object. As Paul Roberts says in an essay called "How to Say Nothing in 500 Words," "All subjects, except sex, are dull until somebody makes them interesting. The writer's job is to find the argument, the approach, the angle, the wording that will take the reader with him."

Another major problem in writing descriptions of objects is the temptation to write from memory rather than from **direct observation**. We are not in the habit of observing carefully; we tend to take familiar objects for granted, thinking we know them well, yet when we try to write about them, we discover large gaps in our knowledge. For that reason, your writing assignment for this chapter requires that you directly observe an object and that you write from that observation.

Let's look further, now, at the process of observing and writing a description of an object so that the end result is a paragraph that both writer and reader can be interested in.

Once you've decided upon an object to describe, you must brainstorm by observing and recording the specific details of that object. Use all of your **five senses**. Look at the object; listen to it; smell it; taste it; touch it. What's it made of? What shape is it? What are its colors, size, and texture? You won't always be able to (or want to) use every sense to describe an object, but in any observation you do, try to use as many of your five senses as you can.

Mike chose to describe a coffee mug that people had commented on and that people disagreed about. Some liked it and called it "unusual" while others hated it and said it was grotesque, so he knew that people found the mug interesting.

For his brainstorming, he chose to do focused freewriting as he directly observed the mug. First he concentrated on the mug for a few minutes. With the coffee mug in front of him, he tried to note as many things as he could that have to do with the senses—seeing, touching, tasting, smelling, and hearing. Since the mug was empty, however, smell and taste were not significant. Here is a freewriting based on what he saw, heard, felt, and thought when he examined this particular mug.

mug isn't very tall—about 3 and a half inches. tapers to
narrow base and holds about what any cup would hold. it's
ugly—ugly mugly, seasick green, worst I've seen. dark
brown inside like coffee, poor little animal struggling from
inside. I'm thirsty, wish I had some hot coffee. poor little animal must get his bottom burned. handle keeps hand from
getting burned—just stuck on—might fall off. Creature
looks like a wombat—what's that? His head and shoulders
and claws are over the side but the rest is inside wishing it
was outside—back legs, tail, body down in the coffee.
Beady eyes and sharp nose stare at me and its head hits
mine when I drink. got this thing at a dog sale, and it's a real
dog. gets a lot of attention, though. It feels heavy to me and
clunks when I set it down. Thick sides, thick bottom thick,
thick, thick, sick, sick, sick. bottom is rough, too, like fine
sandpaper that might scratch the table. rest is smooth but
colors are uneven, roughly vertical bands. I can feel
the ridges as my fingers run down the cup, and when I hit
it with my pen it goes clunk. why do I like this weird, sick,
ugly mug?

This freewrite gives him many clear, specific details about the mug. In
addition, it led him to record some of his thoughts about the mug. This combination of details and thoughts led him directly to an impression of the mug:
it's ugly. The specific information about size (three and a half inches tall) and
the **comparison** of the cup's creature to a wombat are good details that he
will want to use in his paragraph. Such details enabled him to convey a clear
picture to his readers. The few minutes of concentration before he started
writing helped him to see those specific details.

Writing Activity 3.1

- Choose an object that interests you.
- Examine it: touch it, smell it, listen to it, and so on.
- Concentrate on the object for a few minutes, and then freewrite about it.
- Give as many details and impressions of it as you can.

STEP 2:
Write the Topic Sentence

Writing a topic sentence for a descriptive paragraph has two steps. First, you must find a word or idea to control the paragraph. Second, you must write a sentence that identifies what you are describing and that states the controlling idea you chose in the first step. The controlling idea will be your **dominant impression** of what you are describing. Something that is dominant is something that stands out above everything else, and you state your dominant impression when you say, "Maria's dress is colorful," or "That is an intricate puzzle." The dominant impression or controlling idea of the first example is "colorful," and the dominant impression of the second is "intricate." The dominant impression that Mike discovered in his freewriting was "ugly," and that word will become the controlling idea for his paragraph. Here is his topic sentence:

> **A good word to describe my coffee mug is "unusual," but "ugly" comes closer to the truth.**

You may or may not have one dominant impression in your mind as you begin to brainstorm, but once you've completed this step, sit down for a moment and think about the one impression you get. Think about the one major idea that all the specific details seem to add up to. If you began with a clear impression and ended with the same impression, check your brainstorming work carefully. Are there details that might contradict your impression? Look back at the object itself. Can you find anything there that might contradict your impression? This double checking is important because we often overlook details that go against ideas we already hold about something. (Remember William Least Heat Moon's point about the desert on page 24.) Of course your original idea may also be correct, but you need to check. Mike's freewrite, for example, only confirmed his original idea, but the observation gave him details—such as the sound of the mug—that he hadn't noticed before.

Writing Activity 3.2

• Reread your brainstorming and decide on one major or dominant impression you have about the object.

• Think carefully about your audience and purpose. Who are your readers? Why should they be interested in the object you are describing?

• Write a topic sentence that contains your dominant impression.

STEP 3:
Outline the Paragraph

Now that you have a topic sentence, it's time to take the details from your freewrite and put them into an outline. This procedure will ensure that your paragraph will have good unity. Then you'll write your paragraph, developing the details even further and more specifically. It's a good idea to keep the object you describe close by while you outline, since you'll probably want to look at it again and again.

After reviewing his freewrite and topic sentence and examining the mug again, Mike came up with the following outline (remember to turn your topic sentence into a question as you start your outline):

Topic sentence:

A good word to describe my coffee mug is "unusual," but "ugly" comes closer to the truth.

Topic sentence question:

What is ugly about my coffee mug?

Answers:

1. Its colors are seasick green and ugly brown.
2. It has a figure of a creature crawling over the side.
3. It's heavy with thick, uneven sides.
4. It even sounds ugly.

This outline gives him a good beginning for his paragraph and will guide him as he selects details from his freewrite or from further observation.

- Use your material from your brainstorming to write an outline to help plan your paragraph.

- Remember to make a question out of your topic sentence.

- Refer back to pages 9–11 if you need a little more help on outlining.

Step 4:
Write the First Draft

With a brainstorm, a topic sentence and an outline, Mike was ready to write his first draft. Looking at his outline, he saw that the first and fourth answers contained the controlling word, "ugly," but that the second and third did not. He saw a danger, then, that the paragraph might lose unity as he developed the ideas. He was aware that he might, for example, end up just describing the creature rather than by explaining how the creature helped to make the cup ugly. Being aware of the relation between his controlling idea and the details of his outline helped Mike as he wrote his first draft.

His mental picture of a reading audience helped, too, and he chose to write to an audience that had never seen the mug. He knew, though, that people are interested in things that are unusual and that the judgment that something is ugly often arouses people's curiosity. His purpose, he decided, would be to show the reader what there is about the mug that makes him say it's ugly. With that information, readers seeing the mug might agree or disagree with Mike's judgment, but at least they would be able to see why he made that judgment.

Draft 1

A good word to describe my coffee mug would be "unusual," but "ugly" comes closer to the truth. When you first see it, you notice the ugly green color of its unevenly tapered body, or maybe you see the ugly brown stain about a third of the way around from the crooked handle. A little

closer look shows you a little animal that seems to be struggling up over the side after nearly drowning in hot coffee.
The ugly brown stain on the side extends to the inside of the
cup, and the animal's body, back legs, and tail hang down
in the center of the stain. Its sides seem unusually thick, and
you can't set the heavy thing down anywhere without hearing a loud clunk. Usually, if you tap one cup against another
or tap a cup with a pencil or pen, you'll hear a musical clink.
My cup responds with a dull thud. I'm not sure why I keep
my ugly mug, but it certainly does have character.

His first draft, like all first drafts, has some problems. We'll work on those
problems in Step 5.

Writing Activity 3.4

• Write a first draft of your description of an object.
• Set your rough draft aside for a while before you revise it.

STEP 5:
Revise the Paragraph

As you revise your paragraph, remember that while you have directly
experienced the object you are describing, your readers have not. It is only
through the details you choose and the words you write on the page that most
of your readers will ever know the object. You must, then, ask whether you
have included enough sensory details, and you must examine your word
choices to be sure they convey the ideas you want your readers to understand.

One way to examine your word choices in descriptions is to look carefully
at the nouns and adjectives you use. Although we won't spend much time in
this text on grammar terms, we will define two right now, and then we'll look
at how examining nouns and adjectives can help in revising a paragraph.

noun: A word that names a person, place, thing, or concept. Nouns have several important characteristics that help you recognize them. First, noun indicators—words like *a, the, some,* or *those*—often precede nouns and indicate

that the reader can expect to see a noun very soon. In the sentence, "The boy threw a frisbee to the white dog," for example, *boy, frisbee,* and *dog* are nouns and are preceded by noun indicators—*the, a,* and *the.* Second, nouns can be made singular or plural—*aunt* or *aunts, child* or *children.* Third, they can show possession—*Lil's motorhome* or *the Smiths' house.*

adjective: A word that **modifies**—describes or tells more about—a noun. In the sentence, "The boy threw a frisbee to the white dog," *white* is an adjective; it tells us more about the dog. We can add more adjectives to the sentence if we wish, and these adjectives might give the reader a clearer mental picture of what happened. Here's an example: "The handsome, young boy threw a large, red plastic frisbee to the excited white dog."

Look again at Mike's first draft; this time adjectives are underlined once, and nouns have been underlined twice.

> A good word to describe my coffee mug would be "unusual," but "ugly" comes closer to the truth. When you first see it, you notice the ugly green color of its unevenly tapered body, or maybe you see the ugly brown stain about a third of the way around from the crooked handle. A little closer look shows you a little animal that seems to be struggling up over the side after nearly drowning in hot coffee. The ugly brown stain on the side extends to the inside of the cup, and the animal's body, back legs, and tail hang down in the center of the stain. Its sides seem unusually thick, and you can't set the heavy thing down anywhere without hearing a loud clunk. Usually, if you tap one cup against another or tap a cup with a pencil or pen, you'll hear a musical clink. My cup responds with a dull thud. I'm not sure why I keep my ugly mug, but it certainly does have character.

As Mike looked again at his paragraph, he thought that the noun "animal" didn't create a clear enough image in the reader's mind, and he noticed that he had repeated the adjective "ugly" five times. He saw that he had very little description of the animal, and when he reviewed his freewrite he saw several specific nouns and adjectives he could have used to give the reader a clearer image. He decided, then, to be more careful and specific in his word choices as he revised.

As you revise your paragraph, be aware that the nouns and adjectives you choose can often be made more specific. Here, for example, is a list of words that moves from the general to the specific: animal, mammal, pet, dog, Australian Shepherd, Jessica (an Australian Shepherd owned by one of the authors). Notice how a clearer picture is created in your mind with each step down the list. In the move from animal to mammal, we eliminate the need to think about robins or rattlesnakes. In the move from mammal to pet, we exclude elephants and elk. In the move from pet to dog, we get rid of the cats and the gerbils, and Australian Shepherd lets us stop visualizing poodles, spaniels, and St. Bernards. Even if you've never seen Jessica, your mind is focused on a single dog of a single breed, and thus the movement from the general to the specific has improved the communication between writer and reader. A reverse example, movement from the specific to the general, is offered by the main character in James Joyce's *A Portrait of the Artist as a Young Man*. He has written in his geography book:

Stephen Dedalus
Class of Elements
Clongowes Wood College
Sallins
County Kildare
Ireland
Europe
The World
The Universe

Now let's look at what Mike's understanding of specific language did to help his paragraph.

Draft 2

My pottery mug is so ugly that it's almost sickening. When you first see it, you notice the mottled, seasick green color of its unevenly tapered sides, or maybe you spot a dingy brown stain about a third of the way around from the crudely attached, crooked handle. A closer look will show you a desperate, pathetic, wombat-like creature that seems to be struggling over the side after nearly drowning in hot coffee. The sad little varmint is in the center of the muddy splotch that extends into the cup's inside; its thick body, stubby back legs, and scraggly tail hang limply down in-side. Beady eyes on each side of the sharp nose stare help-lessly at me. Although I have used the cup for a year, I still can't pour coffee into it without a feeling of pity for the poor beast and a sense that I ought to go scour the cup to get rid of the animal's germs.

Notice how the addition of an adjective, "sickening," to the controlling word ("ugly") focuses the paragraph more sharply on some particular characteristics of the mug. It led Mike to more adjectives like "desperate," "pathetic," "seasick," and "scraggly." Note, also, how he's given the paragraph more variety by using different nouns to describe the same object: "mug" and "cup"; "stain" and "splotch"; and "creature," "beast," "varmint," and "animal." There are, of course, other changes, but the choices of strong and vivid nouns and adjectives are an important part of what makes Mike's paragraph more effective.

Writing Activity 3.5

• Revise your paragraph.
• Pay particular attention to your choices of nouns and adjectives as you revise. Make them as specific as possible.

Samples from Professional Writers

Our first two professional examples to close this chapter are selected from "My Horse" by Barry Lopez, a widely published writer who specializes in nature and the outdoors.

If you were a Crow warrior and I a young Teton Sioux out after a warrior's identity and we came over a small hill somewhere in the Montana prairie and surprised each other, I could tell a lot about you by looking at your horse.

Your horse might have feathers tied in his mane, or in his tail, or a medicine bag tied around his neck. If I knew enough about the Crow, and had looked at you closely, I might make some sense of the decoration, even guess who you were if you were well-known. If you had painted your horse, I could tell even more, because we both decorated our horses with signs that meant the same things. Your white handprints high on his flanks would tell me you had killed an enemy in a hand-to-hand fight. Small horizontal lines stacked on your horse's foreleg, or across his nose, would tell me how many times you had counted coup. Horse hoof marks on your horse's rump, or three-sided boxes, would tell me how many times you had stolen horses. If there was a bright red square on your horse's neck I would know you were leading a war party and that there were probably others out there in the coulees behind you.

Farther along in his essay, Lopez describes his modern day "horse":

The truck is a van. I call it a truck because it's not a car and because "van" is a suburban sort of consumer word like "oxford loafer," and I don't like the sound of it. On the outside it looks like any other Dodge Sportsman 300. It's a dirty tan color. There are a few body dents, but it's never been in a wreck. I tore the antenna off against a tree on a pinched mountain road. A boy in Midland, Texas, rocked one of my rear view mirrors off. A logging truck in Oregon squeeze-fired a piece of debris off the road and shattered my windshield. The oil pan and gas tank are pug-faced from high-centering on bad roads.

We close with a selection from *The Story of My Boyhood and Youth*, the autobiography of John Muir, one of America's first and greatest conservationists. Muir was born in 1838.

One of my many inventions was a large thermometer made of an iron rod, about three feet long and five eighths of an inch in diameter, that had formed part of a wagon box. The expansion and contraction of this rod was multiplied by a series of levers made of strips of hoop iron. The pressure of the rod against the levers was kept constant by a small counterweight, so that the slightest change in the length of the rod was instantly shown on a dial about three feet wide multiplied about thirty-two thousand times. The zero point was gained by packing the rod in wet snow. The scale was so large that the big black hand on the white-painted dial could be seen distinctly and the temperature read while we were plowing in the field below the house. The extremes of heat and cold caused the hand to make several revolutions. The number of these revolutions was indicated on a small dial marked on the larger one. This thermometer was fastened on the side of the house, and was so sensitive that when anyone approached it within four or five feet the heat radiated from the observer's body caused the hand of the dial to move so fast that the motion was plainly visible, and when he stepped back, the hand moved slowly back to its normal position. It was regarded as a great wonder by the neighbors and even by my all-Bible father.

Other Suggestions for Writing

1. Write about an object that has been made by hand and is especially well-crafted.

2. Write about a machine that doesn't work.

3. Write about an object from memory, and then write about it again with the object in front of you.

4. Write about something you treasure—a trophy, a gift from a special person, something you worked hard to buy.

5. Write about something you bought because it was a fad at the time.

6. Write about an object you have been longing to own but that is unreachable at this time.

PREVIEW FOR CHAPTER 4

Thinking back to that windy day, it was like all my dreams were floating on the tops of the trees.

He was a good coach, though. For the first week of practice he ran us like dogs. I think he did this to see who could handle his practices and who couldn't. After two weeks of practice there were only thirty of us left. But we sure were in good shape.

One of them handed Tim a wadded up $10 bill, and as soon as I saw that I knew what was going to happen. I was sure one of them was going to pull a gun, and he did. "Get down on the floor and don't look at me or I'll shoot you."

"'Come into my parlor,' said the spider to the fly." Tiffany stared suspiciously at Danielle from across the pool. Her small fists were stubbornly clenched at her sides, and her brow furrowed in annoyance.

The wind was blowing so hard that the boat felt as if it were made of styrofoam. The cold salt water washed over the side and drenched everything on deck. Occasionally I looked around to see bodies hanging over the rails. I could hear people cursing as they tried to regain their composure. At one point, I was tempted to pay the captain to take me back to land.

I was upset when my dad backed over my cat Blue Eyes and shocked at the related spanking I got a year later.

4 MORE ABOUT REVISING

SKILLS INTRODUCED

1. Writing interesting openings
2. Developing ideas
3. Connecting ideas
4. Choosing words
5. Writing clear sentences

In Chapter 2 we explored the task of brainstorming, one of the most important of the five steps of the writing process. In this chapter, we will focus on the task of revising. To *revise*, remember, means to "see again" and then to make the changes that you see need to be made. We will show you some ways to "see" your work again so that you can decide what changes will help your audience better understand what you have to say.

You may often be reluctant to go back and change what you have written, but the truth is that most of us seldom do our best job on our first try. Also, as we work on a piece of writing, we develop a kind of "pride of ownership" and, at the same time, an inability to see how something might be said differently. Although it takes time and effort, revision leads to clearer communication, pride in a job well done, and higher grades.

Overview and Example

We have so far presented the five step process—brainstorming, formulating a topic sentence, outlining, writing a first draft, revising—as if it were an orderly set of steps everyone goes through when writing. In truth, though, it is not always that orderly. You may find that you have a clear idea for a subject, so you'll do little if any brainstorming. More likely, though, you'll go through the brainstorming and outline steps, then find as you begin to draft that your ideas have changed, so you'll go back and repeat one or both of the previous steps. Or perhaps as you write, details will come to you that you hadn't thought of at first, so you will still be brainstorming even as you write and revise. Writers call this moving back and forth among the steps a *recursive* process. Be prepared, then, as you revise, to discover that you may have to go back to an earlier step—that you may even have to scrap what you have and start again from the beginning. If that happens, don't think of the time you have spent as "wasted"; it has been time invested in exploring and refining ideas, and such time is never wasted.

As the first step in revision, let your writing get cold before you begin to revise. That is, don't look at it for twenty-four hours before you start your revision. This waiting period lets you approach your work with a fresh eye and mind. Of course, given deadlines and due dates, waiting a day is not always possible, but try to give it at least a few hours' rest.

When your work is cold, reread it and ask yourself whether you are really discussing what you want to discuss. Because the process of writing is a process of discovery, sometimes as you write, you may discover that your ideas have changed. Here, for example, is a paragraph in which a student began with one idea and, after letting her work get cold, saw that she was actually working toward a different, more specific statement about her friend.

P.J.'s First Rough Draft

My friend Desi is an all-around woman. To begin with, she's great looking. She's five feet eight and has a great figure, but her dark, sparkling eyes and the perfect dark skin of her face are what most catch your eye. Her long legs and slim build also make her a fine athlete, so when she's not backpacking or jogging, she's on the tennis courts. Her mind is as good as her body, so she always got good grades in school, and has always been able to do just about anything she sets her mind to. When she was nominated for homecoming queen, she campaigned hard and won.

When she decided to buy a house, she did it and paid it off in only a few years. When she decided to become a bank teller, she achieved that goal too. This all-around woman seems to accomplish whatever she sets out to do.

As we discussed earlier, the steps of the writing process are not separate and linear. The human mind seems not to work in that way. We rethink and refine our ideas as we write, and so writers often discover that what they really want to say about their subject emerges at the end of an early draft. Drafting can help us discover and plan just as brainstorming and outlining do. The trick is to be aware of that and to give yourself time to become conscious of the discoveries your mind makes as you write.

P.J. revised her paragraph, focusing on the idea that emerged at the end of her first draft—her friend can accomplish whatever she wants to.

P.J.'s Second Rough Draft

My friend Desi sets goals and reaches them. In high school, her friends nominated her for homecoming queen. She campaigned very hard, and indeed she reached this goal and was encouraged to aim higher. After she graduated from high school, she applied for and got a job as a secretary with a steel company. She made good money, but it was all going to rent, so she made it her goal to own her own home before she was twenty-five. With a little luck and a lot of work, she managed to buy and pay for her home by the time she was twenty-two. When the house was paid off, she rented it out and moved to California. Nine months later she returned with a new interest; she wanted to be a bank teller. She took out a loan and enrolled in a teller training course. Upon completing the course, she said, "I will be a bank teller by Friday." On Wednesday she was interviewed, and on Thursday she got the job. She is presently a bank teller at a nearby credit union. Desi has a way of doing anything she sets her mind to, and she's not afraid to work for her rewards.

This second draft has some of the same elements as the first draft, but it's a very different paragraph. Having revised her paragraph so that it focused on a more specific and interesting characteristic of her friend, P.J. was ready to begin a more detailed revision.

Writing Activity 4.1

- Using the five-step method that you've practiced in Chapters 1 and 3, write a paragraph describing a person or object.
- Let your paragraph get cold for about twenty-four hours, and then reread it carefully.
- If you can revise it so that it focuses more sharply on some part of your subject, do so.

As we promised, we will show you some ways of deciding what changes will improve your paragraph, so when your paragraph is ready for a detailed revision, begin by doing the following steps:

1. *Listen to it.* There are two ways of listening to your paper. One is to read it aloud to yourself, and the other is to have someone read it to you. Try both of these methods and see which one works better for you. Hearing how your ideas sound in spoken language is an amazingly effective way to find places where you haven't expressed yourself clearly enough. It also helps you spot where you're using stuffy or phony language, rather than writing in your own, natural voice.

2. *Read it with a different eye.* Pretend you are someone whose opinion you respect and would ask for. Spend a few minutes thinking about how that person might look at your paper; then read it as if you were that person. Seeing your writing from a different point of view can help you evaluate it more objectively.

3. *Analyze it.* Review the criteria for judging writing we listed in Chapter 1 (pages 14–15), and read your paper, asking the suggested questions.

As you do these steps, make notes in the margins of your paper about problems you see or things you might change. When you're finished, you are ready to begin the actual revision of your work. As you revise, you will see that when you make one change, others are necessary; these other changes often occur naturally. It is probably not possible to tell you everything you should look for as you revise. Writing is too individual an activity for that. However, we can tell you that good writers often play with their writing. They experiment with words, sentences, and ideas, and that is what you should do. As you experiment, try to

1. Find an interesting opening
2. Develop ideas fully
3. Connect ideas clearly
4. Use effective vocabulary
5. Vary sentence structures

Revise to Find an Interesting Opening

As you revise a piece of writing, think about the effect your opening sentence will have on your readers. People who write for newspapers and magazines call these openings "leads," and they know that a piece without a good lead may not get published and may not get read even if it is published. Here is what one writer says about leads.

> **What is a newspaper lead? It is the first paragraph of a story intended to seduce the reader into finishing the entire piece.** [Note that paragraphs in newspapers and magazines are often much shorter than the kinds of paragraphs you are writing.] **As Thomas Collins of Long Island, N.Y., *Newsday* once wrote, "The lead is to a newspaper writer what a home run is to a ballplayer—the sum total of his art, the feather in his cap, the pat on his back." Here are some examples:**
> **Lead on an article in *Capper's* about a publication that has urged its readers to go in for hugging: "The *Farmer's Almanac* has gone hug wild."**
> **From the Philadelphia *Inquirer*: "After going around in circles, the California Senate decided not to make the square dance the official state dance."**
> **In a *National Geographic* news feature: "To some 15 million Americans who suffer through the agonies of hay fever, pollen is unquestionably something to be sneezed at."**
> **The lead on an article about a reunion of old-time aviators: "Two veteran aviators met here yesterday for the first time in 40 years and discovered that of all the things that fly, time is the fastest."**

The lead is what "grabs" your readers' attention and draws them into your writing. Leads come in many forms. The leads above are mostly plays on words or old sayings, but the one from *National Geographic* also offers us a surprising fact—that 15 million Americans suffer from hay fever. A surprising fact or claim can often be an effective lead. Among other possibilities for leads are beginning at a dramatic moment in the action, describing a scene to help your reader see where events take place, or offering a quotation that sums up the situation or arouses the readers' curiosity. Let's look at some examples of each.

Lewis Thomas opens his essay, "On Warts," with this sentence:

"Warts are wonderful structures."

Since most people dread getting a wart and want to get rid of it as soon as it appears, Thomas' claim is startling—it says the opposite of what many people believe to be true. Guillermo Gomez-Pena opens "Documented/Undocumented" like this:

"I live smack in the fissure between two worlds, in the infected wound: half a block from the end of Western civilization and four miles from the start of the Mexican-American border, the northernmost point of Latin America."

The startling choice of words like "fissure" and "infected wound" draws the reader in.

"What was going on? A roar of laughter coming from the aphasia ward, just as the President's speech was coming on, and they had all been so eager to hear the President speaking. . . ."

That sentence opens Oliver Sacks' "The President's Speech" at the most dramatic moment of the essay, and the reader soon discovers what, indeed, was going on.

A description of a sunrise draws readers into Edward Abbey's "Cliffrose and Bayonets":

"A crimson sunrise streaked with gold flares out beyond Balanced Rock, beyond the arches and windows, beyond Grand Mesa in Colorado."

Gretel Ehrlich's "From a Sheepherder's Notebook" opens like this:

"When the phone rang it was John: 'Maurice just upped and quit and there ain't nobody else around, so you better get packed. I'm taking you out to herd sheep.'"

John's "there ain't nobody else around" tells us that his choice is desperate, so we continue to read to see what will happen to this greenhorn sheepherder.

Writing Activity 4.2

- On a separate piece of paper, write a sentence that might serve as a lead for the paragraph you wrote in Writing Activity 4.1. Make this lead a description of a scene in which the person or object is likely to be seen.

- Write a second possible lead for your paragraph, but make this one a quotation—something the person you are describing often says, something someone has said about the person or object you describe, or a well-known quotation that seems appropriate.

- Write a third possible lead; make a surprising claim or state a startling fact about the person or object you describe.

- When you are ready to do the next full draft of your paragraph, choose one of these leads and include it as your first sentence.

Revise to Develop Ideas Fully

English teachers often write "show, don't tell" on student papers. What they mean is that the student should add details, examples, and comparisons. These additions help your reader to see what you saw, hear what you heard, and so on. If readers are not familiar with your subject, they should be able to say when finished reading, "Oh, so *that's* the way it is." If familiar with your subject, they should be able to say, "Yes, that's *just* the way it is."

Your early drafts of paragraphs will often be full of sentences that just tell, for you will be concentrating on getting ideas onto paper. When you revise, however, you will need to look specifically for places where you might add detail to show. To illustrate, we have rewritten a wonderful paragraph by Rachel Carson, a famous naturalist, and in our rewrite we have left out the details she put in. We have told, while Rachel Carson has shown. Here's our telling version, followed by the paragraph as it originally appeared in the book *The Edge of the Sea*.

Our Version

One of my favorite paths to a rocky seacoast goes through an evergreen forest that I find enchanting. I usually go there in the early morning when it's barely light and slightly foggy. Many of the trees are dead—some standing and some fallen. All of them have moss and lichens growing on them. Moss also covers the ground. It's very quiet because the forest seems to muffle the sounds of nature.

Original Version

One of my own favorite approaches to a rocky seacoast is by a rough path through an evergreen forest that has its own peculiar enchantment. It is usually an early morning tide that takes me along that forest path, so that the light is still pale and fog drifts in from the sea beyond. It is almost a ghost forest, for among the living spruce and balsam are many dead trees—some sagging earthward, some lying on the floor of the forest. All the trees, the living and the dead, are clothed with green and silver crusts of lichens. Tufts of the bearded lichen or old man's beard hang from the branches like bits of sea mist tangled there. Green woodland mosses and a yielding carpet of reindeer moss cover the ground. In the quiet of that place even the voice of the surf is reduced to a whispered echo and the sounds of the forest are but the ghosts of sound—the faint sighing of evergreen needles in the moving air; the creaks and heavier groans of half-fallen trees resting against their neighbors and rubbing bark against bark; the light rattling fall of a dead branch broken under the feet of a squirrel and sent bouncing and ricocheting earthward.

The writer's use of the words "pale," "drifts," and "ghost forest" help show the enchantment of the forest and help to reinforce the controlling idea. She supplies details that help us see the trees more clearly, and she names the lichens and compares them to bits of sea mist, thus allowing us to visualize them more clearly. "Yielding carpet" shows the reader what it feels like to walk on the moss, and "whispered echo," "ghosts of sound," and the specific examples of sounds help to show the reader what sounds of nature are there in this forest.

Writing Activity 4.3

- Using the paragraph you wrote for activity 4.1, find sentences that merely tell.
- As you read, make notes or marks in the margins to identify where you need to make changes or additions.
- Revise your paragraph so it includes the details, examples, and comparisons that show.

Revise to Connect Ideas Clearly

Remember that in written communication, the audience does not have the clues to meaning that an audience has in spoken communication. There are no facial expressions, no voice tones, no gestures. There are only the words and punctuation on the page. As a result, writers use words and phrases whose only purpose is to show the relationships between ideas. These words and phrases are called **transitions**. The following paragraph by Camara Laye, a writer from French Guinea, illustrates several of the kinds of transitions one can use to connect ideas:

> At a sign from my father the apprentices began working two sheepskin bellows. The skins were on the floor, on opposite sides of the forge, connected to it by earthen pipes. While the work was in progress the apprentices sat in front of the bellows with crossed legs. That is, the younger of the two sat, for the elder was sometimes allowed to assist. But the younger—this time it was Sidafa—was only permitted to work the bellows and watch while waiting his turn for promotion to less rudimentary tasks. First one and then the other worked hard at the bellows: the flame in the forge rose higher and became a living thing, a genie implacable and full of life.

In the second sentence, "the skins" is a word repetition telling the reader that the sentence is about the sheepskin bellows. "While the work was in progress" is a time transition, letting the reader know when the described action takes place. "That is" signals the reader that what follows will explain or clarify the previous information. "But" signals a contrast or contradiction, and the "first-then" construction is another time transition.

Each sentence after the first in this paragraph opens with a transition, helping the reader to follow the chain of ideas. In your own writing, use transitions in this way; supply your readers with clear signals so that they can follow the flow of your ideas. This may seem artificial and awkward at first, but look back at our sample paragraph. If you had read it without our initial note or later comments, you probably would never have noticed the transitions. You would only have been aware that the paragraph communicated clearly.

Writing Activity 4.4

- Look at the beginning of each sentence after the first in your own paragraph. Does it contain a word or phrase that ties it to the preceding sentence?
- Supply transitions so that the relationship of each sentence to the one before it is clear.

Revise to Use Effective Vocabulary

The words you choose as you write do a great deal to show not only what you are writing about but also your attitude toward your subject. For example, we might write, "The skinny girl walked in," or "The slender lady glided in," or "The lithe woman slinked in." Each of these sentences could describe the same event, but each shows a different attitude on the part of the writer.

Carefully chosen words can convey actions, ideas, and emotions in very powerful ways. To illustrate, we have again taken the liberty of changing a paragraph, this time one by the well-known author John Steinbeck. Again, we'll first look at our version; then we'll see what made the original more effective.

Our Version

The wind got there when they said it would, and blew hard across the water. It hit like a ton of bricks. The top of a tree blew off, almost hitting the place where we watched. The next gust pushed one of the windows in. I pushed it back and put wedges in the top and bottom with a hand ax. . . . The trees waved and bent, and the water became foamy. A boat got loose and blew up on the shore, and then another.

Original Version

The wind struck on the moment we were told it would, and ripped the water like a black sheet. It hammered like a fist. The whole top of an oak tree crashed down, grazing the cottage where we watched. The next gust stove one of the big windows in. I forced it back and drove wedges in top and bottom with a hand ax. . . . The trees plunged and bent like grasses, and the whipped water raised a cream of foam. A boat broke loose and tobogganed up on the shore, and then another.

Words like "struck," "ripped," "hammered," "crashed," "stove," "forced," "drove," "plunged," "bent," and "tobogganed" certainly show the fury and activity Steinbeck wanted to portray.

As you experiment with words, use a **thesaurus**. A thesaurus is a dictionary-like book that lists words and gives other words with similar and opposite meanings. As a treasure-house of words, it can be an important tool for a writer, but we must offer a caution: be sure to use a dictionary with it. Sometimes the thesaurus will give you a word that means almost the same thing as another, but there may be enough of a difference in meaning to make it inappropriate for the way you want to use it.

Writing Activity 4.5

- Once again look at your paragraph from activity 4.1.
- Underline words that you think could be made stronger.

- Using a thesaurus, find words to replace at least five of those you underlined.
- Be sure to use a dictionary for any word you are not certain about.

Revise to Vary Sentence Structures

Sentences are the basic unit for expressing ideas in the English language. If you are a native speaker of English, you know a tremendous amount about sentences already, and you are often a good judge of whether a sentence is clear. When a sentence is not clear, however, analyzing why it isn't can be a complex task. Most of the sections of our Handbook talk about ways of making your sentences clear, and much of your education as a writer will deal with this problem. Obviously, then, we cannot hope to do more than brush the surface of this important skill in this short section. We can, however, offer the following suggestions:

Sentence Checklist

1. Be sure each of your sentences expresses at least one complete thought. To check a paragraph, write your first sentence on a piece of paper, and read the sentence aloud. This allows your eye to see the sentence as a complete unit. It also converts the written language to the more familiar spoken language, thus allowing you to check the sentence for completeness by hearing it. If it is not a complete thought, revise the sentence until it is. Then skip a line, write the paragraph's next sentence, and read it aloud on its own, revising as necessary. Repeat this procedure for each sentence in your paragraph. For a more detailed discussion of checking your sentences, see the Handbook.

2. Try varying your **sentence structure**. Often an idea becomes clearer when it is paired with other ideas. Take, for example, the following sentences:

My daughter Jennifer hates school. She loves to go downtown. She loves to hang out in the record stores.

We can give the reader that same information more simply and clearly by combining those three sentences into one:

My daughter Jennifer hates school, but she loves to hang out in the record stores downtown.

Often, however, an idea can become clearer when it is set off by itself as a separate sentence instead of included in another. Here's an example:

"All right, young man! If you think you're tougher than your dad, stand up!" shouted my father, so I stood up.

Look at the emphasis the last idea gains when it is set off by itself:

"All right, young man! If you think you're tougher than your dad, stand up!" shouted my father. I stood up.

3. Eliminate **wordiness** and stuffy or phony language. Many people seem to think that using long sentences and big words will make their writing sound good, but when the lengths of the sentences and words interfere with meaning, the writing is ineffective. It doesn't do what it is intended to do. Here is a student example from a recent paper:

It is my sincere hope that my college education will enable me to find employment in the area of education teaching at the fifth-grade level.

Revised, the sentence reads:

I hope that my education will help me find a job as a fifth-grade teacher.

As the next example shows, even professionals fall into the trap of thinking that longer is better. This is the first paragraph from an article in the *Journal of Higher Education*:

The term "computer literacy" has become de rigueur among avant garde educators and public officials. De-

spite its frequent use, however, computer literacy remains an amorphous concept. The purpose of this article is to postulate a planning framework which a college can use to decide what its students need to know about computers.

The words "de rigueur" and "avant garde" are foreign words which have perfectly good English equivalents. "Amorphous concept" and "postulate" are unnecessarily long words. Writers should try to state their ideas clearly and directly, especially in an introduction.

After careful revision, a simpler and more understandable introduction would look like this:

Leading educators and public officials frequently use the term "computer literacy." Despite its frequent use, however, the term is not well-defined. The purpose of this article is to suggest a way in which a college can decide what its students need to know about computers.

4. Make sure the relationship of the ideas in your sentences is clear. The main reason for studying grammar and punctuation rules is to understand how these relationships are shown, and your skill in writing and revising sentences will grow as you learn and apply the rules. For now, we'll show you three sentences with unclear relationships and how they can be corrected.

Swaying in the breeze, I saw the spider hanging by a thin web.

Cover up the words after "I saw." You will see that as the sentence reads, it says that the speaker ("I") was swaying in the breeze. The revision makes clear that the spider, not the speaker, was swaying:

I saw the spider swaying in the breeze, hanging by its thin web.

Here's another example.

My brother told his friend he had a flat tire.

We don't know who had the flat tire. Was it my brother or his friend? The revision makes it clear:

My brother told his friend, "I have a flat tire."

Here's a final example of faulty sentence relationships:

I don't know much about music. I enjoy going to concerts.

There seems to be a contradiction here, and the writer seems not to recognize it. The revision shows that the writer recognizes the apparent contradiction:

Although I don't know much about music, I enjoy going to concerts.

These examples illustrate just a few of the possible problems in showing relationships among ideas. You can learn more about such problems by studying the Handbook, but you'll find that you can spot many problems in your own writing simply by being aware that the relationships need to be clear. Ask yourself, "Just how are those ideas related?" Because you know English, you know a lot about how relationships are expressed. You know, for example, that "but" shows a different relationship between two ideas than does "so." Let your ear guide you.

Writing Activity 4.6

- Refer again to the paragraph you wrote for activity 4.1.
- Write each sentence as described in Step 1 of the Sentence Checklist (page 60) and make any necessary changes.
- Experiment with sentence variety.
- Eliminate any wordiness or stuffy language.
- Check the logical relationships of ideas and make any necessary changes.

Putting It All Together

Because revising is a continuous process, you rarely rewrite a paragraph and fix only one problem at a time. More often, you'll solve several problems at the same time: as you work to improve clarity, you will automatically change vocabulary and sentence structure along the way. Going step by step, however, gives you a definite place to start and helps make sure that you haven't overlooked something important.

As you revise each draft, think first about your lead. Will it grab your readers' interest? What might you do to make it more effective? Next, look at the main points of your paragraph. Have you adequately developed each one? Does your paragraph show rather than tell? Third, look at the transitions between each of your sentences. Have you supplied words or phrases that will lead your readers clearly from one idea to the next? Fourth, check your vocabulary. Do the words accurately show the important points about your subject? Do they accurately reflect your attitude toward your subject? Will your readers find them interesting? Finally, look at your sentence structures. Are they varied? Is your wording clear? Are the relationships of the ideas clear?

To illustrate the process of revision, we'll close this chapter with three drafts of a student paragraph. As you look at each draft, remember that revising is a complex process and that all the steps are related to each other. These revisions illustrate this complexity very nicely.

Three Drafts of a Student Paragraph

One of our students, Dannette, wrote the following three drafts of a paragraph. Notice how in each successive draft she makes important changes until she has created a paragraph that clearly supports its controlling idea and makes the subject come alive for her readers.

Draft 1

There's more to Joe Murphy than meets the eye. He has arthritis, and it has disfigured his hands. His knuckles are big and swollen, but his fingers are long and slender. They're clenched into a permanent loose fist, and you could never tell by looking that his hands have done so much during his life. Although a yellowish film clouds his eyes, they have seen a lot in his lifetime. He saw World War II, the Depression, and the rebuilding of our nation. His big nose shows his fondness for whiskey, but his sense of smell is almost gone. His ears are big, too, and he's losing his hearing, but he's enjoyed a lot of music in his lifetime.

In reviewing her paragraph, Dannette decided she needed a more interesting lead. Most important, she decided, was developing her ideas to show more about Joe Murphy—what the eye sees and what the eye doesn't see. As you can see in the next draft, other improvements took place almost automatically as she blended her changes smoothly into the paragraph.

Draft 2

At first glance you see an insignificant, white-haired Irishman whose frail, slow-moving body hides his past. But there's more to Joe Murphy than meets the eye. The first thing you notice about him is his hands. They lie in his lap, the knuckles swollen by arthritis, curled into a claw-like clench. Those fingers, though, have played the fiddle, worked on hydro-electric dams, harvested forests, and farmed the land. As your eyes move from his hands to his face, they meet his intense blue eyes now clouded by a yellowish film. His eyes may not see you very well, but they saw the Depression, the rebuilding of this country under FDR's New Deal, and the horror of World War II. His dark-rimmed glasses perch on his most prominent feature, his nose. Its red skin and dark blue veins remind everyone of his fondness for whiskey, even though he hasn't drunk for ten years, and sixty years of smoking have destroyed its sense of smell. As swollen and knobby as his nose, his ears, too, have lost their usefulness. He will never again hear the music and laughter that were so much a part of his life.

In this second draft, Dannette has begun with a brief description of her subject and a hint about his past that rouses the readers' curiosity. In improving development, Dannette has also improved her vocabulary and sentence structures. Compare, for example, the description of his hands. In the first draft she *tells* us that arthritis has disfigured his hands, but in the second draft she *shows* us. In the first draft she *tells* us the hands have done many things, but in the second draft she *shows* us. Notice, too, how smoothly the transition, "As your eyes move from his hands to his face," shifts our attention to this new feature.

As Dannette thought about her third draft, she decided to add more detail about Joe's life. She had remembered more as she wrote her second draft, and, as she thought about the fullness of Joe's life, she decided to make her controlling idea more specific.

Draft 3

At first glance you see an insignificant Irishman well past his prime, but the frail, slow-moving body has lived abundantly. The first thing you notice about him is his once powerful hands. Enlarged knuckles seem gigantic compared to his slender, elongated fingers which arthritis has bent into a claw-like clench, his thumbs curling outward like the horn of a horse's saddle. Those hands, though, have played the fiddle and have worked on huge hydro-electric dams and in dark, dusty coal mines. They have helped to raise power lines that stretched over the mountains to the farmers in the valleys below. They have harvested forests and made a living by farming the land. As your eyes move from his hands to his face, they meet his intense, sky-blue eyes, now clouded by a yellowish film. They may not see you very well, but those eyes saw homeless people walking the roads during the great Depression. They saw the many projects of FDR's New Deal, and they saw frightened, angry people massed on every street corner on December 7, 1941. His dark-rimmed glasses sit on a nose covered with large-pored skin, skin like the peel of an orange. Dark blue veins show through the skin reminding everyone of Joe's fondness for whiskey even though he hasn't drunk for a decade, and sixty years of smoking have destroyed his sense of smell. As swollen and knobby as his nose, his ears, too, have lost their usefulness. He will never again hear the music and laughter that were so important a part of his rich and full life.

Notice how the last sentence of the paragraph now echoes the first, bringing the paragraph smoothly to a close. Notice, too, the use of comparisons—thumbs "like the horn of a horse's saddle" and skin "like the peel of an orange." Such comparisons are very effective in creating pictures in a reader's mind.

Some of Dannette's changes were planned, and some were simply suggested by other changes she made, but the effect is a much improved paragraph, one that clearly shows its subject and the writer's point about that subject.

As you have seen, revising is a complex activity, but it can be made less complex by dividing the process into steps. First, let your writing get cold. You'll do a better job of revision when you can see your writing more objectively. Next, do the three reading steps of listening to it, reading it with a different eye, and analyzing it. Finally, begin the actual revision of your paragraph by playing with it. First, experiment with different openings. Second, develop your ideas by showing, not telling. Third, use transitions to connect your ideas within the paragraph. Fourth, experiment with different vocabulary to find the most effective words. Finally, work carefully with your sentence structures. Refer back to this chapter as you work through this book. Revision is a skill that needs to be practiced continually.

Writing Activity 4.7

- Revise the paragraph you wrote for activity 4.1.
- Make as many revisions as you need to reach a final draft.

PREVIEW FOR CHAPTER 5

The in-house suspension room at Rogers High School is in a far corner on the third floor, away from all the classrooms. A heavy metal door closes with a strong hollow thump as the metal frame and door strike against each other. Stark yellow walls have no decorations, and twelve chairs set into booths face the wall. The silence is broken only by the dull, continuous whir of an exhaust fan.

The Mexican market place is full of the most wonderful sights and smells. There are rows of small shops that you can wander in and out of. Leathercrafters, with tools the size of small nails, whittle out patterns before your eyes. A glass blower, who I could watch for hours, blows tubes of glass into wonderful creations. Pottery, from casserole dishes to piggy banks, are hand painted right there, so the smell of fresh paint lingers in the air. Best of all is the bakery where cooks make tortillas and empanada, a pastry filled with fruit.

Our garden grew. The pumpkin plants were magnificent. In no time they covered the fledgling corn and charged blatantly over the radishes. By July, the carrots had fallen asunder and the back lawn was in serious danger. Vines sashayed around the rose bush and embraced the fence. The fruits we thought would be pumpkins began to form and resemble baseballs, white and perfectly round. Eventually these mysterious orbs reached volleyball size.

My memories of Casper, Wyoming, are memories of blustery wind.

5 WRITING ABOUT A PLACE

SKILLS INTRODUCED

Analyzing outlines
Using the observation chart
Showing sense impressions
Using specific detail

"What did your house look like when you were a little girl?" "Tell us about the island where you spent your vacation." People ask questions like these because they are curious about places. Histories and biographies describe places because events are often influenced by the places where they happen. Travel brochures describe places in order to interest prospective tourists. Novelists describe places to help us see the settings in which the actions of the stories occur. People write about places in their diaries or journals because the act of writing helps them remember those places more vividly than they otherwise might. People enjoy reading about places because they can thus experience new scenes or because they can re-experience familiar ones. Understanding the skills involved in describing places can help you create or re-create the experience of a place for yourself and your readers.

This chapter will continue the development of your writing skills by taking you once again through the five steps of the writing process you followed in the first chapter:

1. Brainstorm to discover what you know
2. Write the topic sentence
3. Outline the paragraph
4. Write the first draft
5. Revise the paragraph

Along the way, we'll discuss some of the special things you must keep in mind as you write descriptions of places, but you're ready now to begin step one.

STEP 1:
Brainstorm to Discover What You Know

Before you start writing we will show you an example of a problem that students often encounter. The problem is that of trying to write a description from memory rather than from direct observation. Descriptions from memory can be written, of course, but to write an effective description from memory, you must have done some careful observation at some time in the past. Most of us are not careful observers, however. Our memories are too vague and general to produce vivid descriptive writing. Here, for example, is the kind of brainstorming list that is often created when someone is trying to write about a place from memory.

1. sound of creek
2. lots of trees
3. rocks
4. meadow
5. tents
6. beautiful
7. peaceful
8. away from hustle and bustle
9. hot and sunny
10. mosquitoes

11. birds singing

12. smell of trees and grass

Now to see why that list won't work, let's try to make an outline from it. We feel that "peaceful" is the dominant impression or controlling idea. Here's our outline.

Topic sentence:

The campsite at Cedar Creek is a very peaceful place.

Topic sentence question:

What makes the campsite a peaceful place?

Answers:

1. **It is beautiful.**

2. **It is peaceful.**

3. **It is away from the hustle and bustle.**

4. **The sights are peaceful.**

5. **The sounds are peaceful.**

The problems with this outline come mainly from the fact that the details are too general. It would be difficult to write a paragraph that creates a specific picture in the reader's mind. For example, look at the word "beautiful." This word means many things to many people. What's beautiful to us may not be beautiful to anyone else, so if we used a word like beautiful in our paragraph, we'd have to develop it with specific information about why we think the place is beautiful.

Another problem is the answer, "It is peaceful." "Peaceful" has the same problem as "beautiful" (it is too vague), but it also repeats the controlling word of the topic sentence. In effect we're saying, "The campsite is peaceful because it's peaceful." People who study logic call this "circular reasoning," but it doesn't take a label for us to see that the idea isn't likely to lead us anywhere. The phrase "away from the hustle and bustle" is also too general, and it pulls our attention away from the campsite back to places that aren't peaceful. This idea certainly belongs in the list of details—since that's where we write down anything that comes to mind when we brainstorm about our subject—but it may cause the paragraph to lose its unity if added to the outline. "Sights" and "sounds," like the other words, have little specific information to suggest to us, the writers, what we must do in order to show you, the reader, what's peaceful about the campsite.

The trouble with our list, then, is that there is nothing in it that will help us to be specific. Before we can do an adequate job of developing the paragraph, we'll have to do a direct observation to decide what qualities the place has that make us say it's peaceful and to check whether our impression is accurate.

When you describe a place, you want to create as clear a picture of it as you can in your reader's mind. That means you must spend your brainstorming time getting a clear picture of it in your own mind, and one way to do that is to make a list using an observation chart. Whether you are writing from memory or from direct observation, the chart will call your attention to details you might otherwise overlook. Figure 5-1 is a chart that Jan made as she remembered a kitchen in a house she had visited often as a child.

Writing Activity 5.1

- Choose a place to write about and, using a chart like the one in Figure 5-1, list the details you observe or remember.
- Observe carefully and fully, putting as many details as you can into each column.

Step 2:
Write the Topic Sentence

Remember that your topic sentence must identify the place you are describing, and it must state your dominant impression of that place. The word that states your dominant impression will be the controlling idea of your paragraph. For example, if you write "The intersection of Third and Madison is confusing," you have identified "confusing" as your dominant impression of that place, and the details of your paragraph will show what makes that intersection confusing. "That was the messiest office I've ever seen" is another statement of dominant impression, as is, "This garden is well cared for." "Messy" and "well cared for" are the controlling ideas in the last two examples.

As you review your observation chart, you might discover two or three ideas that can work as dominant impressions for a paragraph, and you'll need

Observation Chart: Farmhouse Kitchen			
Sight	*Sound*	*Smell / Taste*	*Touch / Movement*
old wood cookstove— black top, white front, sides, shelf	aunts and uncles talking	food cooking	warmth
	cats purring	tamarack firewood	heat
two old rocking chairs, one wood with cloth seat, one cloth	clang of stove lids	pungent wood smoke	Polly moving around kitchen, stepping over feet
	pots bubbling on stove	Uncle Jim's pipe	
cats sleeping	water running	turkey roasting	people walking from kitchen to living room
pink and gray roses on flowered wallpaper— green leaves	firewood crackling in stove	pies baking	smoke rising from stove
dirty pink walls pink sooty ceiling			Polly opening oven
never changes			
people standing and sitting			
fir branches outside window			
birds in feeder			
pink floor			
pink counter top			

Figure 5–1

to decide which of these will best suit your audience and your purpose. What interests you most about the place you have chosen? To whom are you writing? What do you want your readers to understand about the place you are describing? As Jan reviewed her chart, she noticed that the idea of warmth appeared several times, and as she thought about the kitchen she decided that she would focus on warmth as her controlling idea. She thought that many of her readers might remember family gatherings in old houses and that they might enjoy hearing about her memories of a special place.

She stated her dominant impression in a complete sentence, and that became her topic sentence:

I remember the warmth of the kitchen in the old farmhouse.

This sentence names the place being described and states the dominant impression.

Writing Activity 5.2

- Review your chart and record your dominant impression.
- Think carefully about your reading audience. Who are your readers? How do you want them to respond to your paragraph?
- Write a possible topic sentence.

With a topic sentence that named the place she would describe and that stated her dominant impression of the place, Jan was ready to outline her paragraph, choosing from her chart details that would show the warmth of the kitchen.

STEP 3:
Outline the Paragraph

Remember that the first step in outlining is to turn the topic sentence into a question that begins with *who, what, when, where, why, how,* or *in what way.* Use the words from your topic sentence to complete your question. This keeps your attention focused on the controlling idea; it helps you be sure that the controlling idea does, in fact, control the paragraph. Here is Jan's question.

What made the kitchen in the old farmhouse warm?

To complete her outline, Jan wrote five answers.

1. **The wood cookstove always had a fire in it.**
2. **People laughed and visited there.**
3. **Comfortable rocking chairs with sleeping cats stood in front of the stove.**
4. **Warm pink colors decorated the floor and walls.**
5. **Warm smells filled the kitchen.**

The answers are all in complete sentences, and each one directly answers the topic sentence question, so Jan can be sure that her paragraph will have unity—that it will focus on the dominant impression of warmth.

Writing Activity 5.3

- Outline your paragraph using details from your observation chart.

STEP 4:
Write the First Draft

In the "Standards for Judging Writing" (pages 14–15), one question about development asks, "Have you provided enough information for your reader to see or feel or understand what you're talking about?" Your task in writing description is to help your reader experience the place as you have experienced it. That means you must include specific sensory detail in your paragraph—the sights, sounds, smells and so forth that you included in your observation chart or that you remembered as you wrote your draft. The focus or controlling idea of Jan's paragraph is warmth. Read over her first draft and see if the details convince you that the old farmhouse kitchen is, indeed, a warm place to be.

First Draft

I remember the warmth of the kitchen in the old farmhouse. I remember most the heat from the old wood cookstove and the smell of food cooking. The kitchen was always full of people with Polly trying to cook around them. Two old rocking chairs sat in front of the stove, and the two cats were always in them. Wallpaper covered the lower half of the dirty, pink, plaster walls, and the color of the ceiling barely showed through the layers of soot. Part of what made it so warm and comfortable was the fact that it hardly changed over the years. Even now, I can hear Polly opening and closing the stove lids to put in another stick of wood, and I can still see and smell the smoke that rose to blacken the ceiling even more.

Jan has used a variety of words and details that suggest warmth. Words like "heat," "comfortable," and "warm" directly suggest or state the dominant impression.

Writing Activity 5.4

- Write a first draft of your paragraph. Try to use words that state or suggest your dominant impression.
- When you have finished your first draft, let it sit for a time before you go to Step 5.

STEP 5:
Revise the Paragraph

As you revise your paragraph, remember that while you have directly experienced the place you are describing, your readers probably have not. It is only through the details you choose and the words you write on the page that you can show your readers the place you are describing and help them relate it to their own experiences. As we said in Chapter 4, it isn't enough to just tell, you have to show. To see sentences that simply tell, let's look back at Jan's first draft and ask some questions:

- Can you smell food cooking? What do you smell?
- Can you see Polly trying to cook? What is she doing?
- Can you hear the stove lids? What do they sound like?
- Can you smell the wood smoke? What does it smell like?
- Can you see the wallpaper? What is its pattern?

Thinking about these kinds of questions, Jan revised her paragraph so that it could show her reading audience what the kitchen was like. After all, to readers who have spent their lives in city apartments, a kitchen in an old farmhouse might be a foreign place, and her job is to show them that place. Here's her revision.

Revised Draft

"Open that oven door and get out of the way," Polly would call, and three aunts would rush to do her bidding. That was a special time full of good memories, but I especially remember the warmth of the kitchen in Polly's old farmhouse. The soft heat radiated from the ancient wood cookstove and the wonderful aromas of turkey roasting and apple and pumpkin pies baking filled the air. On late autumn days the kitchen was always full of uncles and aunts, visiting and laughing as Polly wove among them, moving from stove to sink to refrigerator, stepping over their legs and feet. Two worn rocking chairs sat in front of the stove, and the two cats either dozed on the soft cloth seats or purred in the laps of people who had claimed a greater right to the comfort. Large gray and pink roses decorated the wallpaper that covered the lower half of the dirty, pink, plaster walls, and the pink of the ceiling barely showed through the layers of soot. That was part of what made it so warm and comfortable; it had hardly changed in the years that I'd been going there. Even now, I can hear the clang of

the iron stove lids as Polly opened them to stuff in another
stick of tamarack, and I can still feel the pungent wood
smoke burning my nostrils as it rose to blacken the ceiling
even more. The sights, sounds, smells and love in that old
kitchen are a precious part of my life.

Now the paragraph shows rather than simply tells. Readers are likely to
have smelled turkey or pies cooking, they can see what Polly does as she
weaves around the kitchen, and they can hear the clang of the iron stove lids.
Jan has added a lead, a quote from Polly, to catch her readers' interest.

**Writing
Activity
5.5**

- Revise your paragraph, doing your best to show
  rather than tell.
- Try to make your words as specific as you can.
- Review Chapter 4 to remind yourself of leads and of
  other revising techniques.

As you have probably seen in your work for this chapter, the brainstorming step is especially important. Carefully observing a place or thoroughly
searching your memory allows you to reach a dominant impression that accurately reflects your experience of the place, and referring back to your list of
details will help you develop your paragraph as you write and revise. In other
words, careful brainstorming is the key that helps you show rather than tell
your reader what you are writing about.

Samples from Professional Writers

As you read through the professional examples that end this chapter,
note how clearly they show you the places they describe. The first selection is
from Isak Dinesen's book *Out of Africa*. Dinesen writes from her own experience, having lived in Africa for many years, and the book served as a basis for
a movie of the same name.

The geographical position and the height of the land combined to create a landscape that had not its like in all the world. There was no fat on it and no luxuriance anywhere; it was Africa distilled up through six thousand feet, like the strong and refined essence of a continent. The colours were dry and burnt, like the colours in pottery. The trees had a light and delicate foliage, the structure of which was different from that of the trees in Europe; it did not grow in bows or cupolas, but in horizontal layers, and the formation gave to the tall solitary trees a likeness to the palms, or a heroic and romantic air like fullrigged ships with their sails clewed up, and to the edge of a wood a strange appearance as if the whole wood were faintly vibrating. Upon the grass of the great plains the crooked bare old thorn-trees were scattered, and the grass was spiced like thyme and bog-myrtle; in some places the scent was so strong, that it smarted in the nostrils. All the flowers that you found on the plains, or upon the creepers and liana in the native forest, were diminutive like flowers of the downs,—only just in the beginning of the long rains a number of big, massive heavy-scented lilies sprang out on the plains. The views were immensely wide. Everything that you saw made for greatness and freedom, and unequalled nobility.

The next two selections are from *Invisible Man* by Ralph Ellison, winner of a National Book Award.

It was a beautiful college. The buildings were old and covered with vines and the roads gracefully winding, lined with hedges and wild roses that dazzled the eyes in the summer sun. Honeysuckle and purple wisteria hung heavy from the trees and white magnolias mixed with their scents in the bee-humming air. I've recalled it often, here in my hole: How the grass turned green in the springtime and how the mocking birds fluttered their tails and sang, how the moon shone down on the buildings, how the bell in the chapel tower rang out the precious short-lived hours; how the girls in bright summer dresses promenaded the grassy lawn. Many times, here at night, I've closed my eyes and walked along the forbidden road that winds past the girls' dormitories, past the hall with the clock in the tower, its windows warmly aglow, on down past the small white Home Economics practice cottage, whiter still in the moonlight, and on down the road with its sloping and turning, paralleling the black powerhouse with its engines droning earth-shaking rhythms in the dark, its windows red from the glow of the furnace, on to where the road became a bridge over a dry riverbed, tangled with brush and clinging vines; the bridge of rustic logs, made for trysting, but virginal and untested by lovers; on up the road, past the buildings, with the southern verandas half-a-city-block long, to the sudden forking, barren of buildings, birds, or grass, where the road turned off to the insane asylum.

The next selection describes a reception room.

Beyond the door it was like a museum. I had entered a large reception room decorated with cool tropical colors. One wall was almost covered by a huge colored map, from which narrow red silk ribbons stretched tautly from each division of the map to a series of ebony pedestals, upon which sat glass specimen jars containing natural products of the various countries. It was an importing firm. I looked around the room, amazed. There were paintings, bronzes, tapestries, all beautifully arranged. I was dazzled and so taken aback that I almost dropped my brief case when I heard a voice say, "And what would your business be?"

Other Suggestions for Writing

1. Write about the scenery in the opening of your favorite movie.
2. Write about a place that made you afraid to be there.
3. Write about your favorite hangout—a restaurant, a bowling alley, a tavern, a gallery.
4. Write about a place whose beauty took your breath away.

5. Write about a place you've seen recently after a long absence—an old neighborhood, a former house, your elementary school.

6. Write about a place you worked hard to make your own, to feel comfortable in, to reflect who you are.

PREVIEW FOR CHAPTER 6

At midnight, Boston seemed to come alive. Engines roared, tires squealed, and horns honked as people raced their cars up and down the street near Kenmore square. Sirens shrilled and quavered as fire trucks and ambulances competed with crazy drivers for a space on those crazy streets.

I had watched him from the time he left the top of the Hooter, the toughest run of the Eaglecrest Ski Resort. He had sailed down the slope, attacking each perfectly formed mogul, almost obscured by the powder snow that sprayed from beneath his skis, but now he was at the cliff. Boom! He was in the air, sailing with the wind. Bam! He sank into the soft cushion of powder.

She sat crosslegged, looking from the flower to her sketch pad, her whole being intent on making the drawing perfect. The pencil moved upright as she crafted a line, then sloped almost flat, moving quickly to create some shading. The purple wildflower swayed slightly in the breeze, echoing the movement of her hair.

The flower seller moves three tiny dance steps forward, twirls almost a full circle, and dances back again. With one hand she waves red roses peeking from the green paper that holds them, and with the other hand she beckons, flirting with the traffic, smiling and waving at every car that passes.

6 WRITING ABOUT AN ACTIVITY

You read newspaper descriptions of ball games, horse races, and high-speed chases. You write letters describing the activities of your friends, your children, or your grandchildren. When someone does something that amuses, excites, or upsets you, you share your feelings and impressions with others; you show them some of what is happening in your world and how you react to it. Your readers are people who will probably be interested in the events themselves, in your responses to the events, or both.

Because you are a unique individual, you see any activity from your own **point of view**; what you see and how you respond to it is determined by who you are and what you've experienced. To make your readers see, feel, and understand things from your point of view, you must observe carefully and be aware of your own responses. The brainstorming step of the paragraph you will write for this chapter is your observation of an activity.

STEP 1:
Brainstorm to Discover What You Know

In this section, we show you two observers watching an activity, one using clustering to record her observations, the other listing. Either technique works well; use the one that is most effective for you.

As you brainstorm, try for the right word the first time. You might, for example, make a note that says,

boy runs from first to second

But you might also record,

boy trots confidently from first to second

Note how the second version captures the specific action. If you begin your observations by planning to use the best words to describe what happens and how it happens, you will find yourself watching the action and the actors more closely. Of course your first task is simply to observe and record the action, so you can't spend too much time searching for just the right word. Get in the habit, though, of asking, "What, exactly, did he do?" "How, exactly, did she do that?" "What word can best show that action and attitude to a reader?" The more you practice looking for the right words, the more quickly the right words will come to you, so practice looking at any action through the eyes of a writer, a person who paints pictures with words.

Two kinds of words will be especially important to you: **verbs** and **adverbs**.

> **verb:** A word that shows action or state of being. In the sentence, "The girl danced," "danced" is a verb; it shows action. In the sentence, "The girl was tired," "was" is a verb; it shows a state of being. The Handbook tells you more about verbs.

> **adverb:** A word that modifies—describes or tells more about—a verb, adjective, another adverb, or even a whole sentence. In the sentence, "The boy shouted happily," "happily" is an adverb, and it modifies the verb "shouted." An adverb often answers the question, "How was it done?"

The following two sentences show how careful choice of verbs and adverbs can make a description of an activity more effective.

The dancer lifted her leg off the floor. At the same time, her arm rose over her head.

The dancer stretched her leg slowly, almost painfully, off the floor. At the same time, her arm weightlessly drifted over her head.

The choice of the verb "stretched" instead of "lifted," and the addition of the two adverbs, "slowly" and "painfully," give a far clearer picture of how the action happened. Changing the verb "rose" to "drifted" and adding the adverb "weightlessly" also helps the reader to picture the action more clearly. As you brainstorm, and as you review your brainstorming, be conscious of your word choices.

Finally, remember to use all of your senses. Record not only what you see, but also what you hear, taste, smell, and touch, as well.

As our example for this chapter, we observed Marcia's two small children eating some sweet rolls. We made separate observations, and then we each wrote about the activity without comparing notes. Even though we watched the same activity, each of us brought a different personality and set of experiences to the observation. The difference in point of view is evident even in our observations. See Figure 6-1 for Marcia's cluster of observations and the following list for Ed's observations.

Ed's List of Details

1. Stacey growls and giggles

2. Leans over table—on knees on high chair

3. Holds hands apart and in front, giggles

4. Jeff picks chocolate off, throws back head, comments to Stacey

5. Stacey brushes hair back, takes another bite, licks fingers

6. "There's frosting inside mine"—walks around table, extending finger—Stacey carefully licks his finger clean

7. "I got salt on mine"—leans across table, extending finger—Jeff smacks sugar off her finger

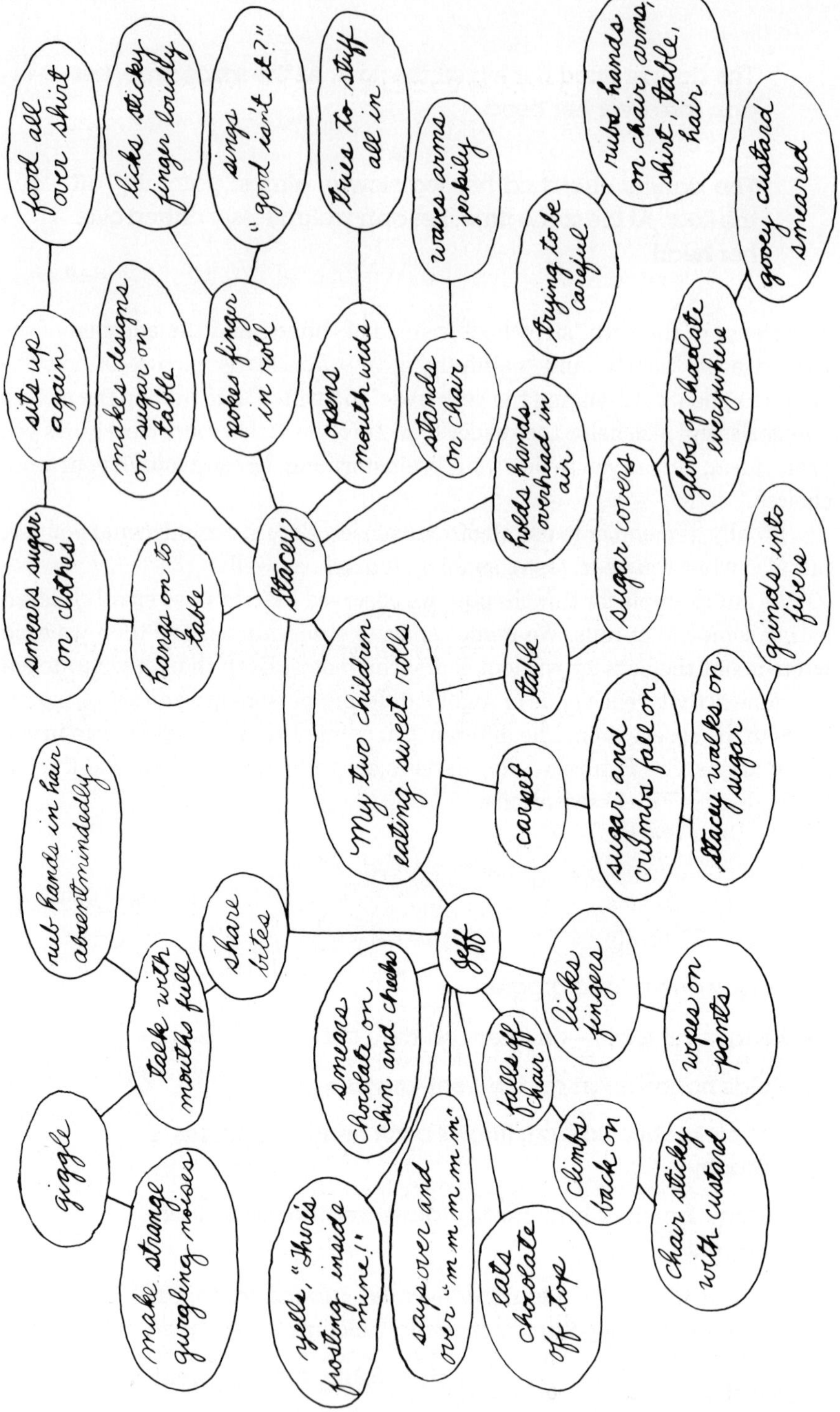

Figure 6-1   Marcia's Cluster: Two Children Eating Sweet Rolls

8. Jeff moves to stool so he can share with Stacey

9. Jeff's eating slows to tasting custard from his, sugar from Stacey's

10. Jeff chatters, Stacey eats, blows a "razzberry" on palm of hand

11. Stacey smears powdered sugar on table, blows another razzberry, looks around to see if she can get a laugh—no laugh

12. Jeff blows razzberry and giggles, Stacey does too

13. Jeff reaches inside and takes custard out with fingers, picks up roll and takes a big bite, roll wraps halfway around his head

14. S. does a little dance in her chair, leans on one elbow on table, licks fingers and giggles

15. J. runs to kitchen, asks for milk

16. Sits on stool, goes over top and falls to floor, bumps head, goes for a kiss, returns, drapes self on stool, takes fingerful of custard, cocks head, puts finger in mouth, rocks on stool

17. Each has roll about half gone, Stacey licks finger, then waves hand

18. Stacey blows a razzberry on hand

19. Stacey settles back, eats meditatively, drinks milk, puts cup down, looks over her shoulder and says, "No monsters behind me." Plays with her shoe.

Looking back over the two sets of details, you can see that different observers see different things. What you observe and how you interpret it will depend on your point of view—who and where you are in relation to the action and the actors. For example, many of the details of Marcia's cluster focus on the mess the kids are making, while details of Ed's list focus on the fun the kids are having.

Differences in point of view have led to the use of instant replays in football games, but as any fan knows, even the instant replays don't always stop arguments about what did or didn't happen. No two people see quite the same thing or interpret what they see in quite the same way, and that fact makes the job of the writer important. If people are to understand each other, they must know that points of view differ; one way they can know that is to see different points of view in people's writing.

Writing Activity 6.1

- Choose an activity you find interesting.
- Carefully observe it, recording the events as you see them happen.
- Use strong verbs and adverbs.
- Use as many of your senses as you can.

STEP 2
Write the Topic Sentence

Looking back at our brainstorming, you can see that Marcia watches the activity from the perspective of a mother and chief cleaner-upper. Her focus, then, is on the mess and the work it creates for her. Her point of view helps shape her topic sentence:

I watched, dismayed, as my two children ate their rolls.

Ed, on the other hand, is a little more neutral or impartial in his observation. It's not his house, he likes the children, and he enjoys watching them have fun. His topic sentence is:

The kids were delighted with their treat.

Sometimes you will quickly form a dominant impression of an event, but sometimes it can be hard to state your dominant impression. If you're having trouble, ask yourself what one word you would use if you were forced to describe the activity with just one word.

Writing Activity 6.2

- Look back at your own brainstorming.
- Write a word that captures the dominant impression of the event you observed.
- Think carefully about your audience and your purpose.
- Write a topic sentence for your paragraph.

STEP 3:
Outline the Paragraph

In the outline step of writing, our individual viewpoints continue to influence which details are included and which are excluded as we plan our respective paragraphs. Each of us focuses only on those points that will convey our unique impression of the activity. Our differences in perspective and focus, therefore, become even more evident in our outlines.

Marcia's Outline

Topic sentence:

I watched, dismayed, as my two children ate their rolls.

Topic sentence question:

Why was I dismayed as I watched my two children eat their rolls?

Answers:

1. **I saw the mess on Jeff and Stacey's faces.**
2. **I saw the mess on Jeff and Stacey's hands.**
3. **I saw the mess in Stacey's hair.**
4. **I saw the mess on Jeff and Stacey's clothes.**
5. **I saw the mess on the table.**
6. **I saw the mess on the chair.**
7. **I saw the mess on the floor.**

Ed's Outline

Topic sentence:

The kids were delighted with their treat.

Topic sentence question:

What did the kids do to show they were delighted with their treat?

Answers:

1. **They laughed and chattered as they ate.**
2. **They stayed close to the table instead of running around.**
3. **They shared various tastes.**
4. **They sometimes took big bites and sometimes savored the good parts.**

At this point in the writing process, it's important to stop, take a good look at the outline, and determine whether it will be a good framework for a paragraph. Do the answers really answer the question? Is there too much in it? Is something missing from it?

Looking at her outline, Marcia decided there is too much information in it. The problem lies in the topic sentence: it is too broad. If she were to fully develop the topic sentence, she would need to write much more than one paragraph. Even before beginning her first draft, then, she limited her subject to Stacey and revised her topic sentence to focus on the mess.

> **I watched an awful mess begin and grow as Stacey devoured her huge, gooey roll.**

By **narrowing the focus** from the entire activity just to the creation of the mess, and by focusing on one child rather than both, Marcia narrowed her paragraph to a manageable size. Also, she shifted her point of view from the entire scene to a specific part of it, much like a movie camera pans in for a close-up. This shift allowed her to supply enough specific details about Stacey for the reader to gain a clear picture of at least part of the event. Obviously, this new topic sentence required a change in both the question and the answers of Marcia's outline. Here's her new one.

Topic sentence:

> **I watched an awful mess begin and grow as Stacey devoured her huge, gooey roll.**

Topic sentence question:

> **How did an awful mess begin and grow as Stacey devoured her roll?**

Answers:

1. She smeared custard and powdered sugar on her hands, face, and hair.
2. Powdered sugar fell to the table top and then to the floor.
3. She lay in the sugar and jelly, making her shirt filthy.
4. She ground the mess into the carpet when she was finished.

Writing Activity 6.3

- Outline your materials from activities 6.1 and 6.2.
- Decide whether or not your outline will work as a framework for a paragraph.
- If your outline seems too broad, narrow your topic sentence and write a new outline.

STEP 4:
Write the First Draft

As you learn to be thorough and careful on the first three steps, the actual writing step will gradually become easier to manage. Writing well will always be hard work, but you're mastering a writing system that you can apply to any kind of writing you may need to do.

After reviewing our outlines, we struggled with our paragraphs about the kids and their rolls and came up with the following rough drafts. As before, we let our outlines guide our selection of details and their order in the paragraphs.

Marcia's First Draft

I watched an awful mess begin and grow as Stacey devoured her huge, gooey roll. It was covered with a fine, white powdered sugar and filled with thick, yellow lemon custard, offering her a variety of activities. She began by opening her mouth wide and stuffing in as much as she could, leaving a ring of white paste around her lips and up one cheek. Next she poked a stubby index finger into the jelly and licked her finger; she continued scooping until the center was empty and her hand was covered with goo. She then wiped a stray strand of hair off her face, and the hair stuck to her forehead. Meanwhile, the powdered sugar fell from the roll and covered the table top, and Stacey began to draw designs in it. She stood up and rubbed her hands, arms, and elbows in the sugar, knocking it to the floor. Soon Stacey lay over the table and rested her chest in the sugar and jelly and then stood up to reveal a shirt ready for the laundry. Having eaten enough, Stacey climbed down, walked over the mess, and ground it into the carpet. I moaned as she skipped by, grinning at me, satisfied.

Ed's First Draft

Stacey picked up her powdered-sugar-covered roll, bit down on it, and growled and giggled while Jeff delightedly picked a large chunk of the chocolate frosting off his roll. They were obviously delighted with their treat. After his first large bite, Jeff shouted, "There's frosting in mine!" and he slowly began taking the custard filling on his fingertip and licking it off. After a couple of tastes, he walked around the table to offer Stacey a taste. She, meanwhile, was standing on her knees in the high chair, leaning over the table, weight on her elbows and forearms, alternately rocking back to take a bite, smear powdered sugar around the table, brush her hair back, blow a razzberry, giggle, or lick her fingers. When Jeff returned, Stacey leaned across the table, and Jeff loudly kissed the powdered sugar from her extended finger. Picking up his roll, Jeff again bit into the custard-filled center. The sides of the roll wrapped nearly halfway around his small head. Stacey, too, again took a big bite, smearing powdered sugar on the lower half of her face. By this time, their chewing had slowed—they were awfully big rolls for small children—but there was no move by either to leave the table. Stacey licked her finger, then blew another razzberry on her palm. Taking a drink of milk, she looked over her shoulder down the hall. "No monsters behind me," she mused, and quietly began playing with her shoe. The half-eaten roll lay safely within reach.

In looking over his paragraph, Ed felt that the paragraph was focused on something other than his topic sentence, but he couldn't say exactly what was wrong. He decided to let it sit for a day before he tried to revise.

It's normal and common for writers to have vague feelings of discomfort about what they have written, and it's important for a writer to learn to pay attention to those feelings. Often those vague feelings are signals that your mind is at work on the problem and that, given time, your mind will probably identify and maybe solve the problem.

Writing Activity 6.4

- Write a first draft of your description of an activity.
- Underline the verbs and adverbs.
- Let your paragraph sit awhile before you begin to revise.

STEP 5:
Revise the Paragraph

When she was ready to begin her revision, Marcia reviewed her paragraph. She had underlined the verbs but noticed she hadn't used adverbs effectively. Here's her first draft.

Marcia's First Draft

I <u>watched</u>, dismayed, as Stacey <u>attacked</u> the huge, gooey roll. It <u>was</u> covered with a fine, white powdered sugar and filled with thick, yellow lemon custard, offering her a variety of activities. She <u>began</u> by opening her mouth wide and stuffing in as much as she could, leaving a ring of white paste around her lips and up one cheek. Next she <u>poked</u> a stubby index finger into the jelly and <u>licked</u> her finger; she <u>continued</u> scooping until the center <u>was</u> empty and her hand <u>was</u> covered with goo. She then <u>wiped</u> a stray strand of hair off her face, and the hair <u>stuck</u> to her forehead. Meanwhile, the powdered sugar <u>fell</u> from the roll and <u>covered</u> the table top, and Stacey <u>began</u> to draw designs in it. She <u>stood</u> up and <u>rubbed</u> her hands, arms, and elbows in the sugar, knocking it to the floor. Soon Stacey <u>lay</u> over the table and <u>rested</u> her chest in the sugar and jelly and then <u>stood</u> up to reveal a shirt ready for the laundry. Having eaten enough, Stacey <u>climbed</u> down, <u>walked</u> over the mess, and <u>ground</u> it into the carpet. I <u>moaned</u> as she <u>skipped</u> by, grinning at me, satisfied.

In her review, Marcia decided that her second sentence should focus more on the action of the event, she saw some other places where changing or adding verbs and adverbs would show the action more clearly, and she saw that she had mentioned sound only in her last sentence.

As you read Marcia's revised paragraph, look at the changes she made in response to the problems she saw, and look for other changes as well. Again, verbs are underlined and adverbs are double underlined.

Marcia's Revision

I <u>watched</u> an awful mess <u>begin</u> and <u>grow</u> as Stacey <u>devoured</u> her huge, gooey roll. Opening her mouth wide, she <u>stuffed</u> in a bite of the powdered-sugar-covered treat and <u>smiled</u> up at me with a clown face—lips and cheeks smeared with white powder. The bite <u>had revealed</u> a lemon custard filling, and Stacey <u>cheered</u> <u><u>loudly</u></u> when she <u>discovered</u> it. She <u>poked</u> a stubby index finger into the jelly and <u>scooped</u> out the filling, <u><u>noisily</u></u> licking her finger. More earnest now, she <u>jammed</u> in her whole hand for the yellow treasure, then <u>paused</u> to wipe a stray strand of hair from her face, glueing the lock firmly to her forehead. As the powdered sugar <u>fell</u> from her roll and <u>covered</u> the tabletop, Stacey <u>began</u> to trace lines and circles with her finger. Pulling herself to her feet, she <u>left</u> sticky lumps of custard on the arms of the chair. Leaning over the table, she <u>used</u> her hands, elbows and arms to draw more elaborate designs and in the process <u>knocked</u> white sugar to the floor. I <u>watched</u> it <u>snow</u> <u><u>quietly</u></u> on the carpet. Oblivious, Stacey now <u>slowly</u> <u>rested</u> the entire top half of her body on the table, rubbing her hair, face, and chest in the mess. She <u>rose proudly</u> to reveal the disastrous results on her head and shirt. <u>Finally,</u> having had enough, she <u>climbed</u> down, <u>walked</u> over the food-covered carpet, and <u>ground</u> the mess <u>expertly</u> into every fiber. I <u>moaned</u> <u>softly</u> as she <u>grinned</u> a satisfied grin and <u>left</u> to see where else she <u>could</u> <u>leave</u> her mark.

Obviously, Marcia has made major changes and additions to her paragraph, and that's what often happens as writers revise. A third draft would probably lead to still more changes, and you will often be asked to do three or more drafts of what you write. You can, however, make each revision more effective by carefully studying the draft you plan to revise.

Recall that when Ed wrote his first draft, he had a vague feeling that something wasn't quite right about it, so he decided to let the work sit before he began to revise. As Ed reviewed his rough draft later, he realized the problem: he wanted to talk about the children's discoveries rather than their delight. He changed his topic sentence so it would speak only of the discoveries the kids had made, and that change gave the paragraph the sharp focus that it had lacked in the first draft.

Ed's Revision

It was wonderful watching Stacey and Jeff discover the marvels of their pastries. Stacey picked up hers, bit down on it, and growled and giggled, scattering powdered sugar on the table. Jeff deliberately scooped up a glob of chocolate frosting and grinned as he popped the finger into his mouth. Satisfied that the roll was going to be as good as he'd hoped, he slowly took a large bite. "There's frosting inside!" he shouted as soon as he could talk. Stacey licked the sugar from her fingers as Jeff scooped custard filling into his mouth, then walked around the table to offer a fingerful to his sister. "There's salt on mine," she observed, and offered a finger to Jeff who loudly kissed off the powdered sugar coating. Completely absorbed in the tastes, the activities, and the pure pleasure of the treat, Stacey knelt on her high chair, sometimes leaning most of her body on the table, sometimes drawing back to take a bite, scoop out some filling, smear powdered sugar around on the table, or giggle and blow a razzberry. Jeff, having eaten his roll into a crescent, was hard at work on the center, the outer edges wrapping nearly halfway around his small head. As their stomachs filled and they realized there would be no new tastes or textures, their chewing slowed, but they made no move to leave their precious goodies. Stacey licked her fingers, then her whole hand, then contentedly blew a razzberry on her palm. She finished her milk and looked back over her shoulder into the hall. "No monsters behind me," she mused and quietly began playing with her shoe. Jeff chewed slowly and quietly. The discovery was complete.

In revising, Marcia narrowed her paragraph at the outline stage by focusing just on the mess and on Stacey rather than on both of the children. Ed narrowed his paragraph in the second draft to focus on the discoveries the children made rather than on their general delight. In each case, the changes made the details sharper and clearer. This sharper focus almost forces the writer to discuss the subject in more detail, and that detail gives life to a piece of writing.

But the focus isn't the only thing that clarifies our picture of the action in these paragraphs. Look again at these two sentences from Marcia's drafts:

First draft

Stacey . . . stood up to reveal a shirt ready for the laundry.

Second draft

She rose proudly to reveal the disastrous results on her head and shirt.

Both sentences show what Stacey did, but the second sentence shows us how Stacey felt about what she had done and how Marcia felt about what Stacey had done. Four words, the verb "rose," the adverb "proudly," the adjective "disastrous," and the noun "results," bring the actions and reactions dramatically to life.

As you revise your description of an activity, be sure that you focus your readers' attention where you want it and that you look for words that will show not only a clear picture of the action but also people's attitudes toward the action.

Writing Activity 6.5

- Revise your paragraph.
- Use the Standards for Judging Writing from Chapter 1 (pages 14–15).
- Look carefully at the focus of your paragraph. Is it too broad or too narrow?
- Choose precise nouns and adjectives.
- Pay particular attention to your choices of verbs and adverbs.

Samples from Professional Writers

Our first professional example to close this chapter is from Philip Caputo's *A Rumor of War*. Caputo served in Vietnam both as a Marine lieutenant and as a newspaper reporter. This selection is a graphic and chilling description of the death of a man in modern warfare.

> What happened next happened very quickly, but in memory I see it happening with an agonizing slowness. It is a ballet of death between a lone, naked man and a remorseless machine. We are ranging in on the enemy soldier, but cease firing when one of the Skyhawks comes in to strafe the tree line. The nose of the plane is pointing down at a slight angle and there is an orange twinkling as it fires its mini-gun, an aerial cannon that fires explosive 20-mm bullets so rapidly that it sounds like a buzz saw. The rounds, smashing into the tree line and the rice paddy at the incredible rate of one hundred per second, raise a translucent curtain of smoke and spraying water. Through this curtain, we see the Viet Cong behind the dike sitting up with his arms outstretched in the pose of a man beseeching God. He seems to be pleading for mercy from the screaming mass of technology that is flying no more than one hundred feet above him. But the plane swoops down on him, fires its cannon once more, and blasts him to shreds. As the plane climbs away, I look at the dead man through my binoculars. All that remains of the third Viet Cong are a few scattered piles of bloody rags.

This next observation of an activity is from John Steinbeck's *Log from the Sea of Cortez*, a book about a collecting expedition that Steinbeck and his marine biologist friend Ed Ricketts made into the Gulf of California.

> Once, passing the boat department of Macy's in New York, where there are duck-boats and skiffs and little cruisers, one of the authors discovered that as he passed each hull he knocked on it sharply with his knuckles. He wondered why he did it, and as he wondered, he heard a knocking behind him, and another man was rapping the hulls with his knuckles, the same tempo—three sharp knocks on each hull. During an hour's observation there no man or boy and few women passed who did not do the same thing. Can this have been an unconscious testing of the hulls? Many who passed could not have been in a boat, perhaps some of the little boys had never seen a boat, and yet everyone tested the hulls, knocked to see if they were sound, and did not even know he was doing it. The observer thought perhaps they and he would knock on any large wooden object that might give forth a resonant sound. He went to the piano department, icebox floor, beds, cedar chests, and no one knocked on them—only on boats.

Our final example is from a children's book, Pearl Buck's *The Big Wave*. Buck, a well-known writer who won the Pulitzer Prize for her 1938 novel *The Good Earth*, lived in both China and Japan.

> In a few seconds, before their eyes the wave had grown and come nearer and nearer, higher and higher. The air was filled with its roar and shout. It rushed over the flat still waters of the ocean and before Jiya could scream again it reached the village and covered it fathoms deep in swirling wild water, green laced with fierce white foam. The wave ran up the mountain side, until the knoll where the castle stood was an island. All who were still climbing the path were swept away—black, tossing scraps in the wicked waters. The wave ran up the mountain until Kino and Jiya saw the wavelets curl at the terrace walls upon which they stood. Then with a great sucking sigh, the wave swept back again, ebbing into the ocean, dragging everything with it, trees and stones and houses. They stood, the man and the

two boys, utterly silent, clinging together, facing the wave as it went away. It swept back over the village and returned slowly again to the ocean, subsiding, sinking into a great stillness.

Other Suggestions for Writing

1. Write about an argument or fight between two people you know.

2. Write about a campus activity organized by students at your school.

3. Write about a noisy event—a rock concert, a child's birthday party, a parade, a block party, an auction.

4. Write about a place full of people doing things—a playground, a roller rink, a factory, an exercise gym, a carnival, an opera house.

5. Write about an activity where tension is high—a hospital emergency room, backstage during a play, an important meeting, a restaurant kitchen on a busy night.

6. Write about a competition—piano, windsurfing, basketball free-throw, chess, dance.

PREVIEW FOR CHAPTER 7

"Are you sure this is what you want to do?" my dad had asked. "You bet!" I said. "This will be great!" When I arrived in San Diego there were about fifty other men waiting for the bus from boot camp. In a few minutes, a big green bus pulled up. We were all talking and laughing and having a good time. A large, sour-looking Marine leapt out of the bus and shouted, "Shut the hell up! Get into the bus! Now!"

I left Vietnam on a boat made to hold sixty people, but when more showed up we could not say no; to do so would have been inhuman. One hundred and twelve people left on that boat around midnight. We started on the River at Can Tho and then entered the sea at Dai Ngai.

I rented scuba diving equipment and an underwater camera and jumped straight into the water. It was warm and clear and I swam easily through it, passing large, colorful fish within reach of my hand and exploring the wonderful underwater constructions of the coral reefs. I was in twenty-foot deep water before I remembered that this was known as an attractive spot for sharks, and I beat a hasty retreat for the shallower water.

I ran to the first car that stopped, a ragged old pickup, and climbed in. The driver seemed strange and nervous, his eyes darting back and forth from me to the road and back again, seeming as afraid of me as I was of him. We rode in silence until he began describing, in a low voice, the gruesome deaths of two local girls. "This is as far as I go," I said, and I got out almost before the pickup stopped.

7 WRITING ABOUT AN EXPERIENCE

SKILLS INTRODUCED

Identifying details of an experience
Ordering events
Varying placement of the topic sentence

Storytelling is an important part of our lives. We grow up listening to stories, and by the time we're able to talk we are telling stories of our own experiences. Our families and our friends are our first audiences, and they listen with varying degrees of attention to our childhood tales. As we grow, we become more selective about what we tell, for we have more experiences from which to choose and our audience has different expectations of what is appropriate for us to share.

In this chapter, you will write about your experiences. Writing that tells the story of an experience is called narrative. Most novels are narrative, as are many other books and magazine articles. To some extent the order of the details in a narrative is already decided for you since events happen in a certain order, one after another. Still, when you write a narrative paragraph you can re-create events in the order that they actually happened or in a different order. In other words, you can control the time line of a narrative. Narratives are often written in strict chronological order, starting at the be-

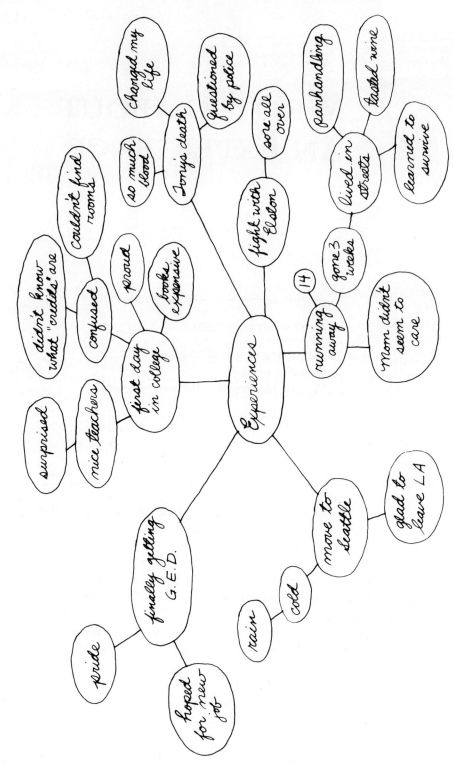

Figure 7-1   Daniel's Cluster: Experiences

ginning and going straight through to the end, just as events happen in real life. But narratives can also begin in the middle of the action or even at the end, and we often see this manipulation of time line in books, movies, and television shows.

This chapter will discuss some of the special techniques you will use as you write narratives, and we will begin by brainstorming.

Step 1:
Brainstorm to Discover What You Know

You have had hundreds of experiences, so your first brainstorming for a topic is an important step. Of all of your experiences, which are worth writing about? Some are dull, some are nobody's business, some are funny, some are exciting, and so on. Figure 7-1 is a cluster that one of our students, Daniel, did as he explored possible topics for this assignment. Even without knowing the details of Daniel's experience, you can see how some ideas suggested others and how the writer thought of details and saw connections as he brainstormed.

Looking at his cluster, Daniel debated whether to write about Tony's death. That time had been a turning point in his life and he knew a reading audience would find the events dramatic, but he wasn't sure that he wanted to revive the painful memories that writing the story would bring. On the other hand, he thought writing might help him understand the experience better, and he finally decided to use it as his subject. To explore further, he wrote a focused list of the events of that night.

1. gathering at Angelo's
2. wrestling with Tony
3. smoking dope
4. talking about girls
5. talking about other gangs
6. Frank said "Who's going to the drive-in?"
7. July 23rd
8. end of a hot day
9. Saturday
10. Sam in town for weekend

11. crowding into Frank's Ford

12. driving with windows open, looking for girls

13. sun going down over city

14. more dope

15. bright drive-in lights

16. leaning on car talking

17. wanting a fight

18. knowing we'd get one, being excited

19. talking with Tony

20. saw car coming slowly—fight time

21. things happening fast

22. four guys

23. shots—3

24. hiding behind car

25. scared, couldn't move

26. heard Tony crying

27. blood, popcorn and trash

28. Tony dead

29. scared

30. wanting revenge

31. why was I there?

32. why was I saved?

33. sirens and lights

34. running from cops

35. hid out for three days

Writing Activity 7.1

- Make a cluster like the one in Figure 7-1 to brainstorm experiences you might write about.

- Work quickly; write down ideas as they come to you, and don't worry about the order in which the ideas occur. Let your brain work freely.

- Next, choose a specific experience from your cluster, and do focused brainstorming on that experience.

• Again, work quickly. Let one idea suggest another, and don't stop to criticize your ideas or worry about the wording. You're trying to discover what's in your memory and nudge it to the surface.

Step 2:
Write the Topic Sentence

When writers tell stories, they don't always directly state the point of the story. If they do state the main idea in a sentence, they often delay that sentence until the end of the story. Thus the rules for placing topic sentences in narrative paragraphs are much more flexible than they are for other kinds of paragraphs.

Still, when you write a narrative, you need to have some sort of controlling idea in mind. You need something to help you select the details that go into the paragraph and to reject those that don't belong. As a result, you will write a topic sentence and do an outline for your narrative, but your final draft may or may not contain that topic sentence.

A narrative creates a mood or impression, so your first step in writing a topic sentence is to ask, "What is the dominant impression I want my readers to have when they have finished reading?" To answer that, you must understand and be able to state your own dominant impression of the event, so that is your starting point. What mood or impression do you have as you look back over your brainstorming and think about the event? Why is the event important to you? Why might other people want to read about it?

As Daniel thought about his experience, he kept coming back to the shock of realizing that Tony had died while he (Daniel) had lived. His dominant impression, then, would be the shock of that realization, and he wrote this topic sentence:

> **Realizing that my life had been spared and my friend's had not was the shock of my life.**

Daniel reasoned that his readers might have experienced situations that began with excitement and ended in tragedy, or that they had read or heard about such situations. For that reason, and because he knew his experience was out of the ordinary for most people, he thought his audience would probably be interested. His purpose would be to show the shock.

Writing Activity 7.2

- Write your own topic sentence about the incident you brainstormed in activity 7.1.
- Be sure you've written a complete sentence and that it focuses on the dominant impression you have of the event.
- Think about why your reading audience will be interested in your experience and what your purpose will be.

STEP 3:
Outline the Paragraph

In outlining a narrative paragraph, remember that only the events that directly focus on your topic sentence will go into the outline and that some things that *must* go into the paragraph will not appear in the outline. When you write your paragraph, you must, of course, set the scene where the action takes place, but that scene-setting will probably not appear in your outline since it does not directly answer the topic sentence question. The outline helps you identify those points that are central to accomplishing your purpose in the paragraph. Here's Daniel's outline:

Topic Sentence:

> **Realizing that my life had been spared and my friend's had not was the shock of my life.**

Topic sentence question:

> **In what way was the realization shocking?**

Answers:

> 1. **I had lost my friend.**
> 2. **I realized that I could have died.**
> 3. **It made me wonder if there was a reason I was saved.**
> 4. **It made me question my life.**

Notice that the outline doesn't provide us with information about how, where, or why the event occurred, but it does show what the writer must discuss in order to show his dominant impression of the event. The outline is not something that most readers will ever see. It is a tool for the writer to use as he plans his paragraph.

Writing Activity 7.3

• Now write your outline from your material of activities 7.1 and 7.2.

STEP 4:
Write the First Draft

Your task in writing about an experience is to recreate for your reader what the experience was like for you. You can do this by showing your reader not just *what* happened but also *how* it happened and how you felt about it. If you've chosen an experience you remember well and have done a thorough job of brainstorming and outlining, you'll be off to a good start. Understanding who your readers are, why they might be interested in your story, and what your purpose is will help, too.

One more thing you must consider before you begin your first draft is where your story will begin and end. Experiences themselves seldom have clear beginnings and endings: there are always things that happened before and after. When you tell a story, however, you must start and stop somewhere; your purpose for writing the paragraph will help you determine where to start and stop. For his story, Daniel chose to start at the drive-in just a few minutes before the central event and not to discuss much of what happened after. Here is his first draft:

First Draft

Realizing that my life had been spared and my friend's had not was the shock of my life. It had started out like a normal weekend night at the drive-in. We were hanging out, waiting for a fight, and my friend Tony and I were standing at the rear of the car. I saw another car coming up slowly. I tried to see who was in the car, but all I saw was four guys, and then a gun, and then the flashes of three shots. I leaped over the back end of the car and hid. The other car raced away. I heard Tony crying, but I could not move. When I did get up, I saw the blood all over him and the ground. I could see that Tony was dead. I was mad, confused and crying, wanting to get even. Then the thought came that it could have been me dead. Why was I even there? I wanted out of the gang. I wanted to know why I was saved. There must have been a reason for it to work out this way. The drive-in lights were very bright. I still see them every time I think about that night.

This draft has clear starting points, but it lacks the details that might really make it come to life for his readers. Daniel was there and experienced the events, but his readers were not, so Daniel must put them directly into the action if he is to accomplish his purpose of having his readers experience the shock that he felt. Readers need to see what Daniel saw, hear what Daniel heard, and feel the emotions that Daniel felt, before, after, and during the shooting.

Writing Activity 7.4

• Write the first draft of your paragraph you've outlined in activity 7.3. Remember that you were there, but your readers weren't.

• Use your brainstorming to remind yourself about the small details which are still in your head. You might take these images for granted, but your readers need them in order to understand the event.

STEP 5:
Revise the Paragraph

Daniel looked back at his brainstorming list and decided that he needed to relive the experience. He knew it would not be easy, but he decided to freewrite just about the time he was at the drive-in. He concentrated for a few minutes, then wrote for ten minutes without stopping:

> Bright lights and blood all over the popcorn and the trash and Tony doubled up dead on the ground. I cried for the first time in a long time. We were young and stupid and out for a fight, craving a fight, wanting to show what big men we were but we were nothing but kids and now Tony was a dead kid. And I was scared—more scared than I'd been before or since, and the cops came with their red lights flashing over everything and I ran. I should have gone to Tony when I heard him crying but I couldn't move because I was scared. Why did they shoot him and not me? It could have been either of us or both of us or somebody else but it was just him. They didn't know us and we didn't know them, but I guess they wanted the same kind of excitement we did. Why are kids so stupid? But I wanted to get even. Tony was on the ground, not breathing, his face contorted and his blood everywhere. I don't know if I even heard the shots, but I heard the car's engine, the squealing tires, and the kids in the drive-in yelling and screaming. And then I heard the sirens and I was still scared but I didn't know what I was scared of. My friend was dead and instead of bragging about how well he'd done in a fight, he'd be buried and I'd never see him again.

You can see that Daniel's freewrite helped him recall specific details of the event, details that would help him make the event more real for his readers. As he worked through his various revisions, Daniel experimented with time order and with the placement of his topic sentence. We'll show you three revisions, any one of which could be a final draft.

Revision 1

> As I ran, all I could picture were the bright lights of the drive-in, the flashing red lights of the police cars, the young

kids running and screaming, and Tony's blood on the ground mixed with popcorn and trash. I still see that scene every time I relive the shock of knowing that my friend had died and my life was spared. It was just another weekend night at the drive-in. Six of us were hanging out, high and craving a fight, leaning on the car, waiting for some action. My friend Tony and I were talking at the back of the car when I spotted another car coming slowly through the dusk. "Here we go," I said. I saw four guys, and then a gun, and then the flashes of three shots. Leaping over the back end of the car, I hid by the tire, listening to the other car race away. Then I heard my friend crying, and I knew he'd been shot. Still, I couldn't move. When I did get up and walk around the car, the crying had stopped, and I could see that my friend was dead. I was mad, confused and crying, wanting to get even. Then it hit me. It could have been me dead. Why was I even there? I wanted out of the gang. I wanted to know why I was saved. There must have been a reason. I've been working on a reason ever since.

This revision begins at the end of the action with the narrator running away. A flashback like this can sometimes be an effective lead because it arouses the reader's curiosity. The topic sentence, **"I still see that scene every time I relive the shock of knowing that my friend had died and my life was spared,"** has been revised to fit more smoothly into the paragraph, but it still focuses the readers' attention on the dominant impression of the paragraph, shock. The action begins in the middle of the paragraph, and while the writer doesn't show us the arrival of the police, the lead helps us picture it. The next revision follows the more common pattern of beginning at the beginning.

Revision 2

It started out like every other weekend night at the drive-in. A few of the guys and I were hanging out, waiting for a fight. We were tough and we knew it, so we leaned against the cars, passed a joint, and waited. It was getting late and we craved a fight, but we knew it would come. My friend Tony and I were leaning on the trunk lid when I spotted another car cruising up slowly. It was dusk and we were high and here came our fight. I could see four guys, and I nudged Tony with my elbow, and then I saw a gun and the flashes of three shots. I vaulted over the trunk and huddled by the tire. The other car's engine roared and its tires squealed, and then I heard Tony crying softly. Looking underneath the car, I could see my friend lying on the ground, and I could see blood. But I could not move. Young kids were running and screaming, but my legs just wouldn't move. I saw people's feet come and stand around Tony, and I realized he'd stopped crying and I had to get up. When I looked at him his contorted face told me my friend was dead. The bright lights of the drive-in reflected from Tony's blood mixed with popcorn and trash, and I was mad, confused and crying, wanting to get even. Then the thought hit me that I could be the one lying there dead. It was a shock that changed my life. Why was I even there? Why was I spared and Tony not? There had to be a reason for it to work out this way. I've been working on a reason ever since.

The lead for this revision sets the scene. We move into the action about a third of the way through the paragraph, and the controlling idea (**"It was a shock that changed my life"**) isn't stated until the end of the paragraph. The topic sentence works well in that position, though, because the action of the paragraph builds up to it, showing the way that the writer felt the shock during the experience. The third version of the paragraph puts us immediately into the main part of the action.

Revision 3

High and craving a fight, my friend Tony and I leaned arrogantly on the trunk of the car, waiting, watching the other car coming up slowly through the dusk. When the bright yellow glow of the drive-in lights showed us four guys in the car, it was too late. A shiny black gun poked out of the back window, and three shots flashed, bright even in the glare of the drive-in. Leaping over the back end of the car, I crouched by the tire as the other car screeched away. My friend cried, a kind of a whimper I'll never forget, but fear pinned me down. My legs wouldn't take me to him. When I finally found the strength to move, blood covered Tony and the ground, and my friend lay there, his face contorted in death. The shock hit me, and I barely heard the young kids screaming as I realized that it could be my blood mixing with popcorn and trash. Sirens screamed, and the white drive-in walls reflected red flashes of police car lights as the sirens closed in. I ran, hating the creeps who'd killed Tony, hating the gang for being at the drive-in looking for a fight, and wondering why I was alive when Tony was dead.

Here again the writer builds to his dominant impression, stating the topic sentence (**"The shock hit me . . ."**), just past the middle of the paragraph. But regardless of where the topic sentence is placed, each of the three versions of this paragraph keeps its focus on the dominant impression of the writer's shock when he realizes that he has lived while his friend has died. That focus is one of the elements that makes this a powerful and effective paragraph.

Writing Activity 7.5

- Revise your paragraph.
- Review your rough draft and ask yourself whether it begins at the time you want it to and ends when you want it to. Remember that you can present the events in a different order from the one in which they actually happened, but it is probably best to use chronological order, at least until you have a detailed draft you're satisfied with. Then you can start to play with the order of events to make it more exciting.
- Be sure your dominant impression is evident throughout your paragraph. In other words, be sure that your controlling idea controls what goes into the paragraph and what stays out.
- Finally, be consistent in your point of view. Obviously, you are telling the story, but are you telling it as you saw it then or as you see it now?

Samples from Professional Writers

We end this section with three selections by professional writers. The first is by Joseph Conrad, a Polish-born sea captain and famous novelist to whom English was his third language. It is from his short story "Youth."

Next day it was my watch on deck from eight to twelve. At breakfast the captain observed, 'It's wonderful how that smell hangs about the cabin.' About ten, the mate being on the poop, I stepped down on the main deck for a moment. The carpenter's bench stood abaft the mainmast: I leaned against it sucking at my pipe, and the carpenter, a young chap, came to talk to me. He remarked, 'I think we have done very well, haven't we?' and then I perceived with annoyance the fool was trying to tilt the bench. I said curtly, 'Don't, Chips,' and immediately became aware of a queer sensation, of an absurd delusion—I seemed somehow to be in the air. I heard all round me like a pent-up breath released—as if a thousand giants simultaneously had said Phoo!—and felt a dull concussion which made my ribs ache suddenly. No doubt about it—I was in the air, and my body was describing a short parabola. But short as it was, I had the time to think several thoughts in, as far as I can remember, the following order: 'This can't be the carpenter—What is it?—Some accident—Submarine volcano?—Coals, gas!—By Jove!—We are being blown up—Everybody's dead—I am falling into the afterhatch—I see fire in it.'

The coaldust suspended in the air of the hold had glowed dull-red at the moment of the explosion. In the twinkling of an eye, in an infinitesimal fraction of a second since the first tilt of the bench, I was sprawling full length in the cargo. I picked myself up and scrambled out. It was quick like a rebound. The deck was a wilderness of scrambled timber, lying crosswise like trees in a wood after a hurricane; an immense curtain of soiled rags waved gently before me—it was the mainsail blown to strips. I thought: the masts will be toppling over directly; and to get out of the way bolted on all fours towards the poop ladder. The first person I saw was Mahon, with eyes like saucers, his mouth open, and the long white hair standing straight on end round his head like a silver halo. He was just about to go down when the sight of the main deck stirring, heaving up, and changing into splinters before his eyes, petrified him on the top step. I stared at him in unbelief, and he stared at me with a queer kind of shocked curiosity. I did not know that I had no hair, no eyebrows, no eyelashes, that my young mustache was burnt off, that my face was black, one cheek laid open, my nose cut, and my chin bleeding. I had lost my cap, one of my slippers, and my shirt was torn to rags. Of all this I was not aware. I was amazed to see the ship still afloat, the poop deck whole—and, most of all, to see anybody alive. Also the peace of the sky and the serenity of the sea were distinctly surprising. I suppose I expected to see them convulsed with horror.

Our second professional selection is part of a story about a lesson in courage. It is from Maya Angelou's autobiography *I Know Why the Caged Bird Sings*.

When I was around ten years old, those scruffy children caused me the most painful and confusing experience I had ever had with my grandmother.

One summer morning, after I had swept the dirt yard of leaves, spearmint-gum wrappers and Vienna-sausage labels, I raked the yellow-red dirt, and made half-moons carefully, so that the design stood out clearly and mask-like. I put the rake behind the Store and came through the back of the house to find Grandmother on the front porch in her big, wide white apron. The apron was so stiff by virtue of the starch that it could have stood alone. Momma was admiring the yard, so I joined her. It truly looked like a flat redhead that had been raked with a big-toothed comb. Momma didn't say anything but I knew she liked it. She looked over toward the school principal's house and to the right at Mr. McElroy's. She was hoping one of those community pillars would see the design before the day's business wiped it out. Then she looked upward to the school. My head had swung with hers, so at just about the same time we saw a troop of the powhitetrash kids marching over the hill and down by the side of the school.

I looked to Momma for direction. She did an excellent job of sagging from her waist down, but from the waist up she seemed to be pulling for the top of the oak tree across the road. Then she began to moan a hymn. Maybe not to moan, but the tune was so slow and the meter so strange that she could have been moaning. She didn't look at me again. When the children reached halfway down the hill, halfway to the Store, she said without turning, "Sister, go on inside."

I wanted to beg her, "Momma, don't wait for them. Come on inside with me. If they come in the Store, you go to the bedroom and let me wait on them. They only frighten me if you're around. Alone I know how to handle them." But of course I couldn't say anything, so I went in and stood behind the screen door.

Before the girls got to the porch I heard their laughter crackling and popping like pine logs in a cooking stove. I suppose my lifelong paranoia was born in those cold, molasses-slow minutes. They came finally to stand on the ground in front of Momma. At first they pretended seriousness. Then one of them wrapped her right arm in the crook of her left, pushed out her mouth and started to hum. I realized that she was aping my grandmother. Another said, "Naw, Helen, you ain't standing like her. This here's it." Then she lifted her chest, folded her arms and mocked that strange carriage that was Annie Henderson. Another laughed, "Naw, you can't do it. Your mouth ain't pooched out enough. It's like this."

I thought about the rifle behind the door, but I knew I'd never be able to hold it straight, and the .410, our sawed-off shotgun, which stayed loaded and was fired every New Year's night, was locked in the trunk and Uncle Willie had the key on his chain. Through the fly-specked screen-door, I could see that the arms of Momma's apron jiggled from the vibrations of her humming. But her knees seemed to have locked as if they would never bend again.

She sang on. No louder than before, but no softer either. No slower or faster.

The dirt of the girls' cotton dresses continued on their legs, feet, arms and faces to make them all of a piece. Their greasy uncolored hair hung down, uncombed, with a grim finality. I knelt to see them better, to remember them for all time. The tears that had slipped down my dress left unsurprising dark spots, and made the front yard blurry and even more unreal. The world had taken a deep breath and was having doubts about continuing to revolve.

Our final selection is from Ernest Hemingway's *The Old Man and the Sea.*

He remembered the time he had hooked one of a pair of marlin. The male fish always let the female fish feed first and the hooked fish, the female, made a wild, panic-stricken, despairing fight that soon exhausted her, and all the time the male had stayed with her, crossing the line and circling with her on the surface. He had stayed so close that the old man was afraid he would cut the line with his tail which was sharp as a scythe and almost of that size and shape. When the old man had gaffed her and clubbed her, holding the rapier bill with its sandpaper edge and clubbing her across the top of her head until her colour turned to a colour almost like the backing of mirrors, and then, with the boy's aid, hoisted her aboard, the male fish had stayed by the side of the boat. Then, while the old man was clearing the lines and preparing the harpoon, the male fish jumped high into the air beside the boat to see where the female was and then went down deep, his lavender wings, that were his pectoral fins, spread wide and all his wide lavender stripes showing. He was beautiful, the old man remembered, and he had stayed.

Other Suggestions for Writing

1. Write about a time when you lost your best friend—to another person, when you moved, because of a misunderstanding.
2. Write a humorous story of a bad experience—"date from hell," "vacation from hell," "moving day from hell."
3. Write about a time when the weather made all the difference.
4. Write about a time you were lost, a time you had a close call, a time you were a victim, a time you had to struggle.

5. Write about a time you met your goal, came out on top, won first prize, showed them all.

6. Write about a time when you did something wrong and didn't get caught (or when you did).

PREVIEW FOR CHAPTER 8

Nurses are required to do more complex tasks today than ever before. They need to have increased technical knowledge in addition to basic nursing skills.

Alzheimer's disease is incurable, gnarling the brain tissue, robbing its victims of dignity, self-esteem, and sanity. Victims become child-like, often unable to walk, talk, or perform the most basic of needs. Alzheimer's disease has become the fourth leading cause of death among the elderly.

In the 1980s quilt making has become an important form of artistic expression. Quilts have moved from the bedroom to the art museum.

The Displaced Homemakers program at the Institute for Extended Learning is funded through a five-dollar tax on state marriage licenses. It is designed for women who have primarily been homemakers and who want to return to the working world and become self-supporting.

Alcoholism can make the whole family as ill as you are. Your husband will lose his respect for you, and when that happens his love for you starts to die. There are always fights over your drinking and the money it wastes. The children hear the fights and react to them, failing in school and starting to ignore you.

8 WRITING THE EXPLANATORY PARAGRAPH

So far in this book you have been practicing your skills on descriptive and narrative paragraphs, but there are other kinds of paragraphs that you will be expected to write in many of the courses you take. These are **expository** or explanatory paragraphs, paragraphs that explain. The basic principles and the process of writing do not change for these paragraphs. In fact, you have already been using many of the specialized techniques you will learn in this chapter.

When you explain something, as you will do in most of the writing you do in college, the way you choose to explain will depend on your subject, your audience, and your purpose. For our introduction to the types of explanatory paragraphs, let us suppose you are in a film class where the teacher has assigned a paper asking students to discuss their experiences with monster movies. Obviously the experiences and interests of the class members will differ greatly, and it is likely that a teacher who gives this kind of assignment expects to see many different kinds of responses. Everyone in the class will be writing about the same subject, monster movies, and everyone will be writing for the same audience, the teacher and the other members of the class. The purposes of the writers will be the main difference.

Phuong has seen several monster movies and is interested in what effects make a movie frightening. She decides to write a paper giving examples of scenes and special effects—sounds, lighting, and so forth—that have frightened her. Her paper will be an **example** or **illustration** paper, developed by the use of examples that support, clarify, or explain the controlling idea.

José is interested in filmmaking and animation, and he knows quite a bit about how the monsters are made to seem real. Further, he has a good library of books and magazines that will help him understand more, so he chooses to write about how to make a realistic-looking monster. José's paper will be a **process** paper, the sort of paper one writes in order to show how to do or make something. It will show in sequence the steps one goes through to make a monster.

Alicia has seen only two monster movies, so she doubts that she can do a good job on the paper. As she brainstorms about those two movies, however, she realizes that she remembers some important differences between the two movies and that there were some important similarities as well. Her paper will undoubtedly be a **comparison/contrast** paper that shows her readers what the movies have in common as well as how they differ.

Janusz has a ten-year-old son who recently saw a monster movie and who woke three nights in a row afterward with nightmares. He decides to go see the same movie and to talk with his son about the nightmares to learn whether or how the movie caused the nightmares. His paper will follow the **cause and effect** pattern, a pattern that shows the results (effects) of some action or incident (cause).

Maria has never seen a monster movie. She doesn't even know what one is for sure. She decides that she will talk with her classmates, do some reading, and go to see one or two of the movies. Her paper, she thinks, will tell readers who know little about the subject just what a monster movie *is*. Her paper, then, will be a **definition**. It will explain what the term "monster movie" means.

Tom has seen many monster movies. He and his friends used to go to one every Saturday night and talk about the movies all week long, so he is an expert on the subject. What interests him most is the different types of monsters that the movies are built around—human-like monsters, animal monsters, and alien beings. What Tom will end up writing is a **division/classi-fication** paper. His paper will divide the subject into three different parts and discuss the characteristics of each part.

Chandra has seen enough monster movies to know that she hates them and never wants to see another, so she plans to write an **opinion** paper. She'll explain in detail why she dislikes these movies.

None of these people would set out to write a paper with a specific pattern in mind. What dictates the pattern is the writer's purpose, and what dictates the purpose is the writer's interest in the subject. Still, knowing about the various methods of development that a writer can use is most helpful when one is trying to decide how to explain something. The remainder of this chapter, then, will discuss and show examples of the kinds of paragraphs described here. The writing activities give you a chance to further develop your writing skills.

Writing the Example Paragraph

Sometimes an idea can be best explained by using examples, and in such cases the writer must be sure that the examples do, in fact, illustrate the controlling idea. If, say, you want to show readers that your Aunt Elizabeth is stingy, you might write something like this: "Last night at the restaurant, my Aunt Elizabeth left a twenty-five cent tip for a ten-dollar meal." If you were writing a paragraph about Aunt Elizabeth, you would develop your controlling idea with several such examples.

In Ben's paragraph, the controlling idea is that his good luck charm brings him luck only after he's used it for something. He uses examples to convince his readers that the charm really does seem to bring him luck.

Ben's Paragraph

Not many people have army can openers, especially one as beat up as mine, and not many can openers are good luck charms. The really strange thing about my good luck charm, though, is that it only works after I've used it for something. For example, one time my truck wouldn't start in front of Safeway, so I pulled out my good luck charm and used it to scrape and tighten the battery cables. Sure enough, the truck started. Satisfied that I could get home, I went into the store, did my grocery shopping, and bought a couple of lottery tickets. When I was back outside, I looked at my numbers and saw I had won 2,000 dollars! Another time, when I was in the army, I did not receive an expected promotion. After using my can opener to open a lot of beer cans that night, I was promoted to corporal the next day by some special orders from our headquarters. I never did find out why those orders were issued. I think that if I use my can opener a lot more, good luck will just follow me around.

Our professional model of the example paragraph is the opening paragraph of David Binder's "Brotherhood of the Inept."

> Probably it runs in the family, this clumsiness, not as a river but at least as a stream enveloping one of us each generation. My father held on to a garage door handle after he had pulled it down. It slammed on his thumb. He fell off a bicycle and broke his arm. Once, when my mother threw a dress-up luncheon party in our backyard for his business colleagues, a tablecloth concealed a large irregularity on the edge of our rustic table. It was at this spot that my father, wearing a white suit, placed his plate of spaghetti with tomato sauce. It toppled into his lap. He changed into another white suit, sat down at the same place and spilled a second plate. Changing again upstairs, he dropped his pocket watch on the tile floor of the bathroom. It stopped.

Suggestions for Writing

1. Write a paragraph giving examples of rituals that members of your family perform—morning rituals, holiday rituals, mealtime rituals.

2. Write a paragraph giving examples of people's behaviors that irritate you—people's driving habits, the ways people talk to children, the ways shoppers treat store clerks.

3. Write a paragraph giving examples of things you do for entertainment—watching television, hiking, reading.

Writing the Process Paragraph

When you want to explain to readers how to do something, a process paragraph is your only choice. There are two chief things to keep in mind as you write a process paragraph: first, tell your readers what process you are describing, and, second, give every necessary step in the order in which it occurs. Use clear transitions (first, second, third, next, finally, and so on) to let your readers know when you are moving from one step to another.

Vic lets readers know immediately that he will show the process of making a baby laugh. Then he shows the steps to take, starting with the simplest cases and moving to the most extreme. Vic uses clear transitions such as "after that," "at this point," and "with this maneuver" to keep us moving through the process. Also, he consistently uses the second person "you" throughout the paragraph because he is giving directions specifically to his readers.

Vic's Paragraph

A most rewarding experience is making a baby laugh. The process involves a small amount of mental preparation. You must understand that it is okay to act goofy in front of a baby. After that knowledge is firm in your head, you should mold a grand ear-to-ear smile. The smile should be accompanied by a vast variation of facial contortions. A few examples are lifted eyebrows, wiggling ears, and a great look of surprise. If baby has not yet laughed, you can quickly develop a repertoire of strange but lively sounds. Hoots, beeps, barks, shrieks, and squeaks all work rather well. You must experiment with the particular pitch and tone which may tickle the individual baby's fancy. At this point the baby should be laughing. If so, keep up the good work; however, in some extreme cases all of the above might not affect that unresponsive child. These cases will require physical action because there are areas on everyone that react to the tickle of a finger. Some of these key locations are under the arms, on the tiny tummy, or on the bottoms of the feet. They may vary with different models. With this maneuver the baby will be laughing gleefully, and everybody's happy with a joyful baby. This is the true reward for your efforts.

Process descriptions are most often used in instruction manuals, and our professional example is from an automobile maintenance manual subtitled "A Guide for the Compleat Idiot."

> The pump should deliver more fuel than the engine can use. Let's measure it. The fuel return line is the large braided metal hose (rubber hose in U.S. made Rabbits) that begins at the base of the fuel distributor. It is connected by two captive nuts to a thin metal line running back to the gas tank. Loosen and pull apart the return line connection (two 17mm wrenches). Stick the end of the hose into your graduated container. Pull the big central wire from the coil to prevent the car from suddenly starting, and have Friend turn the starter over for 30 seconds. No more, no less. You should get at least 758cc (3/4 qt) of gas. Much less than this (500cc–1/2 qt–or so) with at least 11.5 volts to the pump (Procedure 1, Step 3) means that the pump is shot or the fuel filter or fuel lines are clogged. If you didn't get any gas, do Procedure 1 to check that the pump is working! I suspect the filter, so let's check it in Step 2. Lotsa gas? Reconnect the gas line to the fuel distributor and empty the gas into your fuel tank. Jump to Procedure 5.

Suggestions for Writing

1. Write a paragraph explaining how to do something that not many people know how to do—set the timing on a car, build a model airplane, prepare a flaming dessert. (Avoid the obvious, such as how to bake a cake or change a car's oil.)

2. Write a paragraph that explains to a recent immigrant how to apply for a driver's license.

3. Write a paragraph that shows a new student the process of registration at your college.

Writing the Comparison Paragraph

Sometimes when we write, we find ourselves focusing on how things are alike, and in cases like that, we might choose to develop the entire paragraph in the comparison pattern. The comparison paragraph shows similarities, and the contrast paragraph shows differences, but "comparison" is often used to refer to paragraphs that show either similarities or differences. In writing comparison (or contrast), you must first state what two things are being compared. You must know which specific points you plan to compare, and you must arrange the details in a logical order.

Details in a comparison paragraph may be arranged either in **point-by-point** or in **block style**, and the two paragraphs that follow show those two styles. The first example, David's paragraph, is point-by-point; it compares a jet mechanic and a surgeon on six points, and it completes its discussion of one point before it goes to the next. The second example, Frank's paragraph, uses the block style; it compares people who climb Mount Everest with people who eat in the school cafeteria, and it discusses the climbers completely before it discusses the eaters. In something as short as a paragraph, the block style is often smoother and more effective than is the point-by-point.

As you read David's paragraph, notice that the comparison is well-balanced. Each point he makes about the mechanic he also makes about the surgeon. Words like "just as" and "both" help to keep the reader's mind sharply focused on the comparison.

David's Paragraph

Being a jet mechanic is a lot like being a surgeon. First, the jet mechanic has to examine an engine just as carefully as a surgeon examines a person when something is wrong. After diagnosing the problem, both the surgeon and the mechanic have to take on the intricate and complicated job of fixing it. Jet mechanics use expensive instruments and tools, just as surgeons do, and both are required to know everything about their profession or the operation could be a failure. The work is intricate, hard, and time-consuming in both jobs; however, the mechanic and the surgeon both feel a certain satisfaction when the job is completed, when the jet engine works properly, or when the cured patient walks out the hospital doors.

As you read Frank's paragraph, notice that both parts are about equal in length and that the second part deals with each point that is brought up in the first part. The discussion, then, is balanced. The phrase "like the climbers" is an effective transition between the two parts because it clearly lets us know that the first part has ended and the comparison has begun.

Frank's Paragraph

Eating lunch in the school cafeteria is surprisingly like climbing Mount Everest. To get to the mountain, climbers have to travel a long way through the foothills. When they arrive at the mountain, they start up a route they've decided on ahead of time, but they'll usually find some problem that makes them change their plans. As they get closer to the top, the climbers face great hardship and danger, but the few who reach the top experience a thrill that can't be matched. Like the climbers, cafeteria diners begin with a long trip since lines are always long and slow. Once they get to the steam tables, diners' plans, like those of the climbers, usually change because of unexpected problems. Maybe the cooks have run out of a main dish, or maybe the food just doesn't look good. As the diners near their goal, they too face hardship and danger. First they must somehow find the money to pay for what they've chosen, then comes the death-defying act of eating the food. The comparison ends there, though, because the only thrill in finishing a cafeteria lunch is knowing that you won't have to go back again until the next day.

The professional comparison example appears as two paragraphs in Robert Pirsig's *Zen and the Art of Motorcycle Maintenance*.

You see things vacationing on a motocycle in a way that is completely different from any other. In a car you're always in a compartment, and because you're used to it you don't realize that through that car window everything you see is just more TV. You're a passive observer and it is all moving by you boringly in a frame.

On a cycle the frame is gone. You're completely in contact with it all. You're in the scene, not just watching it anymore, and the sense of presence is overwhelming. That concrete whizzing by five inches below your foot is the real thing, the same stuff you walk on, it's right there, so blurred you can't focus on it, yet you can put your foot down and touch it anytime, and the whole thing, the whole experience, is never removed from immediate consciousness.

Suggestions for Writing

1. Write a paragraph comparing two things that seem very different from each other—love and a disease, a friend and a place, studying for a test and a color.

2. Write a paragraph comparing two teachers or two textbooks you have had.

3. Write a paragraph comparing a high school class and a college class.

Writing the Cause–Effect Paragraph

Sometimes it is useful to explain why things happen; the cause–effect paragraph does just that. If you don't study for a test and you fail the test, your failure is the effect, and your lack of study is the cause. If you burn your hand on your coffee cup and then drop and break it, the burn is the cause, and the broken cup is the effect. Of course it wouldn't take a paragraph to explain either of these two incidents, but explaining something like why the sky appears blue or why you have certain feelings can require a paragraph or much more.

When you write a cause–effect paragraph, you must analyze your subject very carefully. Be sure that what you identify as a cause is, in fact, a cause. Ask, "Does that really cause this? Is this really an effect of that?" Be careful not to jump to conclusions.

In Paige's paragraph, she explains that dandelions make her happy because they remind her of her grandmother. Dandelions are the cause; happy thoughts of her grandmother are the effect.

Paige's Paragraph

On my way home from school yesterday, I saw a yard full of dandelions, and suddenly I felt very happy. As I thought about that, I realized that I felt happy because dandelions always remind me of my grandmother. Gram used to tell me that dandelions were her favorite flower, even though the rest of the neighborhood folks spent time and money trying to rid their lawns of the hated weed. When I see them, I can hear her voice saying, "I sure despise that old, cold winter more than these pretty, bright yellow flowers. I'm glad they're finally here." Also, they make me remember the warmth of her hugs when I'd pick a large bunch and run into the house with them. She'd find a vase to hold them and give them a place of honor on the mantle, and that made me feel special, for I felt that I'd given her something special. The joy that was always on her face is the thing I remember best about Gram, and dandelions always bring back the vision of that face. It's no wonder that dandelions make me happy.

The professional example of a cause and effect paragraph is from Sheila Tobias's book *Overcoming Math Anxiety*.

A common myth about the nature of mathematical ability holds that one either has or does not have a mathematical mind. Mathematical imagination and an intuitive grasp of mathematical principles may well be needed to do advanced research, but why should people who can do college-level work in other subjects not be able to do college-level math as well? Rates of learning may vary. Competency under time pressure may differ. Certainly low self-esteem will get in the way. But where is the evidence that a student needs a "mathematical mind" in order to succeed at learning math?

Consider the effects of this mythology. Since only a few people are supposed to have this mathematical mind, part of what makes us so passive in the face of our difficulties in learning mathematics is that we suspect all the while we may not be one of "them," and we spend our time waiting to find out when our nonmathematical minds will be exposed. Since our limit will eventually be reached, we see no point in being methodical or in attending to detail. We are grateful when we survive fractions, word problems, or geometry. If that certain moment of failure hasn't struck yet, it is only temporarily postponed.

Suggestions for Writing

1. Write a paragraph explaining how a boss's attitudes toward employees can cause a job to be pleasant or unpleasant.

2. Write a paragraph that shows some of the major effects of having children.

3. Write a paragraph that shows how your decision to go to college has affected your life.

Writing the Definition Paragraph

We often use words such as "freedom," "success," "pleasure," or "love," but these words usually require some definition because they mean different things to different people. They are highly abstract. Also, common, apparently simple words can have unusual meanings for some people, and these unusual meanings need to be explained or defined. When you write a **definition paragraph** to define an abstract term or give a special definition to an ordinary term, you must show your reader, as exactly as you can, what that term means to you. Both of our sample paragraphs do this well.

As you read Maryanne's paragraph, notice that she begins with a general definition of "success." She follows that general definition with specific examples. The examples help us to understand exactly what she means by "success." We can look at a person in a certain situation and say, "Maryanne would (or would not) call that person a success."

Maryanne's Paragraph

To some people, success can be measured in dollars, but to me success is the feeling that I've done the best job I can do at something I enjoy doing. Last fall, for example, I had decided that my effort at raising sheep would be successful if I could win a ribbon at the county fair, but even though I didn't win a ribbon, I still call the experience a success. I know I did the best I could, I made some new friends, I learned from the winners how to do better next time, and I returned home feeling successful. I'm not the only person who defines success this way, either. My friend Fred was what most people would call a successful businessman, but he never woke up feeling happy. Two years ago, he quit his job and is now making a lot less money, but he is enjoying his new job. Both of us would call him a success because he enjoys what he is doing, and he feels he does it well.

As you read Tammera's paragraph, you will see that she begins with a specific definition of "fad" and goes on to explain what, in her experience, has led her to define "fad" as she does. There is no doubt in our minds about what Tammera means by the word "fad." The paragraph is also wonderfully humorous, largely because Tammera is able to laugh at herself.

Tammera's Paragraph

To me, the word "fad" means almost the same thing as "fade" because fads fade away. It always seems that by the time I've caught on to a fad, it's dissolved. The fashion fads have fooled me most often. Last spring when mid-calf pants were in, I too, wanted to be in. Therefore, I proceeded to cut the bottom six inches off every pair of pants that I owned. They all still fit half a year later, but not one pair was in style. You'd think I would have learned. A few months later, I saw the trendy movie *Flashdance*. The clothing styles in the film were uniquely different. Once again, I cut the arms and collars off every sweatshirt and T-shirt in my closet. When the movie dropped from the top ten, so did the fad, and I was foiled again. Now I have learned my lesson. I won't be fooled again by these spurious, fleeting fads. I just purchased a pair of pink, plastic shoes. . . .

Gretel Ehrlich's definition of a cowboy is from her essay "About Men" in *The Solace of Open Spaces.*

A cowboy is someone who loves his work. Since the hours are long—ten to fifteen hours a day—and the pay is $30 he has to. What's required of him is an odd mixture of physical vigor and maternalism. His part of the beef-raising industry is to birth and nurture calves and take care of their mothers. For the most part his work is done on horseback and in a lifetime he sees and comes to know more animals than people. The iconic myth surrounding him is built on American notions of heroism: the index of a man's value as measured in physical courage. Such ideas have perverted manliness into a self-absorbed race for cheap thrills. In a rancher's world, courage has less to do with facing danger than with acting spontaneously—usually on behalf of an animal or another rider. If a cow is stuck in a boghole he throws a loop around her neck, takes his dally (a half hitch around the saddle horn), and pulls her out with horsepower. If a calf is born sick, he may take her home, warm her in front of the kitchen fire, and massage her legs until dawn. One friend, whose favorite horse was trying to swim a lake with hobbles on, dove under water and cut her legs loose with a knife, then swam her to shore, his arm around her neck lifeguard-style, and saved her from drowning. Because these incidents are usually linked to someone or something outside himself, the westerner's courage is selfless, a form of compassion.

Suggestions for Writing

1. Write a paragraph that defines the term "good mother" or "good father."

2. Write a paragraph that defines a term like "gifted athlete" or "talented artist."

3. Explain the meaning of a phrase or saying—"A bird in the hand is worth two in the bush," "Too many cooks spoil the broth," "When the going gets tough, the tough get going."

Writing the Division/Classification Paragraph

If you want to divide a subject into its parts so that your readers can better understand it, or when you want to group people or things into classifications or categories, the **division/classification** pattern is your choice. With division, you start with a single subject and identify its parts, examining each one in turn. With classification, you take many subjects and sort them into groups or classes according to the characteristics they share. For example, you might classify horror movies as monster movies, slasher movies, ghost movies, and so forth.

Connie divides her day into four parts, discussing what happens in each part.

Connie's Paragraph

As a student and a single mom, I find that my day has four distinct parts. The early mornings are preparation time. I crawl out of bed, cook breakfast, get the kids ready for school, fix their sack lunches, find their socks or hair ribbons, round up their books and homework, write permission slips, and find out who needs a ride to or from basketball practice. When the kids are on their way, I get myself ready for school and race to my first class. The second part of my day is school time. Three classes fill the rest of the morning. I spend a few hurried minutes with my own sack lunch and then run to the library to study or do research. I study until about 1:30, then hustle to the math center for tutoring. I arrive home three minutes before my kids get home unless I have to stop at the grocery store, and I usually do. Time to go to the bank, pay a bill, license my car or whatever has to be stolen from school time. I call the third part of my day "maintenance time." Jennifer has to be consoled because Shelly isn't her best friend anymore and has vowed to hate her forever. Bill has to explain why the teacher yelled at him in science class. And of course I have to see that they do their homework. I fix supper, throw a load of clothes in the washer, do the dishes, throw the clothes in the dryer, hoping it won't fall apart before the load is done, and do whatever cleaning is absolutely necessary. When the kids are tucked in, it's study time. By midnight or one I fall into bed, exhausted, and check the alarm to make sure it's ready to start me on part one of another hectic day.

"Can People Be Judged by Their Appearance?" by Eric Berne is the source of our professional model for the division/classification paragraph.

We can thus say that while the average human being is a mixture, some people are mainly "digestion-minded," some "muscle-minded," and some "brain-minded," and correspondingly digestion-bodied, muscle-bodied, or brain-bodied. The digestion-bodied people look thick; the muscle-bodied people look wide; and the brain-bodied people look long. This does not mean the taller a man is, the brainier he will be. It means that if a man, even a short man, looks long rather than wide or thick, he will often be more concerned about what goes on in his mind than about what he does or what he eats; but the key factor is slenderness and not height. On the other hand, a man who gives the impression of being thick rather than long or wide will usually be more interested in a good steak than in a good idea or a good long walk.

Suggestions for Writing

1. Write a paragraph dividing your friends into groups—close friends, social friends, casual acquaintances.

2. Write a paragraph classifying the people you might see in the grocery store—the bargain hunters, the impulse shoppers, the list fillers.

3. Pour the items from your "junk drawer" onto a table and separate them into groups that have something in common. Write a paragraph explaining how you decided upon the categories and how you determined which items belonged in which categories.

Writing the Opinion Paragraph

Everyone has opinions, and most of us don't hesitate to express them, at least to our friends. Opinions, though, vary from person to person, and some opinions deserve more consideration than do others. The opinion of an expert mechanic about what caused an airplane crash is more likely to be accurate than is the opinion of an untrained eyewitness. In events that directly concern us, though, we are all experts in some way or another, and our opinions are important.

When you write an **opinion paragraph**, write about something that is important to you and that you know about from your direct, personal experience. State clearly what your opinion is, and be sure you explain why you hold that opinion.

Kirsten wrote her opinion paragraph as one of her assignments, but she later rewrote it as a letter to the editor of the local newspaper, where it was published. The letters to the editor column is one of the most widely read sections of any newspaper, and it is an important place for citizens to share their opinions about matters that concern them.

Kirsten's Paragraph

On March 3, the Spokane Falls Community College girls' basketball team won the state championship for the second year in a row. Since that was our second consecutive state title, one would think that *The Spokesman–Review* would print a large article announcing this achievement. Turning to the sports section of Sunday's paper, I noticed large pictures and lengthy articles on the girls' state "B" basketball championship game and another article announcing that the Spokane Community College men's team had finished fifth in its state tournament. Mention of the Spokane Falls girls' team championship didn't appear until three pages into the sports section. This article had no pictures. Being a member of this talented team, I am disappointed to find so little mention of our successful team.

Here is Kirsten's letter as it was published in the Spokane, Washington, *Spokesman–Review*. The editor has made some changes because editorial-page editors like letters to be brief, to the point, and about one specific issue.

They may sometimes edit letters by omitting sections or by correcting spelling and punctuation, and they will almost always make the paragraphs shorter.

Kirsten's Letter

"Your Views"
The Spokesman–Review
Spokane, WA 99210

Dear Editor:

On March 3, the Spokane Falls Community College girls' basketball team won the state championship for the second year in a row.

Since that was our second consecutive state title, one would think that *The Spokesman–Review* would print a large article announcing this achievement.

Turning to the sports section of Sunday's paper, I noticed large pictures and lengthy articles on the girls' state "B" basketball championship game and another long article announcing that the Spokane Community College men's team had finished fifth in its state tournament.

Mention of the Spokane Falls girls' team championship didn't appear until three pages into the sports section, and this article had no pictures. Being a member of this talented team, I am disappointed to find so little mention of our successful team.

Kirsten Riegel

This paragraph by Martin Luther King, Jr., "Letter from Birmingham Jail," is a clear and compelling statement of the reasons he believes that black people should wait no longer for desegregation.

We have waited for more than 340 years for our constitutional and God-given rights. The nations of Asia and Africa are moving with jetlike speed toward gaining political independence, but we still creep at horse-and-buggy pace toward gaining a cup of coffee at a lunch counter. Perhaps it is easy for those who have never felt the stinging darts of segregation to say, "Wait." But when you have seen vicious mobs lynch your mothers and fathers at will and drown your sisters and brothers at whim; when you have seen hate-filled policemen curse, kick, and even kill your black brothers and sisters; when you see the vast majority of your twenty million Negro brothers smothering in an air-tight cage of poverty in the midst of an affluent society; when you suddenly find your tongue twisted and your speech stammering as you seek to explain to your six-year-old daughter why she can't go to the public amusement park that has just been advertised on television, and see tears welling up in her eyes when she is told that Funtown is closed to colored children, and see ominous clouds of inferiority beginning to form in her little mental sky, and see her beginning to distort her personality by developing an unconscious bitterness toward white people; when you have to concoct an answer for a five-year-old son who is asking, "Daddy, why do white people treat colored people so mean?"; when you take a cross-country drive and find it necessary to sleep night after night in the uncomfortable corners of your automobile because no motel will accept you; when you are humiliated day in and day out by nagging signs reading "white" and "colored"; when your first name becomes "nigger," your middle name becomes "boy" (however old you are) and your last name becomes "John," and your wife and mother are never given the respected title "Mrs."; when you are harried by day and haunted by night by the fact that you are a Negro, living constantly at tiptoe stance, never quite knowing what to expect next, and are plagued with inner fears and outer resentments; when you are forever fighting a degenerating sense of "nobodiness"—then you will understand why we find it difficult to wait. There comes a time when the cup of endurance runs over, and men are no longer willing to be plunged into the abyss of despair. I hope, sirs, you can understand our legitimate and unavoidable impatience.

Suggestions for Writing

1. Write a paragraph expressing and supporting your opinion about the grading system used at your college or by a specific instructor.

2. Write a paragraph expressing and supporting your opinion on a specific zoning or land use issue in your neighborhood or community.

3. Write a paragraph expressing and supporting your opinion about a rule or set of rules your parents established for you when you were growing up.

This chapter marks the end of our discussion of general paragraph writing skills. The rest of this book discusses the kinds of writing you're likely to have to do for other college courses and how you can apply the principles of good writing you've learned so far. As you may have already discovered, the more you write and practice these skills, the more confident you become each time you write.

PREVIEW FOR CHAPTER 9

Frank had once been an avid gardener. A self-taught botanist, he tended flowers as a mother nurtures her small children. The numerous hours in the hot sun withered and wrinkled his skin, and now his deadly disease was draining the life from him.

His wife had always been the party girl. Lately, however, the afternoon bull sessions with cocktails, the girls from work, and the odd joint floating around had turned into all-night cocaine sessions and seedy liaisons with punk coke dealers. As her habit grew, her personality changed. She flailed constantly at her children. "I wish I'd never made the mistake of having you. I'm counting the days until you're out of my hair."

There it was in black and white. The <u>Silver Valley News Press</u> had printed an article about my hit-and-run accident.

It may not have been as fast or as sleek as a Corvette. It may not have had the beauty and luxury of a Lincoln. It may not have been able to go as far off the road as a Jeep. Nothing was more practical, however, than my beat-up old Ford pickup.

There are few jobs where you may see the miracle of birth, the horror of serious trauma, the tragedy of a cancer patient in life's last stages, and the joy of a patient discharged after successful major surgery all in one day's work.

9 WRITING THE ESSAY

SKILLS INTRODUCED

Writing the essay:

1. Outline and plan the essay
2. Write body paragraphs
3. Write the introductory paragraph
4. Write the concluding paragraph
5. Revise the essay

The paragraphs you have been writing have allowed you to explore single ideas, but if you want to discuss a subject in more breadth or depth than the paragraph allows, or if you want to explore more complex topics, the essay permits you to do this. An essay is a collection of paragraphs that focuses on and develops a single idea. Like a paragraph, an essay has a controlling idea; for an essay, we call this controlling idea the **thesis statement**. The type of essay we will discuss usually has five or six paragraphs. The first or **introductory paragraph** introduces the subject of the essay and contains the thesis statement. It is a different kind of paragraph from those you have been writing, and you will study introductions in this chapter. The following paragraphs, the **body paragraphs**, are the kinds that you have been writing. Each one supports or explains some part of the thesis statement. The final or **concluding paragraph** brings the essay smoothly to an end, and it, too, is a special kind of paragraph that you will study. Figure 9-1 shows a diagram of an essay.

The process of writing an essay is similar to the process of writing a paragraph. It is a little more complex because the ideas are often more complex and because the essay is longer than the paragraph, but most of your college writing will be in the essay form.

STEP 1:
Brainstorm to Discover What You Know

The techniques for brainstorming don't change at all from those discussed in Chapter 2. In choosing a subject for the essay that we use as an example, our student Annette used listing to explore possible topics. Here is her list:

1. working at fast food restaurants
2. trip to Mexico
3. friendship with Vicki
4. high school graduation
5. winning basketball championship
6. camping with the gang
7. fifth grade teacher
8. grandma

The list is short because when Annette got to the last item, she knew that her grandmother was what she wanted to write about. Her grandmother had recently visited, so memories were fresh in Annette's mind. She knew that other people have and appreciate relatives with unusual habits, and she knew she could entertain a reading audience with tales of her grandma. Her audience, then, would be anyone old enough to understand that one can be amused and annoyed by someone's habits, yet still love that person. Her purpose would be to entertain her readers by sharing with them that combination of emotions.

Choosing a subject that you know and care about will ensure that you have enough information to develop your subject adequately and will help you to write honestly and in your own voice. Knowing your audience and your purpose will help you identify and select specific details, appropriate methods of development (see Chapter 8), interesting vocabulary, and so forth.

INTRODUCTION
(contains thesis)

BODY PARAGRAPH
(has topic sentence that supports thesis, and details of
paragraph support and develop topic sentence)

BODY PARAGRAPH
(has topic sentence that supports thesis, and details of
paragraph support and develop topic sentence)

BODY PARAGRAPH
(has topic sentence that supports thesis, and details
of paragraph support and develop topic sentence)

CONCLUSION
(brings essay smoothly to close)

Figure 9-1   The Essay in Diagram Form

After Annette had chosen her subject, she spent some time freewriting in order to help herself recall some of the details that would go into her essay and make it come alive for her readers. Here is her freewriting:

> I wonder if I'll belch when I'm eighty. If I do I hope I'll at least recognize it when I do. Poor old dear, but it doesn't seem to bother her. Oh, well. I wonder what color her hair really is. Or if she talks to her hairdresser the way she talks to those clerks. Why does a sales clerk need to know that her son's an engineer, that she was brought up in Montana, that her dad owned a grocery store, that she thinks sales tax is a rip-off, and on and on and on. And the snoring—maybe now that she's gone back home I can get some sleep and Mom can ride in the front seat again. Will we ever get the smoke smell out of the house and car? I doubt it. How does she live with—oh, she can't smell, but why the perfume? Habit, I guess, just like wearing a size twelve because she's always worn a size twelve and she knows darned well that her metabolism is so high she can't have gained weight. God, am I doomed to try to be forever young and tell dirty jokes and write the same letter week after week and annoy my grandchildren? I hope they love me as much as I love her. Strange how much I miss her when she's gone and how much she bothers me when she's here. I can hear my tv show now, but I miss laughing with her and at her, and I even miss the stories about when my dad was a boy—I've only heard them all a dozen times or more, but I wonder if I'll remember them when my kids ask questions. I guess I'd better write her a letter and tell her I love her.

With her freewriting and her memories of her grandmother's recent visit, Annette thought she was ready to start the first draft of her essay.

Writing Activity 9.1

- Brainstorm to explore possible subjects for an essay.
- Choose a subject, and then explore it thoroughly by using one of the brainstorming methods you have

learned. If you need to, review Chapter 2 for brainstorming methods.

• Think carefully about your audience and your purpose.

STEP 2:
Write the Thesis Statement

Like the topic sentence of a paragraph, the thesis statement of an essay
names the subject and says something about that subject; it states the controlling idea of the essay. Just as a topic sentence is a one-sentence summary
of the paragraph, the thesis statement is a one-sentence summary of the essay. The thesis statement will usually be included in the introductory paragraph of the essay, often as the last sentence of that first paragraph. The
thesis will control what details go into the essay and what details stay out.
Even in an essay you won't have room to say all that can be said about a
subject, and the thesis acts as your guide to selecting those details that must
be included if your essay is to accomplish its purpose.

Remember that your thesis, like the topic sentence of a paragraph, must
be a complete sentence; it must state a complete thought. "My first date," for
example, cannot work as a thesis, for it doesn't state a complete thought. It
merely names the subject of the essay. "My first date was a disaster," however,
works well, for it names the subject and states a complete thought about it.
Similarly, "How to build a doghouse" or "The time I was mistaken for a movie
star" cannot be thesis statements. "Building a doghouse requires five important steps" or "Being mistaken for a movie star was one of the funniest experiences of my life" can work as thesis statements, for they state complete
thoughts.

For her thesis, Annette wrote this sentence:

**Grandma's quirks are sometimes difficult to deal with, but I
still find them endearing.**

Annette's thesis reflects the ideas she had when she first decided upon
her subject, but that is not always the case. Sometimes writers change their
minds as they brainstorm and arrive at ideas that are quite different from
those they started with, so don't be alarmed if this happens to you. It's simply

part of the process of discovery that brainstorming is designed to encourage. As you outline, draft, and revise your essay, your thesis may change even further, becoming more and more specific as your ideas become clearer and more sharply focused.

Writing Activity 9.2

- Write a thesis statement that reflects the ideas you have discovered and explored in your brainstorming.
- Be sure your thesis statement is a complete sentence.
- Since this is such an important step, you may want to share your thesis with your instructor and revise it if necessary before going on to Step 3.

STEP 3:
Outline the Essay

Outlining an essay is similar to outlining a paragraph in that you write your thesis statement, turn it into a question, and answer the question. When you write your essay, the thesis will be one of the sentences (often the last one) in your introductory paragraph, and your answers to the thesis question will become the topic sentences of the essay's body paragraphs. Let's look at Annette's outline.

Ideas for Introduction:

Talk about a typical grandma and contrast her with mine.

Thesis:

Grandma's quirks are sometimes difficult to deal with, but I still find them endearing.

Thesis Question:

How are Grandma's quirks difficult to deal with, and why do I find them endearing?

Answers:

1. Her letters always say the same thing.
   Examples:
   hairdressers
   new pantsuits
   weather

2. One of her favorite pastimes is beer drinking, which causes her to belch.

3. She loves to tell the same stories over and over.
   Examples:
   talks when tv is on
   talks when I'm reading the paper

4. Her cigarettes fill our house with fumes that linger long after she leaves.
   Examples:
   curtains to the cleaners
   driving with car windows open for days

5. Riding in the car with her is an ordeal.
   Examples:
   Mom in back seat
   non-stop smoking
   I can't roll down window

6. Shopping trips are considered necessary.
   Examples:
   search for pantsuit and handbag
   finding a big enough size 12
   returning purchases to store
   she tells our life history

Ideas for conclusion:

She loves me and gives me advice. She helps me out when I need it. She's special to me.

Note that as she wrote answers to her thesis question, Annette jotted down ideas and details that she might use in developing her body paragraphs. She also jotted down ideas that she might use in her introduction and conclusion, and it is clear that she intended to use her conclusion to develop the idea that she loves her grandmother in spite of her quirks.

It's a good idea to make such notes to yourself as you outline. They can serve as a kind of shorthand way of outlining your body paragraphs.

Writing Activity 9.3

- Outline your essay.
- Be sure your question contains the important words from your thesis.
- Be sure your answers do, in fact, answer the thesis question and can work as topic sentences for the body paragraphs they will control.
- Jot down details to use in developing your body paragraphs.

STEP 4:
Write the First Draft

Some writers like to begin the first draft by starting with the introductory paragraph, and some like to use the thesis all by itself as the introduction while writing the first draft. Our usual advice is to begin with the paragraph that seems easiest to write, which is usually one of the body paragraphs. If you have any doubts about how to start your essay, write your thesis as a one-sentence introductory paragraph, and then write your first answer to your thesis question as the first sentence of body paragraph one. After that, write your first body paragraph, then go to the second, following the same procedure you did for the first. If you have trouble developing your body paragraphs, try outlining them in the way that you have studied.

Because Annette began with good ideas for her introduction and her body paragraphs, her rough draft begins with an introductory paragraph, and its body paragraphs are already well developed.

First Draft: Oddball Grandma

Most people, when thinking of grandma, picture a little, bent-over, white-haired lady, who makes the best chocolate chip cookies in the nation. Not I. The only grandmother I have ever known is an eighty-year old, chain-smoking, beer-drinking, retired party lover, who enjoys telling off-color jokes. Grandma's quirks are sometimes hard to deal with, but I still find them endearing.

My grandma dearly loves to write letters. Since she lives alone in another state, written communication is one of the few ways she can stay in touch with her son and grandchildren. Her letters arrive at our home at least twice weekly and are extremely predictable. She generally writes about her newest hairdresser or a pantsuit she has recently bought. Staying young looking is one of her main concerns; hence, I have never seen her natural hair color nor her cheeks without rouge. And she always wears a favorite perfume, even though she can't smell.

Another of my grandma's favorite pastimes is beer drinking. She tends to open a can after lunch and to sip on it all afternoon. By dinner time, she'll have consumed two beers and built up enough gas in her stomach to let out a couple of good-sized belches. Surprisingly, this doesn't deter her one bit; she'll just continue to simultaneously chew and speak, as if nothing had occurred.

Many events have transpired in my grandma's lifetime and she loves to talk about them. I never worry if I don't catch the whole story the first time through as it is sure to be heard at any possible occasion. Two of her favorite moments for story telling are when the television is on or when someone is trying to read the newspaper. She is even noisy while sleeping as she has a tendency to snore continually throughout the night. When confronted with this fact, however, she absolutely denies there is any truth to it.

Truthfully speaking, my grandma's most annoying habit must be smoking cigarettes. When she comes to see us, our entire house becomes infiltrated with fumes, and they linger on after her departure for home. After one of Grandma's visits, even the curtains must be taken to the cleaners to remove the offensive odor. Furthermore, it takes days of driving with the windows open for the family car to once again become fresh smelling.

Riding in the car with my grandmother is always an ordeal. To begin with, my mother must disgruntledly take the back seat so my dad's mother may sit next to her son. Then, after installing herself next to my father, she lights a

Kent and consecutively inhales one after another, throughout the entire excursion. Unfortunately, she must also exhale the smoke, and it does not hesitate in meandering to the back end, where I proceed to get violently carsick. An obvious solution to the dilemma would be to roll down a window, but this action is considered taboo as it could result in disarraying her painstakingly arranged hair.

When Grandma comes to visit, shopping trips are considered necessary. My mother is the expert in this field and she habitually proceeds to chauffeur Granny from one shopping center to the next. A new polyester pantsuit with matching handbag and shoes must be acquired to make her visitation a success. The stressful part of this situation is trying to find a sufficiently ample size twelve suit to fit her. She refuses to wear anything larger as it is believed that her high metabolism amazingly prevents her from gaining weight. My grandmother is often displeased with her purchases, so they have to be returned to the stores. This can become quite embarrassing as she always makes sure she tells every salesperson our life history, her son's occupation, and that she is from Montana and there's no sales tax over there.

One might wonder how I could possibly find any of my grandmother's notorious quirks endearing. However, the fact remains that she loves me and shows her affection in various manners. If I ever want guidance, she is anxious to give advice. And if I need something, she is the first one to help me out. Furthermore, although her actions become at times truly frustrating, she is the only grandmother I'll ever have. Because of these reasons, and for many others, my grandma is special to me and I will always remember her with love.

Writing Activity 9.4

- Write a rough draft of your essay. Write an introductory paragraph if you wish, or just use your thesis as a one-sentence introductory paragraph. Pay careful attention to structuring and developing each body paragraph.

• Write a brief concluding paragraph that will bring your essay to a close.

Write the Introductory Paragraph

The introductory paragraph serves three main functions. First, it captures your reader's interest—it serves as a lead or "grabber." In Chapter 4 (pages 53–54) you studied examples of openings that grab the reader's interest, and Annette's introduction does that well. Second, the introductory paragraph contains the thesis or controlling idea of the essay and shows the writer's attitude toward the subject. You have studied a great deal about how controlling ideas work in paragraphs, and the thesis is not significantly different from a topic sentence; it controls a collection of paragraphs rather than just one. Third, the introduction often shows the order in which the main ideas of the essay will be discussed.

The introduction should be brief but still grab the reader's attention. Commonly used openings are

- An anecdote or brief story. This might give your reader a brief glimpse of something or someone you will discuss later in your essay.
- A quotation. A line from a song or a well-known statement by a famous person can be an excellent attention grabber.
- A question or startling fact. Arousing your reader's curiosity is the best attention grabber of all, but your question or fact must be carefully chosen. Be sure it will, in fact, make your reader curious about what you will say in the paper.
- Background information. Sometimes the reader needs just a little background to really understand an essay, and the introduction is an excellent place to provide this.
- Scene setting. Especially in descriptive essays, it is often effective to paint a verbal picture that will put your reader in the place you want to describe.

Your introduction should be appropriate for the essay you write, and there's no way to give you a formula for choosing a type of introduction to use. If you can't decide how to introduce your essay, write two or three possible introductions based on our suggestions and choose the one you like best.

Write the Concluding Paragraph

The conclusion brings the paper smoothly to a close. It should be short, and it should leave your readers with a sense of completeness. Annette's conclusion is typical in that it restates the thesis. Many of the same techniques you use for introductions can be used to conclude your essay. Common conclusions are

- A restatement of the thesis with a summary of the main points.
- A statement of the importance of your subject.
- A quotation or an anecdote that seems to illustrate your main point and leave the reader with something to ponder.
- A personal note or a lesson that can be learned from your essay.

As for an introduction, there is no set formula for a conclusion. Think of your reading audience, and think about the idea that you want to leave in your readers' minds. The important thing is that your readers feel that the essay has not just stopped but has come naturally to an end.

Writing Activity 9.5

- Write at least two possible introductions for your essay from activity 9.4.
- Write at least two possible conclusions for your essay.

STEP 5:
Revise the Essay

As Annette looked back over her outline and her first draft, she saw some problems with organization. The first two body paragraphs didn't seem to have topic sentences that controlled them; both the paragraph about smoking and the paragraph about riding in the car seemed to be mostly about Grandma's smoking; finally, the essay didn't seem to focus on her claim that she finds Grandma's quirks endearing. In thinking about it, Annette decided that it wasn't the quirks that endeared her grandmother to her, so she decided that she would have to change her thesis. She looked at the details of her essay and decided that her grandmother's quirks really fit into three categories: her noisiness, her desire to look young, and her smoking. With that analysis, she began to revise. Here's her final draft:

Final Draft: Oddball Grandma

Most people, when they think of a grandma, picture a little, bent-over, white-haired lady who makes the best chocolate chip cookies in the nation. Not I. The only grandmother I have ever known is an eighty-year-old, chain-smoking, beer-drinking, retired party-lover who enjoys telling off-color jokes. She's definitely an oddball, but while her quirks are often hard to live with, I still think she's the dearest grandma in the world.

Sometimes I think Grandma must be one of the noisiest people alive. Every time she visits, she loves to tell and re-tell the stories of her life, especially when I'm trying to watch television or read the newspaper. If she's telling a story that's new to me, I don't worry if I don't catch it all the first time through; I know I'll hear it again and again, probably during one of my favorite shows. Right after lunch, Grandma will open a can of beer and sip on it as she tells her stories or shares her latest jokes, roaring with laughter at the punch lines. By supper time she'll have consumed two beers and built up enough gas in her stomach to let out two or three deafening belches. She doesn't seem to notice,though, and just keeps chewing and talking as if nothing had happened. She is even noisy when she is sleeping, as she snores continually through the night. When we mention it, though, she absolutely denies that it happens.

Sometimes I wish Grandma would admit her age, but she's committed to staying young-looking. I have never seen her natural hair color nor her cheeks without rouge, and even though she's lost her sense of smell she can't live without Emeraude, her favorite perfume. When she's at home, her twice-weekly letters always have some information about a new hairdresser or a new pantsuit she's bought, and when she comes to visit, she can't wait to go to the malls and see the newest styles. No visit can be a success unless Grandma acquires a new polyester pantsuit with matching handbag and shoes. My mother dutifully chauffeurs Grandma from one shopping center to the next, following her from store to store. The stressful part of shopping is trying to find a sufficiently ample size twelve suit to fit her. She refuses to wear anything larger, for she's convinced that her high metabolism has prevented her from gaining any weight in the past ten years. While we're looking, Grandma tries to make friends, especially with the young salespeople, telling them our family's history, her son's occupation, and that she's from Montana where they don't have a sales tax. After we've finally been successful and returned home, Grandma finds something wrong with the purchases, so back we go to exchange them. By the end of the day I'm exhausted, but Grandma's ready to put on her new clothes and go dancing.

I have to admit that my grandma's smoking annoys me most. When she comes to visit, our entire house becomes permeated with fumes that linger on after her departure, and riding in the car with her is a special ordeal. My disgruntled mother takes the back seat so Grandma can climb in next to her son. Immediately, Grandma lights a Kent; she'll inhale one after another throughout the entire excursion. Unfortunately, she also must exhale, and the smoke meanders back to enshroud my mother and me. It makes me violently carsick, and an obvious response would be to roll down the window, but that's taboo. The breeze might disarray Grandma's painstakingly arranged hair.

One might wonder how I could possibly love this noisy, vain, cigarette-puffing woman, but I do. The fact is that she loves me and shows her affection in many ways. If I ever want advice, she is happy to give it. And if I need something, she is the first one to help me out. In spite of her quirks and habits, she's the only grandmother I'll ever have, and I'll always welcome her and remember her with love.

Annette made many good changes as she revised, and her final draft is a strong one. The thesis does a much better job of controlling, the body paragraphs show that Grandma's quirks are hard to live with, and the concluding paragraph shows that Annette does, indeed, love her grandmother in spite of the quirks. Her readers almost certainly know people who have annoying habits, yet are likeable people, so they can identify with Annette's feelings. Part of Annette's purpose is to show how irritating Grandma's quirks can be, and she certainly achieves that purpose but in an amusing enough way so that the reader is entertained.

In her first body paragraph, Annette took details from the first, second, and third body paragraphs of her first draft, using the word "noisy" from her third body paragraph as the controlling word for the paragraph. For her second body paragraph, she took details from the first and sixth body paragraphs of her rough draft, using the idea of staying young-looking to form the topic sentence. Her third body paragraph combines the fourth and fifth body paragraphs of her rough draft. The result is a more tightly focused essay that develops its thesis with specific examples.

Another Student Example

As a final student example, let's look at the drafting and revision process that Nick used as he wrote a paper about a truly unforgettable experience—a rough, dangerous ocean voyage. Read this essay before you begin your own revision.

Nick used listing as a brainstorming technique for this paper, and his list led him to the following outline:

Thesis:

> **My last voyage as a crew member on an ocean-going oil tanker turned out to be an unforgettable, miserable experience.**

Thesis question;

> **How was my last voyage unforgettable and miserable?**

Answers:

> 1. **My friend and shipmate Jim was severely injured while attempting to cross the walkway on the deck to reach the bridge.**
> 2. **The injuries I suffered while searching for Jim, although only temporary, were very painful.**

3. Although the weather started to show improvement,
there were still more troubles ahead for all of us.

Because the experience was so vivid in Nick's memory, he didn't include
specific details in his outline, as Annette had. As he wrote, Nick was careful to
follow the outline format and to use each of his answers as a topic sentence.
While this is generally good practice, notice as you read the rough draft that it
makes his exciting story too stiff and formal.

First Draft: My Last Voyage

Many people cross the ocean for pleasure, but for some
the crossing of the ocean is their occupation. It's a dangerous way to make a living. The ship's mighty turbines
were operating at dead slow. The ship's autopilot, electronic
gyro and radar were all turned off, and only the magnetic
compass was available for navigation. The helmsman at
the wheelhouse was struggling to maintain the heading ordered by the captain. Although it was a cold night, he was
sweating profusely. With waves up to 60 feet high and
winds well over 100 miles per hour, his attempts to maintain
the correct heading proved to be an impossible task. We
were in the middle of a typhoon. At this point it was all too
clear to us that the ship and crew were at the mercy of the
Pacific Ocean. My last voyage as a crew member on an
ocean-going oil tanker turned out to be an unforgettable
experience.

My friend and shipmate Jim was severely injured while
attempting to cross the walkway on the deck to reach the
bridge. It was one hour before midnight, and Jim and I were
standing in the hallway behind a tightly sealed steel exit
door. Looking through the window with the phone receiver
pressed to my ear I waited for the all clear signal from the
bridge to open the door. We were talking about the lousy
weather when the man on the other end of the phone said,
"Now." I pulled the steel bar on the door to the open position,
and I flipped the high power light switch on. Jim, without
saying a word, stepped out and engaged the hook of his
safety belt to the rails. I pulled the door shut and locked it,
engaging all locking bars. I immediately looked through

the window and saw him being swept away by the crashing waves. He was thrown clear off the walkway against the steel tank openings on the deck. I pulled the alarm switch, the powerful loud electronic siren came on, and the entire crew reported to the exit within seconds. Using all available safety gear, we started searching for Jim. Three hours later we found him jammed between two steel pipes. He was frozen stiff and unconscious. But we soon discovered our troubles were not over yet.

The injuries I suffered while searching for Jim, although only temporary, were very painful. Wearing my leather safety belt, the minimum amount of clothing and secured to a nylon rope held by five crewmen, I was lowered onto the deck. I started searching for Jim, but it was a very slow process. The high wind forced me to crawl. Using the steel pipes on the deck I pulled myself forward a few feet at a time. The waves were another problem; millions of gallons of sea water were crashing on top of me. Sometimes I was thrown against a steel wall, and the pain in my back was unbearable. As I was attempting to get up and move to another area, I was hit on my side by a swinging crane beam. That hit catapulted me about fifteen feet and five feet up. Luckily for me, the deck was under three feet of water at that time, so when I came down, I didn't suffer any more injuries. By that time I wasn't feeling any pain, only numbness, so I kept searching for Jim. When the search was over, I went inside, my body started to warm up, and the pain in my back and side was more than I could stand.

Although the weather started to show improvement, there were still more troubles ahead for all of us. Twelve hours later the worst had passed, but we found ourselves in a new predicament. The wind subsided, the sea was calmer and the sky was clear. The change of the weather allowed us to turn on the navigation instruments. It didn't take long for us to discover that we were eighty miles off course and one hundred miles back from our last known position. This was of no help at all for Jim's condition. It would take five days to get back to our last position and about ten more days before we could get any medical help for Jim. Our troubles appeared to have no end. We discovered our drinking water was contaminated with salt, oil and rust. Immediately we focused our attention to the fresh water converter unit. This unit converts sea water to drinking water. It was a relief to discover it was in working order. By that time we were saying "enough is enough." But to make our situation even worse, it was discovered one of the oil tanks was leaking. It wouldn't have been so bad if it had been crude oil leaking, but the leaky tank was holding the oil used to operate the boilers. Without it we couldn't go anywhere. After several hours and a lot of hard work, the oil was transferred to another tank, and we continued our voyage toward our final destination.

Take my advice, next time you decide to cross the ocean, take a submarine. It could be safer. We reached our final destination with no more problems, but upon a physical examination, Jim's head injuries were diagnosed as severe and permanent. He was sent home immediately. The injuries I received were temporary and needed only time to heal. I was hospitalized for only a few days. The day I got off the ship was the last I saw of crew and ship. The ship was a disaster inside and out. It was sent to a dry dock for a complete overhaul. As for me, the experience helped me make up my mind never again to cross the ocean on a ship.

When we learn that this essay will be about an experience, we expect to see the events in the order in which they actually happened. The topic sentences that appear in the outline, however, caused the writer to jumble the order of some of the events. For example, in the first body paragraph of the first draft the writer discusses how Jim got lost and ends that discussion with finding Jim. The topic sentence of the next paragraph is about the writer's own injuries, but he has to go back in time and talk about the search for Jim in order to show how those injuries occurred. There seems to be no good reason for these shifts in time.

Sometimes an outline can lock a writer into a pattern that is not the best way to develop a subject. Use your outline as a tool to help you plan the paper, but don't let it hurt your paper. Even before he began his revision, Nick had a feeling that the topic sentences didn't fit and were forcing him to do some things he didn't want to do. The outline had helped him decide which events of the experience were most important, but when he revised his paper to show the events in the order in which they actually happened, Nick found that while the ideas didn't change, the manner in which they were expressed improved greatly. Here's Nick's final draft.

Final Draft: My Last Voyage

Many people cross the ocean for pleasure, but for some the crossing of the ocean is their occupation. It's a dangerous way to make a living, and it isn't always pleasant. My last voyage as a crew member on an ocean-going oil tanker turned out to be an unforgettable, miserable experience.

The ship's mighty turbines were operating at dead slow. The ship's autopilot, electronic gyro and radar were all turned off, and only the magnetic compass was available for navigation. The helmsman at the wheelhouse was struggling to maintain the heading ordered by the captain. Although it was a cold night, he was sweating profusely. With waves up to 60 feet high and winds well over 100 miles per hour, his attempts to maintain the correct heading proved to be an impossible task. We were in the middle of a typhoon. At this point it was all too clear to us that the ship and crew were at the mercy of the Pacific Ocean.

It was one hour before midnight, and Jim and I were standing in the hallway behind a tightly-sealed steel exit door. Looking through the window and pressing the phone receiver to my ear, I waited for the all clear signal from the bridge to open the door. We were talking about the lousy weather when the man on the other end of the phone line said, "Now." I pulled the steel bar on the door to the open position, and I flipped the high power light switch on.

Jim, without saying a word, stepped out and engaged the hook of his safety belt to the rails. I pulled the door shut and locked it, engaging all locking bars. I immediately looked through the window and saw Jim being swept away by the crashing waves. He was thrown clear off the walkway against the steel tank openings on the deck. I pulled the alarm switch; the powerful, loud electronic siren came on, and the entire crew reported to the exit within seconds. Using all available safety gear, we started searching for Jim.

Wearing my leather safety belt and a minimum amount of clothing and secured to a nylon rope held by five crewmen, I was lowered onto the deck. I started searching for Jim, but it was a very slow process. The high wind forced me to crawl. Using the steel pipes on the deck, I pulled myself forward a few feet at a time. The waves were another problem: millions of gallons of water were crashing on top of me. Sometimes I was three feet under water. All of a sudden it happened. I was thrown against a steel wall, and the pain in my back was unbearable. As I was attempting to get up and move to another area, I was hit on my side by a swinging crane beam. That hit catapulted me about fifteen feet along the deck and five feet in the air. Luckily for me, the deck was under three feet of water at that time, so when I came down, I didn't suffer any more injuries. By that time I wasn't feeling any pain, only numbness, so I kept on searching for Jim. Three hours later we found him jammed between two steel pipes. He was frozen stiff and unconscious. When the search was over, I went inside. My body started to warm up, and the pain in my back and side was more than I could stand.

Twelve hours later the worst of the weather and my pain had passed, but we found ourselves in a new predicament. The wind subsided, the sea was calmer and the sky was clear. The change of the weather allowed us to turn on the navigation instruments. It didn't take long for us to discover that we were 80 miles off course and 100 miles back from our last known position. This was of no help at all for Jim's condition. It would take two days to get back to our last position and about ten more days before we could get any medical help for Jim. Our troubles appeared to have no end. We discovered our drinking water was contaminated with salt, oil and rust. Immediately we focused our attention on the fresh water converter unit. This unit converts sea water into drinking water. It was a relief to discover it was in working order. By that time we were saying, "Enough is enough." But to make our situation even worse, it was discovered one of the oil tanks was leaking. It wouldn't have been so bad if it had been crude oil leaking, but the leaky tank was holding the oil used to operate the boilers. Without it we couldn't go anywhere. After several hours and a lot of hard work, the oil was transferred to another tank, and we continued our voyage toward our final destination.

Take my advice: next time you decide to cross the ocean, take a submarine. It could be safer. We reached our final destination with no more problems, but upon a physical examination, Jim's head injuries were diagnosed as severe and permanent. He was sent home immediately. The injuries I received were temporary and needed only time to heal. I was hospitalized for only a few days. The ship was a disaster inside and out. It was sent to a dry dock for a complete overhaul. This experience helped me make up my mind never again to cross the ocean on a ship.

Nick's shortened introduction gets right to the point, and the second paragraph of his essay sets the scene, using information from the longer introduction to his first draft. Most important, he has dropped the topic sentences from his paragraphs and has, instead, presented the events in the order that they happened. The events, then, move more like the actions of a short story or a novel than like the thoughts and ideas of an essay, but all of the necessary information is there. Nick's purpose is to show his readers that the voyage was unforgettable and miserable, and the revisions let the readers live the experience more fully.

You may never have had an experience this exciting, but your experiences, whatever they are, are unique. Only *you* have seen your experiences from your point of view. If you write about things that are significant to you or that stand out in your memory for some reason, and if you explore your subjects to understand why they are important to you, your readers will come away from your essay with a new understanding.

Writing Activity 9.6

• Write a revision of your essay.
• Look first at your thesis and the topic sentence of each body paragraph. Do the topic sentences clearly support or develop the thesis?
• Look carefully at your body paragraphs. Are they well unified? Fully developed? Would each one be a strong paragraph as judged by the standards you used to

judge your earlier paragraphs? Should some of your paragraphs be combined or separated? Should the details of your essay be grouped differently?

• When the body of your essay is in good shape, work on your introduction and conclusion.

Sample from a Professional Writer

In closing this chapter, let's look at an essay titled "Clever Animals" written by Lewis Thomas, a medical doctor. Dr. Thomas's sense of wonder at the mysteries of science gives a special character to many of his essays and is reflected in this one.

Clever Animals

Scientists who work on animal behavior are occupationally obliged to live chancier lives than most of their colleagues, always at risk of being fooled by the animals they are studying or, worse, fooling themselves. Whether their experiments involve domesticated laboratory animals or wild creatures in the field, there is no end to the surprises that an animal can think up in the presence of an investigator. Sometimes it seems as if animals are genetically programmed to puzzle human beings, especially psychologists.

The risks are especially high when the scientist is engaged in training the animal to do something or other and must bank his professional reputation on the integrity of his experimental subject. The most famous case in point is that of Clever Hans, the turn-of-the-century German horse now immortalized in the lexicon of behavioral science by the technical term, the "Clever Hans Error." The horse, owned and trained by Herr von Osten, could not only solve complex arithmetical problems, but even read the instructions on a blackboard and tap out infallibly, with one hoof, the right answer. What is more, he could perform the same computations when total strangers posed questions to him, with his trainer nowhere nearby. For several years Clever Hans was studied intensively by groups of puzzled scientists and taken seriously as a horse with something very like a human brain, quite possibly even better than human. But finally in 1911, it was discovered by Professor O. Pfungst that Hans was not really doing arithmetic at all; he was simply observing the behavior of the human experimenter. Subtle, unconscious gestures—nods of the head, the holding of breath, the cessation of nodding when the correct count was reached—were accurately read by the horse as cues to stop tapping.

Whenever I read about that phenomenon, usually recounted as the exposure of a sort of unconscious fraud on the part of either the experimenter or the horse or both, I wish Clever Hans would be given more credit than he generally gets. To be sure, the horse couldn't really do arithmetic, but the record shows that he was considerably better at observing human beings and interpreting their behavior than humans are at comprehending horses or, for that matter, other humans.

Cats are a standing rebuke to behavioral scientists wanting to know how the minds of animals work. The mind of a cat is an inscrutable mystery, beyond human reach, the least human of all creatures and at the same time, as any cat owner will attest, the most intelligent. In 1979, a paper was published in *Science* by B. R. Moore and S. Stuttard entitled "Dr. Guthrie and Felis domesticus or: tripping over the cat," a wonderful account of the kind of scientific mischief native to this species. Thirty-five years ago, E. R. Guthrie and G. P. Horton described an experiment in which cats were placed in a glass-fronted puzzle box and trained to find their way out by jostling a slender vertical rod at the front of the box, thereby causing a door to open. What interested these investigators was not so much that the cats could learn to bump into the vertical rod, but that before doing so each animal performed a long ritual of highly stereotyped movements, rubbing their heads and backs against the front of the box, turning in circles, and finally touching the rod. The experiment has ranked as something of a classic in experimental psychology, even raising in some minds the notion of a ceremony of superstition on the part of cats: before the rod will open the door, it is necessary to go through a magical sequence of motions.

Moore and Stuttard repeated the Guthrie experiment, observed the same complex "learning" behavior, but then discovered that it occurred only when a human being was visible to the cat. If no one was in the room with the box, the cat did nothing but take naps. The sight of a human being was all that was needed to launch the animal on the series of sinuous movements, rod or no rod, door or no door. It was not a learned pattern of behavior, it was a cat greeting a person.

The French investigator R. Chauvin was once engaged in a field study of the boundaries of ant colonies and enlisted the help of some enthusiastic physicists equipped with radioactive compounds and Geiger counters. The ants of one anthill were labeled and then tracked to learn whether they entered the territory of a neighboring hill. In the middle of the work the physicists suddenly began leaping like ballet dancers, terminating the experiment, while hundreds of ants from both colonies swarmed over their shoes and up inside their pants. To Chauvin's ethological eye it looked like purposeful behavior on both sides.

Bees are filled with astonishments, confounding anyone who studies them, producing volumes of anecdotes. A lady of our acquaintance visited her sister, who raised honeybees in northern California. They left their car on a side road, suited up in protective gear, and walked across the fields to have a look at the hives. For reasons unknown, the bees were in a furious mood that afternoon, attacking in platoons, settling on them from all sides. Let us walk away slowly, advised the beekeeper sister, they'll give it up sooner or later. They walked until bee-free, then circled the fields and went back to the car, and found the bees there, waiting for them.

There is a new bee anecdote for everyone to wonder about. It was reported from Brazil that male bees of the plant-pollinating euglossine species are addicted to DDT. Houses that had been sprayed for mosquito control in the Amazonas region were promptly invaded by thousands of bees that gathered on the walls, collected the DDT in pouches on their hind legs, and flew off with it. Most of the houses were virtually stripped of DDT during the summer months, and the residents in the area complained bitterly of the noise. There is as yet no explanation for this behavior. They are not harmed by the substance; while a honeybee is quickly killed by as little as six micrograms of DDT, these bees can cart away two thousand micrograms without being discommoded. Possibly the euglossine bees like the taste of DDT or its smell, or maybe they are determined to protect other insect cousins. Nothing about bees, or other animals, seems beyond imagining.

Other Suggestions for Writing

1. Write a feature news article about an interesting person, a noteworthy event, or an unusual place.

2. Write an essay explaining how or why a specific incident helped make you who you are today.

3. Write an essay about a problem that directly involves you. Choose a problem you see in your neighborhood, your school, your job, etc., and explain how it should be solved.

4. Write an essay in which you describe an encounter with a foreign culture and its effect on you.

5. Write an essay about some aspect of your family—your place in the family, your lack of involvement with your family, the influence your family has had on you.

6. Write an essay about some aspect of your job—why it's important, why you chose it, what it's really like, what it requires of you, why you'd like to leave it.

PREVIEW FOR CHAPTER 10

My wife is also going to school. She's a junior at the University now, and it seems a lot different from community college. She's writing paper after paper after paper. It seems all she's been doing is reading and writing with very little time for herself or family.

What really showed me the artist Alan Cober's artistic abilities were his drawings of himself while bedridden. At first he drew himself looking resigned and placid with a determined-to-sit-this-out kind of look that showed in his tightly pursed lips. Later he drew himself looking wild and stir crazy, his eyes wide and bulging, his eyebrows deeply creased.

You asked us about personal experience with alcohol abuse. The last one I had nearly cost me my life. I let Sam drive because he seemed sober enough, but all of a sudden he plunged into his own distorted little world. I thought it was funny until I saw the sign that said "Slow 15 MPH." I realized that we were going to wreck, and I knew it was going to be bad.

This article was interesting because it showed me three factors that work against any dieter. First, the body reacts to a lower intake of food by lowering its metabolic rate, so it resists burning off fat. Second, the early weight loss is mostly water, not fat. Third, a dieter who consumes less than 1200 calories loses muscle tissue as well as fat and thus becomes even fatter than before.

My own experience on public assistance shows that welfare actually discourages welfare recipients' eventual freedom from the system.

10 WRITING FOR COLLEGE CLASSES

SKILLS INTRODUCED

Responding to college writing assignments:

1. Read and understand the assignment
2. State the controlling idea
3. Organize and draft the response

Reasons for College Writing

You have two major reasons for writing about the material you study in any college class you take. First, writing is an important way in which you can explore and learn about ideas. As you write to explain an idea, either to yourself or to someone else, you begin to see connections you may not have seen before. Also, you identify for yourself the things you don't know so that, when you have time, you can learn about those things by asking, reading, or simply thinking about them.

The second reason for writing is to show your understanding of the subject to your teacher. Teachers need ways of finding out whether their students are learning what they should, and responses to writing assignments show them what their students have learned. No test can reveal the extent or lack of knowledge as fully as can a writing assignment. Because the reasons for writing are so clear, we can be very specific in talking about purpose and audience for writing that you do in college classes.

Your purpose is either to help yourself understand material or to demonstrate your understanding of material. In either case, your writing must be clear and direct. If you leave things out because you do not understand them, or use vocabulary that you do not fully understand, your grade will suffer.

Your intended reading audience will be either yourself or your teacher, but here we run into a couple of snags. If you write only for yourself, you might be tempted to skip over material and thus miss some important points. If you see only your teacher as reading audience, you might skip over important details, thinking, "Oh, she knows that, so I don't need to include it." But your teachers are interested in seeing what *you* know and whether you understand the logical structure of the material. You might be better off in either case, then, picturing your reading audience as a reasonably intelligent person who has never taken the class or read a book on the subject about which you are writing. Explain the material, for example, in such a way that a high school sophomore with B's and C's in related subjects will understand your explanations.

"But," you protest, "some subjects are just too complicated to explain that easily." We doubt that. Look, for example, at how Louise B. Young, in her book *Earth's Aura*, describes something as complex as the birth of the universe.

> **We really don't know exactly *when* the universe was created, but most cosmologists believe that they have a conceptual picture of *how* it was created. They think that it began with a concentration of matter and energy so enormously compacted that all the stuff of the present universe was consolidated into one large lump. At time zero, the lump exploded with a force so great that the pieces are still hurtling away from each other in all directions. The fragments of the original "egg" were as finely divided as matter can be—not even whole atoms, just pieces of atoms. This intensely hot plasma pushed outward into space and the random forces of the explosion distributed it into clouds of varying density. Time passed and the plasma cooled; simple atoms like hydrogen were able to form, making up the dust clouds which gradually filled the universal space. In regions of greatest density these clouds began to contract under the force of gravity. They formed whirlpools and eddies. As they continued to contract they rotated faster (just as a figure skater spins faster as she moves her arms closer to her body). From these clouds of collapsing gas a first generation of stars was born, and the gas that was left over from**

this star formation settled into disks or spheres of rotating particles. As the first stars became more and more compacted by gravity they heated up, and when the internal temperatures reached a critical value, fusion processes began to occur, turning hydrogen into helium with the production of impressive amounts of energy. This process is believed to take place in all stars, including our own sun, and is the source of the enormous amounts of energy they pour forth so prodigally over eons of time.

Notice what makes this explanation clear. The vocabulary is simple, designed to explain, not to impress. The sequence of events is clear. The writer uses the analogy of the figure skater to help us visualize what happened. And finally, Young's word choices help convey her own sense of awe at the size and power of this event: "enormously compacted," "impressive amounts of energy," "enormous amounts of energy they pour forth so prodigally over eons of time."

This is the same sort of clarity you have been working toward in your earlier writing, and you have also been working on letting your sense of audience and purpose guide you, so now you are ready to look at the steps of writing for your college classes.

STEP 1:
Understand the Assignment

Most college writing assignments are sentences that tell you what to do, and they commonly use direction words—usually verbs—that tell you what information to include in your answer. Because the direction word tells you exactly what to do, you must be able to identify direction words and know what they mean. Here is a list of some of the most common direction words and a description of what each tells you to do.

DIRECTION WORD	WHAT IT TELLS YOU TO DO
Discuss	Tell in detail what you know about all important aspects of the subject.
Compare	Talk about the similarities. Sometimes instructors will also expect you to talk about differences, so if you have any doubts, ask.

DIRECTION WORD	WHAT IT TELLS YOU TO DO
Describe	Tell in detail how something looks or happens, or show in detail what occurs.
Explain	Show your understanding by giving specific information, including examples, illustrations, and reasons.
Trace	Start from the beginning and go to the end in chronological order.
List	Write a list. A numbered list is usually sufficient as a response to this direction word.
Define	Give a definition of a word or concept.
Evaluate	Make a value judgment about the subject. Explain why it's good or bad, strong or weak, important or unimportant.
Illustrate	Give examples to demonstrate or clarify.
Summarize	Write a summary that states the main points about the subject.
State	Tell the specific fact or idea that the question asks for.

STEP 2:
State the Controlling Idea

Most assignments require a paragraph or a short essay in response, but some do not. A question like this, for example, would not require a paragraph:

List five digestive enzymes and state the type of food that each digests.

Two parallel lists, one naming the digestive enzymes and one naming the type of food that each digests, would be an adequate answer.

When a paragraph or short essay is the only appropriate response, your statement of the controlling idea (the topic sentence of a paragraph or the thesis statement of an essay) will be the most important sentence in your response. Because it controls what goes into the paragraph and what stays out of the paragraph, your topic sentence will help you be certain that you do exactly what the direction word of a question tells you to do.

Let's look at some examples:

> Compare the main characters of *The Catcher in the Rye* and *A Separate Peace* to show how they are examples of troubled youths.

The direction word is "compare," and it requires you to write about what the two characters have in common. The last part of the question focuses or limits the assignment even more sharply, for it requires that you discuss only the similarities that show how the characters are "troubled youths." The best way to be sure that your answer does exactly what the assignment asks is to change the question into your topic sentence or thesis statement of your answer. This step is simply the reverse of what you do in the paragraph outline when you turn your topic sentence into a question. Be sure to use as many of the words from the assignment as you can. Here, for example, is a possible topic sentence or thesis for a response to the above assignment:

> **Holden Caulfield in *The Catcher in the Rye* and Gene in *A Separate Peace* have four main similarities that show how they are examples of troubled youths.**

The word "similarities" shows that the writer will compare, and the writer has specifically stated what the comparison will show.

Here is a question from a biology class:

> Describe what happens when a bear goes into hibernation.

The direction word "describe" means to show in detail. In this case, you must show what happens to the bear when it goes into hibernation. Since your answer will be detailed, your topic sentence should be a general statement that controls the paragraph. Here's an example:

> **There are several major changes that take place when a bear goes into hibernation.**

This topic sentence would help you be sure that you describe or show in detail only the changes that take place when a bear hibernates.

A history exam might ask this question:

> Trace the major events of the late 1930s and early 1940s that
> led to America's entry into World War II.

The direction word "trace" requires that you start from the beginning and go to the end of the period in question, showing how the events relate to one another. If you were not immediately certain about which events to include, your topic sentence could be general:

> **Several major events beginning in the late 1930s and end-
> ing in the early 1940s led to America's entry into World
> War II.**

If you were more certain of what your answer should contain, your topic sentence could be more specific:

> **Major events of the late 1930s and early 1940s that led to
> America's entry into World II began with Hitler's rearming of
> Germany and ended with Japan's attack on Pearl Harbor.**

Either of these two topic sentences gives a specific focus on the time period being covered and on the fact that the writer will state and discuss the events in chronological order. Each sentence limits the answer to the *major* events.

Often you will see questions with more than one direction word, and you must be sure that you do what each of the direction words tells you to do. Here, for example, is a test question from a class on human sexuality:

> What determines whether a child will be a boy or a girl? Explain
> and discuss.

The first direction word is implied, not directly stated. It is "state." Your first task, then, would be to state a direct answer to the question:

> **The sex of a child is determined by the presence or absence
> of a Y chromosome in the sperm that fertilizes the ovum.**

The second direction word, "explain," requires that you tell *why* or *how* the presence or absence of a Y chromosome determines the child's sex. The third direction word, "discuss," gives you a chance to talk about why and how these facts are important. Two paragraphs would be an appropriate response to this assignment: one that states and explains, and one that discusses. The topic sentence of the explaining paragraph will immediately follow the sentence that states the direct answer, and it would be something like this:

> **The female's cells carry two X chromosomes, but the male's cells carry one X and one Y chromosome; if the Y chromosome happens to be in the sperm that fertilizes the ovum, the child will be male.**

The paragraph will consist of several sentences that explain how and why the Y chromosome may or may not be present in the sperm that fertilizes the ovum.

"Discuss" is a direction word that usually leaves you a great deal of freedom, so what you include in the discussion paragraph is largely up to you, though it must deal with the subject in some important way. Class discussions, lectures, your outside reading, and so on will tell you what kinds of things you might discuss. The topic sentence of the discussion paragraph could be,

> **Up to now, having a boy or a girl has been mostly a matter of luck, but some medical researchers are trying to give people the ability to choose the sex of their children.**

Or it could be,

> **According to the laws of chance, there should be an equal number of males and females in the world, but the numbers are not equal for several reasons.**

There are many more possibilities, of course, but the discussion paragraph would contain several sentences to develop the topic sentence.

You must be certain that you do what every direction word in an assignment tells you to do because ignoring or overlooking a direction word will cost you points.

Some assignments can be very complex. Here, for example, is a question from a history course with the direction words underlined:

> <u>Compare</u> the New England, Middle, and Southern colonies as to the types of *economies* they developed. In so doing, <u>explain</u> how the New England colonies solved their balance of trade problem of buying large quantities of manufactures and other products from England, especially as difficulties emerged in lumbering. <u>Explain</u> why Pennsylvania was such an economic success, why land-jobbing was not the biggest part of the economy of the

Middle colonies, and why the Middle colonies evolved craft production. For the Southern colonies, <u>explain</u> why tobacco evolved in Virginia and rice in South Carolina, how the development of slavery differed in these two colonies and why.

The main direction word for this question is "compare," but the instructor announces in class that he wants students to discuss both similarities and differences. The word "explain" is repeated three times within the assignment, and the teacher is very exact about what he wants the students to explain.

Your thesis statement, then, would need to say something about the similarities and differences among the economies. Remember that the main direction word is "compare," and that the word "economies" puts strict limits on what is to be compared. Here is a sample thesis:

> **While the underlying economic activity of most Americans in all colonies was self-sufficient agriculture, the three groups of colonies differed in important ways. The New England colonies specialized in commercial activities, the Middle colonies specialized in crafts, and the Southern colonies specialized in cash crop production.**

Writing Activity 10.1

- Write a topic sentence for a possible answer to each of the following questions. Be as specific as possible.
  1. Trace the process of writing a paragraph.
  2. Discuss the ways in which your writing has improved since you began this course.
  3. Explain why brainstorming is an important step in the writing process.

STEP 3
Explore and Plan the Answer

Step 3 combines focused brainstorming and outlining; the topic sentence you write in Step 2 provides your focus for brainstorming. For example, consider this assignment from a psychology class:

Discuss the main limitations of intelligence tests.

The direction word "discuss" and the rest of the question ask you to tell all you know about the *main limitations* of intelligence tests. To focus your thinking, then, you might turn the question into this topic sentence:

Intelligence tests have _____ main limitations.

Or this one:

Intelligence tests have two main limitations.

Or this one:

The main limitations of intelligence tests are language handicaps and cultural differences.

Any one of these three topic sentences about limitations of intelligence tests will provide an excellent guide for planning your answer. Even the first sample topic sentence,

Intelligence tests have _____ main limitations.

provides a sharp focus by reminding you that you need to discuss some number of main limitations of intelligence tests, even if you're not sure how many there are. To get yourself thinking clearly about them, you might list, cluster, or freewrite around the idea of limitations of intelligence tests. If you were sure enough of the limitations to write something like the third sample topic sentence,

The main limitations of intelligence tests are language handicaps and cultural differences.

you might need only to focus your brainstorming on the details about language handicaps and cultural factors. If, however, you were already completely sure of your facts and details, you might not need to write anything at all in Step 3.

How much brainstorming or outlining you do for an assignment will depend on how well you know the material and how much time you have. List, freewrite, or cluster to help yourself remember. If you're not sure how to organize the answer, outline it by turning your topic sentence into a question and answering that question. If you have a pretty good idea of the content of the answer, you might simply jot down a list and let that serve as your outline. For example, an outline of an answer to the question about intelligence tests might look like this:

> **Language handicap—differences in vocabulary or language, physical/psych. problems.**
> **Cultural factors—experiences, what's important in home and society.**

The more complex assignment about the colonial economics would, of course, require a more complex outline. You would surely plan to write at least a paragraph about the New England colonies, a paragraph about the Middle colonies, and a paragraph about the Southern colonies. Each of the sentences containing the direction word "explain" would guide and limit the topic sentence for the main body paragraphs.

Because the question and the thesis are complex, and because the parts of the question are so specific, the best approach in planning the answer to this question is to plan four parts to your essay, one to discuss the basic similarity of the colonies (self-sufficient agriculture) and one each to discuss the specific economic characteristics of each of the three groups of colonies. Controlling ideas for the four parts might be stated as follows:

1. **The basic reason why the colonies were able to specialize is that agriculture allowed families and communities to support themselves while they engaged in other activities.**

2. **The New England colonies developed a commercial economy, and they solved their balance of trade problem by creating a trade surplus with the West Indies that enabled them to pay off their trade deficit with England.**

3. **Land-jobbing was not a large part of the economy of the Middle colonies because land had been granted to specific individuals, but the colonies were an economic success because their favorable rents, religious freedom, and geographic advantages attracted both farmers and craftsmen.**

4. **In the Southern colonies, tobacco and rice, both large-income crops, were natural crops for the respective lands and climates of Virginia and South Carolina, and each colony's geographic characteristics, together**

with the origins of their settlers, also contributed to the fact that slavery was much harsher in South Carolina than in Virginia.

Writing Activity 10.2

- Choose one of the topic sentences you wrote for Writing Activity 10.1 and plan your answer for it.

STEP 4:
Draft the Response

Writing your response is no different from writing the kinds of paragraphs you have already studied. All you need to do is write down the topic sentence, follow that with a sentence that states your first main point, and write one or more sentences that develop or explain that main point. Next, state and develop your second main point, and so on.

Here is our student's response to the question, "Discuss the main limitations of intelligence tests."

> The main limitations of intelligence tests are language handicaps and cultural differences. Language handicaps may result if a person grows up in a home where English is not spoken or where an unusual English vocabulary is used. A person may also have a physical or psychological problem that will affect his use of language. As a result, he can't understand or respond to the questions even though he may know the answer, and therefore his intelligence is not being tested. Cultural factors can also interfere. If a child has grown up in a home or society that doesn't give him the experiences that most American children have, he might not do well on a test that includes those experiences. Someone growing up on New York City streets develops a different set of skills from those of an Iowa farm boy. Different things are important in the two cultures, and intelligence tests do not always allow for these cultural differences.

Notice especially how the student relates her details back to the idea of limitations: "his intelligence is not being tested," "he might not do well on a test," and "tests do not always allow for these cultural differences." She clearly shows the instructor that she remembers and understands the material.

Writing Activity 10.3

- Using your work from Writing Activity 10.2, write an answer to the question you have chosen.

STEP 5:
Revise and Check Your work

How much revising or proofreading you do depends upon the time you have. If you are writing an in-class assignment, you may have little time, but if you are writing an out-of-class response you should allow yourself plenty of time. Even in an in-class exam, an answer that is clearly stated and properly spelled and punctuated is likely to earn a higher grade than one in which the teacher has to guess at meanings. Pay special attention to the spellings of words, names, or terms that are important to the course.

Writing Activity 10.4

- Check the work you did in Writing Activity 10.3
- Make necessary additions or corrections.

Two Sample Responses to Class Assignments

We close this chapter with two student responses that earned high grades in the courses for which they were written. The first is an essay by Donna in response to this assignment from a political science class:

In the America of the 18th century Benjamin Franklin played a dramatic role in shaping the thoughts and actions of his fellow colonials. In many ways he was the ideal man of the 18th century. Explain how Franklin exemplified the 18th century as we have come to know it.

Donna's research came from a single book about Ben Franklin that had been assigned as one of the course texts. The students were expected to read it on their own. The course text and lectures had discussed the characteristics of the 18th-century man. The instructor wanted to see that her students had read and understood the book about Franklin, that they had understood the characteristics of people in the 18th century, and that they had the thinking skills necessary to see how a person's actions could reflect the values of the time in which he lived.

Donna's paper takes the information from her reading and her course work and presents it in such a way as to show her teacher that she has learned both the information and the thinking skills.

Benjamin Franklin was a revolutionary man in a revolutionary age. He had visions of a prosperous future for a growing nation. He is a perfect example of the characteristics for which the 18th century is known.

The 18th century saw the development of small, fast ships that made traveling long distances in a relatively short time a possibility. Franklin was a traveler in this new age of travel. By the time he was nineteen, he had sailed to England with plans to purchase needed materials to set up his own printing business in Philadelphia. Later in his life he spent years in England trying to persuade the British government and the English people of the benefits of a free and democratic America. He also traveled to France to win that country's sympathy for his emerging nation. He signed the alliance with France that was crucial to our success in the revolution, and he signed the Treaty of Paris that ended the revolution and doubled the size of our country. Because of his travels and knowledge of foreign languages, he became America's ambassador to Europe.

The 18th century sparked the glimmer of what was to become, in the 19th century, the industrial revolution.

The revolution of politics between England and America demanded that the people of the colonies make and grow what they needed. Benjamin Franklin encouraged the growth of this independence. He sponsored apprentice printers in setting up their own shops, and in doing so he was always careful to arrange precise contracts between himself and his partners so as to avoid future problems.

The 18th century was a time of vision and a belief in reason. Franklin wrote, "I have always thought that one man of tolerable abilities will work great changes and accomplish great affairs among mankind." Franklin's signature is on both the Declaration of Independence and the Constitution. He opened the first public library in the United States. His newspaper was written with the goal of encouraging thought and discussion among the common people. He was civic-minded and was always busy with projects which would benefit all—from the lowly activity of devising a method of keeping the streets clean and the street lamps unsmoked to the lofty accomplishment of founding the American Philosophical Society and the academy which later became the University of Pennsylvania. Ben Franklin worked to improve the quality of man's life.

The 18th century was the age of enlightenment. Modern scientific ideas were being developed and acknowledged, and Benjamin Franklin was America's first scientist. He discovered and proved that electricity has both negative and positive charges. He noticed that light colors reflect heat and that dark colors absorb it, so he experimented by placing swatches of black and white fabric in the snow and saw that the black fabric sank as the snow melted under it. He also invented or developed many mechanical devices. He worked to develop a stove which would burn more efficiently. He invented the odometer for measuring the distance a wagon traveled. He invented the glass harmonica, a mechanical hand (for getting books off a high shelf), and the bifocal eyeglasses. He refused to patent his inventions because he felt, as many in this "age of enlightenment" did, that knowledge should be shared. He wrote, "As we enjoy great advantages from the inventions of others, we should be glad of an opportunity to serve others by any invention of ours; and this we should do freely and generously."

> Benjamin Franklin was truly a man of the 18th cen-
> tury—a man of revolutionary vision and reason, a man with
> a whole world approach to the social, political, economic,
> scientific, and practical problems of his day.

Donna's opening paragraph clearly states her controlling idea, and it gets right to the point. It directly responds to the assignment. Her first body paragraph states a major point in support of her thesis by stating one way in which Franklin was an example of the characteristics of the 18th century. She develops the paragraph with specific examples from Franklin's life. She does the same thing in her second, third, and fourth body paragraphs. Her concluding paragraph ties the paper together by restating her thesis and summarizing her main points.

Instructors may read a paper like this as one of forty or fifty papers on the same subject, and they want to see quickly whether the student has discussed all the main points. A well-organized paper will permit your instructor to see that you have learned the course material.

This sample is a response to an assignment from a nutrition class:

Read an article from a current nutrition journal. Write a summary of the article (approximately half a page), and then write your personal response to the article (same length).

Here is Diane's summary and response:

"Sulfites: FDA Drags Heels While Toll Rises"

> In this September 1984 Nutrition Action article, author
> Mitch Zeller points out that the average person is unaware
> of the use of sulfites in our foods. This article discusses the
> use and effects of sulfites. With the use of sulfites in our food,
> beverages and drugs, many people are having reactions
> such as tightness in the chest, wheezing, loss of conscious-
> ness, or even death. Sulfur dioxide and sodium bisulfite are
> used the most in our foods to keep them fresher looking,
> more appealing to the eye, and to give them a longer shelf
> life. This is a very inexpensive method; therefore, most res-
> taurants have used them for their fresh vegetables and
> fruits, especially when they have a salad bar. Even though
> the FDA has been sent petitions for the past two years to ban
> the use of sulfites, the only thing it has accomplished is to set

up two advisory committees to study the situation. Mr. Zeller feels that this is just a "delaying tactic to avoid having to make a decision." The FDA has considered putting the information about sulfites on the labels of foods, but this would not help the people who eat in restaurants or drink wine which Mr. Zeller says, "are the most dangerous sources."

Personal Response

Before I read this article, I knew that sulfites were a problem, but I hadn't thought much about the problem of public awareness. Since this article was published, people have been made somewhat more aware of the side effects related to the use of sulfites, and I'm glad that this is happening. I read in the paper that restaurants were told to stop using sulfite on fresh vegetables, especially on the salad bars. I cannot help but wonder if the restaurants are being checked for use of sulfites on the baked potato that has become such a popular fad at the fast food restaurants. Due to the fast pace of our society, many more people are eating in restaurants, and that makes the use of sulfites even more dangerous because the consumption is greater. I realize that it is a difficult problem to keep foods safe and still be able to have every type of food in every season. As the article points out, it takes a very long time to have the FDA take any action on the use of dangerous additives to our foods, but if the public were made more aware of how the FDA is run, there may be more pressure put upon them by the consumer instead of by the politician and the manufacturer. I feel that we would all be more aware if there were more publications dealing with food and nutrition. I was unable to find Nutrition Today and many of the other recommended magazines on the shelves of bookstores. The only place they were available was the library, and not too many people are going to take the time to go to the library for magazines.

In a summary and personal response assignment, a teacher expects to see evidence that you can read, understand, and state the major details of an article about the subject being studied. The summary shows that you have these abilities. (Chapters 11 and 12 give you instruction and practice in writing summaries.) The teacher also expects to see that you understand how the concepts of the article relate to everyday life, and this is where the response comes in. The response may include your emotions as well as your thoughts.

To write a personal response, think about what you knew before you read the article and what you thought and felt as you read and thought about what the article had to say. Think about the main points that the article makes about the subject. Why did you choose this article in the first place? Why does the subject interest you? Does the article discuss a problem? Why is it a problem? How does it affect you or those you care about? What might happen in the future if the problem continues? These and other questions can lead you to a statement about your response to the article, and that statement can become a topic sentence for a paragraph that discusses your response.

When you write a response to an assignment, your purpose is to show your reading audience—your teacher—that you have the information and the thinking skills that the course is designed to teach. Preparation is critical: you must have and understand the information before you begin to write. Planning, too, is critical: you must do exactly what you are told to do. The rest is not easy, for writing and thinking are always hard work, but the writing skills that you are developing can help you be sure you accomplish your purpose. State your controlling idea, and make an outline as necessary to be sure your response will include all the required information. Write your answer and check it to be sure you have done what you set out to do and that you have expressed yourself clearly. Revise when you have time, since no first draft is ever perfect, and check the mechanics of your writing.

The fact that a writing assignment comes from a history course or a music course doesn't change the fact that you must communicate your ideas clearly and effectively. Because you know a process you can use in any writing task, you can approach any college writing assignment with confidence.

Other Suggestions for Writing

1. List and describe the steps followed in writing a paragraph.
2. Explain why unity is important to a piece of writing.
3. Define "lead" as it applies to writing.
4. Compare the elements of a paragraph to the elements of an essay.
5. State the differences between proofreading and revising.
6. Illustrate your preferred process of brainstorming.

11 WRITING A SUMMARY

In this chapter, you will be working on your reading skills as well as your writing skills. You will be identifying and writing down the ideas of other writers. You'll be writing **summary** paragraphs.

A summary condenses information. It makes a little out of a lot. You summarize when you take notes at a lecture or meeting, or when you tell someone about your vacation. News articles or letters home are summaries of events; a topic sentence is a summary of a paragraph. For this chapter, you'll summarize, or retell, what other people have written. When you write a summary, you look for the main points that the original writer makes and then state them in your own words. You shorten the original without changing its meaning.

Knowing how to write effective summaries is a skill useful in and out of college. Writing a summary of a textbook chapter will help you to review before an exam. An instructor may ask for a summary to see that you have read and understood an article, story, or textbook chapter. Sometimes you will have to summarize someone else's ideas for a longer paper you're writing.

And, as in a book or movie review, your summary might encourage someone to read the original piece, or it might let someone know that the piece will not be useful. Finally, writing summaries can improve your own writing by making you more conscious of how other writers put ideas together. Summaries thus help you discover new ways of combining ideas in your own writing. For all of these reasons, summary writing skills are important skills to know.

MAJOR STEPS IN SUMMARIZING

There are five basic steps to summarizing another piece of writing. These steps differ a little from the steps in the writing you have done so far, but you may notice a few similarities. The steps are

1. Understand the original
2. State the controlling idea
3. Identify supporting details
4. Write the first draft
5. Revise the summary

In this chapter, you'll first practice summary writing on some short pieces; then you'll practice on longer pieces, which, of course, are what you will usually summarize. In summarizing a single paragraph, you will see that Steps 4 and 5—drafting and revising—are shortened and combined because your summary will be only a single sentence. When you summarize longer pieces, however, you'll write a complete paragraph, so you'll need to do Steps 4 and 5 separately. But no matter what length the piece is, the first thing you must do is understand what the author is saying.

Step 1:
Understand the Original

Good summary writers are, above all, careful readers. To be a careful reader, you must first preview the writing to see what it will offer you. Then you must thoroughly read it—sometimes several times—to get a good handle on what the author says. This process of preview and careful reading leads to a complete understanding of the original that will prepare you for writing a good summary.

Preview Checklist

- Look at the title of the work and try to predict what you'll read about. Turn the title into a question and try to answer it as you read.
- Flip through the article to see how long it is, whether it's divided with headings and subheadings, and whether it has pictures, charts, graphs, or other aids to understanding.
- **Skim** the entire article (read it once through *quickly*) to get a general idea of its meaning and organization. Read the first and last paragraphs completely since these often contain important clues to meaning and purpose.

When you've finished your preview, read the article carefully, several times if necessary, until you understand it thoroughly. Here are a few guidelines to help you in this step:

Reading Checklist

- On your first careful reading, underline any important ideas you see. If you find yourself underlining most of the sentences, you're underlining too much. At this point, you should simply be trying to see the big picture.
- Circle any words whose meanings you are not sure of. Look up the words in a dictionary. Write the meanings of those words in the margins.
- On your next careful reading, make notes in the margins or on a separate piece of paper. Pretend you're talking to the author. Write down questions you have or any other observations.
- Carefully read the article as often as necessary until you understand the author's meaning.
- Close the book, and then, in your own words, write a short statement of what the article says. If you feel comfortable with this one-sentence comment, you're probably ready to go to Step 2.

STEP 2:
State the Controlling Idea

You're used to stating the controlling idea—the topic sentence—in your own writing, but now you'll need to find and state the controlling idea of someone else's writing. Because the topic sentence guides both the writer and the reader, when you read something to summarize, you must identify the author's controlling idea and let it guide your understanding. In turn, when you write your summary, you must clearly state the author's controlling idea so that it can guide your reader's understanding of your summary. There are three things you can do to help you identify and state the controlling idea:

Controlling Idea Checklist

- Ask yourself what the subject of the article is. Be as specific as you can. Is the article about cars, or is it specifically about Mustangs? Is it about Mustangs, or is it specifically about body designs in Mustangs?

- Ask yourself what the article says about the subject. What point is the author making? Is the author saying that body designs in Mustangs have improved over time?

- Write a complete sentence that contains the subject of the article and states the author's point. This is the author's controlling idea. It will also become the controlling idea of your summary.

We examine the following example in light of this checklist.

Example 1

Although an egg appears fragile, its shell is remarkably strong. This is because its oval shape embodies the same principle as an arched bridge. Eggs will bear extremely heavy weights on their rounded sides before breaking. Scientists have found that the average weight needed to crush a fowl's egg is 9 pounds. They had to pile 13 pounds on a turkey's egg before it gave way, 26 pounds on a swan's egg, and 120 pounds on an ostrich egg before it broke.

The subject of this paragraph is eggs or, more specifically, the shells of eggs. (We could be more specific still and say it is the shapes of eggshells.)

What the author says about eggshells is that their shape makes them remarkably strong.

The controlling idea, then, can be stated like this:

The shape of eggshells makes eggs remarkably strong.

Let's find the controlling idea of one more example.

Example 2

Eggs are not all shaped alike. Birds that lay their eggs in sheltered places (in nests or hollow trees or underground burrows) usually lay oval or spherical eggs. But many seabirds, which nest on rocky ledges, lay pear- or cone-shaped eggs that taper sharply from the broad end. The guillemot, an arctic bird, makes no nest and often lays its single egg on the flat ledge of a cliff. If the egg were spherical, it might be knocked over by the birds or blown off by the wind. Because the egg is pear-shaped, it does not roll when bumped but swings around in circles. Birds that lay many large pear-shaped eggs arrange them with the narrow pointed ends inwards and almost touching, so as to pack as many as possible under the mother's breast.

The subject of this paragraph is eggs or, more specifically, the shapes of eggs.

What the author says about the shapes of eggs is that they vary according to where the birds nest.

The controlling idea for this paragraph, then, might be stated as follows:

The shapes of birds' eggs vary according to where the birds nest.

Note that the controlling idea was stated clearly in the first example but implied, or suggested, in the second. **Implied topic sentences** are more difficult to find than are stated topic sentences, but they are equally important because they guide what the paragraph or article is about.

In the upcoming writing activity, you will state the controlling idea of this next paragraph:

Example 3

There is another big difference in the eggs laid by various birds. The quarter-inch-long eggs of hummingbirds go sixty to the ounce; a single ostrich egg may weigh three pounds. Between these extremes is the domestic hen's egg of 2 to 2½ ounces. A naturalist once found that an empty ostrich egg shell would hold up to 18 hens' eggs. Ostrich eggs are small stuff, however, compared with the eggs of the now extinct elephant bird. Some eggs of this huge, flightless bird discovered in Madagascar are 13 inches long. You could break 6 ostrich eggs or 150 hens' eggs into one of them.

Writing Activity 11.1

- Write the subject of the Example 3 paragraph.
- Write what the author says about the subject.
- Write your statement of the controlling idea.
- Check your work against our sample printed at the end of this chapter (page 207). Are you close? There are, of course, many ways of saying any one idea, so don't be concerned if your words differ somewhat from our answer.

STEP 3:
Identify Supporting Details

When you outlined your own paragraphs in previous chapters, the answers to your topic sentence question were the supporting details. They supported and clarified your controlling idea. When you write a summary, you'll identify the supporting details in the material you are reading; as you write those details down, you'll actually be outlining your summary.

Let's look at how Steps 1–3 can be applied to a short paragraph.

Example 4

Suspect silver coins can be tested in four ways. First, the ridges, or "reeding," on the edges of bad coins are usually uneven or missing in places. Second, the bright ringing sound is absent when the fake is dropped on a hard surface. Third, a bad coin almost always feels greasy to the touch. Finally, there is an "acid test" in which a drop of acid solution blackens any coin without a rich silver content.

The subject is testing suspect (that is, possibly counterfeit) silver coins. The author says they can be tested in four ways.
The controlling idea is directly stated in the first sentence:

Suspect silver coins can be tested in four ways.

The supporting details are clearly identified by the words "first," "second," "third," and "finally." As we discussed in Chapter 4, authors commonly use transitions, or signal words, like these to identify main points. Having identified the controlling idea and supporting details, we are ready to outline our summary. We'll start by turning our statement of the controlling idea into a question.

Controlling idea:

Suspect silver coins can be tested in four ways.

Controlling idea question:

What are the four ways to test suspect silver coins?

Answers:

1. **check the edges**
2. **drop them on a hard surface**
3. **feel them**
4. **drop acid on them**

The answers to the question are the **major supporting details** for the paragraph you have read.

STEPS 4 AND 5:
Write the Summary

When you write a summary of something as short as a paragraph, you need only state the controlling idea and the major details in a single sentence.

A summary of the Example 4 paragraph, then, could be:

> **Suspect silver coins can be tested by checking their edges, dropping them on a hard surface, feeling them, and dropping acid on them.**

Further Practice

Our next example paragraph is a little more complex, for it has both major and **minor supporting details**. Just as major details support and clarify the controlling idea, minor details support and clarify major details. We include the major details in a summary, but not the minor details. Let's first identify the subject and controlling idea of the following paragraph, and then we'll look more closely at the major and minor details.

Example 5

The theater audience in a horror movie can be divided into three groups. First of all, there are the gigglers. Members of this group may giggle out of nervousness, or they may find the scenes really funny. Then there are the hand grabbers. This group seems to think it can get through anything as long as there is something to hold. The last group contains the talkers. They always have a comment to make. For example, when the horrible-looking monster comes into view, they turn to a neighbor and say something clever like, "He's certainly attractive, isn't he?"

The subject is the theater audience in a horror movie.
The author says the audience can be divided into three groups.
Our statement of the controlling idea:

> **The theater audience in a horror movie can be divided into three groups.**

Again, the controlling idea we identified is identical to the author's topic sentence.

The clues to finding the major supporting details are the transitional words, "first of all," "then," and "the last group." While the Example 4 paragraph simply stated each major detail in a single sentence, this paragraph explains each of its major details with at least one additional sentence. These explanatory sentences contain minor supporting details that are not needed in a one-sentence summary. Our summary outline will therefore look like this:

Controlling idea:

> **The theater audience in a horror movie can be divided into three groups.**

Controlling idea question:

> **Into what three groups can a horror movie audience be divided?**

Answers:

> 1. **gigglers**
> 2. **hand grabbers**
> 3. **talkers**

Again, we can write a one-sentence summary of the paragraph by stating the controlling idea and the major details. Using our outline of the supporting details, we summarize Example 5 as follows:

> **The theater audience in a horror movie can be divided into the gigglers, the hand grabbers, and the talkers.**

In Writing Activity 11.2 you will practice identifying the details in the following paragraph.

Example 6

Good preparation for a speech is essential, and there are several things you can do to prepare. First, you must select an appropriate topic. The best topic is one that will interest both you and your audience. Next, you need enough good material to present. It would be embarrassing to run out of things to say in just a short time, and being overprepared can prevent this. Another idea is to plan the order in which you will present your material. Last, practice your speech. The more you practice, the less nervous you will be on your big day.

△ **Writing Activity 11.2**
- Write the subject, what the author says about the subject, and your statement of the controlling idea of the paragraph in Example 6.
- Turn your statement into a question.
- Using the outline format, answer the question with the major supporting details of the paragraph.
- Write a one-sentence summary of the paragraph.
- Check your answers against our sample at the end of this chapter (pages 207–208).

PRACTICING ON LONGER PIECES

Now that you've prepared a one-sentence summary of a paragraph and have learned the general techniques, it's time to summarize longer, more complex material.

STEP 1:
Understand the Original

The following article is from *Reader's Digest*. Before you read it, remember to preview the article by following the Preview Checklist on page 185. When you preview this article for a summary, turn the title into a question: "How can TV be hazardous to children?" After you preview the article, we'll talk more about what a first look reveals about the work.

Warning: TV Can Be Hazardous To Children

By Vance Packard

In recent years, television has made it a lot more difficult to be a good parent. While the evidence grows that heavy, indiscriminate TV watching can damage a child's development, television is more pervasive than ever before.

If I were raising a child today I would be a lot tougher about what he or she watched than 90 percent of today's parents are. I say this because I spent five years studying the changing world of children.

Television is a major part of that world. I think the sheer amount of time children now consume watching TV is a national scandal. They spend about as many hours a year in front of the tube as they spend in front of teachers. Nielsen surveys show that nearly 3 million children ages 6 to 11 are still watching TV between 10 and 11 p.m. About 380,000 of these watch past midnight. If the home has cable, they could be catching R-rated shows.

If I were a parent of young children today, I wouldn't allow any of my kids under 15 to have a television set in his or her room. Having a set so readily available simply puts too much pressure on children to watch excessively.

Don't get me wrong. I wouldn't put the TV set in the attic. Much of what's on TV can delight young viewers, provided they are given proper guidance. But I would be very uneasy if my children had unsupervised access to television, for the following reasons:

1) I would be concerned that TV was turning my children into materialistic cynics, distrustful of adults.

The typical youngster finishing high school has been the target of several thousand *hours* of commercials on TV. This selling barrage does more than influence children's brand preferences. It helps shape their concept of life.

Much of the advertising aimed at children is designed to make them effective naggers. One children's programming director was quoted in *Advertising Age*: "If you truly want big sales, use the child as your assistant salesman. He sells, he nags, until he breaks down the resistance of his mother or father."

Close to total believers in what adults tell them, very young children are uniquely vulnerable to the verbal curves tossed at them by TV pitchmen. By age seven to ten, according to a report in the *Harvard Business Review*, children are bothered by misleading or exaggerated ad messages. And by the time youngsters reach 11 or 12, they have become cool cynics.

Some studies also indicate that frequent exposure to the plotting, hoodwinking and manhandling depicted on TV may be eroding the very important sense of trust a child learns from loving parents.

2) I would wonder whether heavy viewing was making my children passive and less imaginative.

An essay called "The Electronic Fix" in the U.S. government publication *Children Today* cited two similarities between drug-taking and heavy TV viewing: both blot out the real world and promote passive states.

In general, studies show that children whose TV viewing is heavy score much lower than light viewers do on national reading tests. Does their viewing cause them to go easy on homework? Does it limit their reading for pleasure and thus their literacy? TV viewing over long stretches is not nearly as challenging mentally as reading is.

Preschool kids play less if they are heavy viewers—and that is bad. Play is important for growing children. It helps stretch their imaginations and ease anxieties. Interacting with playmates not only improves verbal skills but also teaches children how to have arguments and still be friends. I'd hate to have kids without those talents.

3) If my children showed frequent signs of being restless or tired, I would wonder whether heavy TV viewing was responsible.

The flickering screen gives a swirling view of the world. On commercial TV, most sales pitches come in 30-second bursts, many even shorter. Evening-news segments average only about two minutes. Some experts worry that a heavy-viewing child is more prone to have a short attention span. The whirl of scenes can also tire the mind. T. Berry Brazelton, the noted Harvard pediatrician, has observed that children under five are likely to show signs of exhaustion if exposed to more than one hour of TV a day.

If television became a strong influence in my children's lives, I would make sure their viewing was a life-enhancing force, not an insidious one. How would I do this? As much as possible I would guide my youngsters away from shows likely to generate distrustfulness or emotional upset, shows that make buffoons of law officers, and programs larded with ads specifically geared to seduce kids. Every week I'd go through a program guide with my children and we would look for shows that might prove interesting and rewarding:

— Shows involving exploration or experiments. It was good news when Mr. Wizard, who uses every-day objects to help youngsters understand science, was brought back by Nickelodeon.

— Shows that stimulate the imagination. Charlie Brown specials, Jim Henson's Muppet characters and the Disney Channel often do this.

— Shows in which adults and kids are shown doing things together. A disturbing trend of our times has been the growing isolation of youngsters from adults.

— Shows that promote thought about the special problems of growing up or about conditions in the world. For example, I have been much impressed with "CBS News Sunday Morning." In general, today's news programs give young viewers a better understanding of the world than I ever had at their age.

After reviewing the week's possibilities with my children, I'd help them draw up a viewing schedule. If they were of school age and under 14, I would let them choose up to ten hours of programming from the list—an hour a day Monday to Thursday, two hours a day on Friday, Saturday and Sunday. Pre-schoolers would be limited to seven hours—one hour a day. If my youngster wanted to watch a two-hour show on a school night, he'd have to skip TV the next night.

At an early age, say by four, my kids would know that commercials are different from regular programming. I would explain the purpose of ads. We'd talk about any overstatement or slickness.

Children are tremendously influenced by the way their own folks behave, so I would try to be a model for them. If I had young ones today, I wouldn't slouch hour after hour in front of the tube. I would spend my spare time reading, helping in some way to make my community a better place—and most of all, playing with my kids.

In our preview, we saw that the article covered about two and a half pages in the magazine. We saw three numbered statements of concern written in italics, and we noticed that the last section was set off with extra space between paragraphs.

After skimming it for meaning and organization, we decided the article had an introductory section, a section that lists and discusses the author's concerns, and a section that lists and discusses what the author would do to reduce television's ill effects on his children. The preview done, we were ready to read the piece carefully, looking for important ideas and referring to the Reading Checklist on page 185 as necessary. In our first reading, we underlined the major details, and we defined unfamiliar words, writing the meanings in the margins. In our second reading we made notes in the margins in the form of a **block diagram**. A block diagram sections off the article into chunks of material to reveal its organization, which is, of course, more complex than that of the sample paragraphs we reviewed earlier. Diagramming this way helps you to see an article's organization more clearly.

Warning: TV Can Be Hazardous To Children

By Vance Packard

In recent years, television has made it a lot more difficult to be a good parent. While the evidence grows that heavy, <u>indiscriminate TV watching can damage a child's development,</u> television is more pervasive than ever before.

indiscriminate = not controlled

pervasive = present everywhere

If I were raising a child today I would be a lot tougher about what he or she watched than 90 percent of today's parents are. I say this because I spent five years studying the changing world of children.

Television is a major part of that world. I think the sheer amount of time children now consume watching TV is a national scandal. They spend about as many hours a year in front of the tube as they spend in front of teachers. Nielsen surveys show that nearly 3 million children ages 6 to 11 are still watching TV between 10 and 11 p.m. About 380,000 of these watch past midnight. If the home has cable, they could be catching R-rated shows.

introduction

If I were a parent of young children today I wouldn't allow any of my kids under 15 to have a television set in his or her room. Having a set so readily available simply puts too much pressure on children to watch excessively.

Don't get me wrong. I wouldn't put the TV set in the attic. Much of what's on TV can delight young viewers, provided they are given proper guidance. But I would be very uneasy if my children had unsupervised access to television, for the following reasons:

1) I would be concerned that TV was turning my children into materialistic cynics, distrustful of adults.

The typical youngster finishing high school has been the target of several thousand *hours* of commercials on TV. This selling barrage does more than influence children's brand preferences. It helps shape their concept of life.

Much of the advertising aimed at children is designed to make them effective naggers. One children's programming director was quoted in *Advertising Age*: "If you truly want big sales, use the child as your assistant salesman. He sells, he nags, until he breaks down the resistance of his mother or father."

Close to total believers in what adults tell them, very young children are uniquely vulnerable to the verbal curves tossed at them by TV pitchmen. By age seven to ten, according to a report in the *Harvard Business Review*, children are bothered by misleading or exaggerated ad messages. And by the time youngsters reach 11 or 12, they have become cool cynics.

Some studies also indicate that frequent exposure to the plotting, hoodwinking and manhandling depicted on TV may be eroding the very important sense of trust a child learns from loving parents.

2) I would wonder whether heavy viewing was making my children passive and less imaginative.

	introduction
	controlling idea for this section
	author's first concern
	cynics = scornful, distrustful people
	barrage = outpouring or bombardment
	makes children nag
	vulnerable = likely to be hurt
	children become cynical
	may destroy trust
	author's second concern

An essay called "The Electronic Fix" in the U.S. government publication *Children Today* cited <u>two similarities between drug-taking and heavy TV viewing</u>: both blot out the real world and promote passive states.

makes children passive

In general, <u>studies show that children whose TV viewing is heavy score much lower than light viewers do on national reading tests.</u> Does their viewing cause them to go easy on homework? Does it limit their reading for pleasure and thus their literacy? TV viewing over long stretches is not nearly as challenging mentally as reading is.

heavy viewers score lower in reading

<u>Preschool kids play less if they are heavy viewers</u>—and that is bad. Play is important for growing children. It <u>helps stretch their imaginations and ease anxieties</u>. Interacting with playmates not only <u>improves verbal skills</u> but also <u>teaches children how to have arguments and still be friends</u>. I'd hate to have kids without those talents.

children play less

3) If my children showed frequent signs of being restless or tired, I would wonder whether heavy TV viewing was responsible.

author's third concern

The flickering screen gives a swirling view of the world. On commercial TV, most sales pitches come in 30-second bursts, many even shorter. Evening-news segments average only about two minutes. Some experts worry that a <u>heavy-viewing child is more prone to have a short attention span</u>. The <u>whirl of scenes can also tire the mind.</u> T. Berry Brazelton, the noted Harvard pediatrician, has observed that children under five are likely to show signs of exhaustion if exposed to more than one hour of TV a day.

short attention span

tired minds

If television became a strong influence in my children's lives, <u>I would make sure their viewing was a life-enhancing force, not an insidious one.</u> How would I do this? As much as possible I would guide my youngsters away from shows

controlling idea for this section

insidious = harmful, evil

likely to generate distrustfulness or emotional upset, shows that make buffoons of law officers, and programs larded with ads specifically geared to seduce kids. Every week I'd go through a program guide with my children and we would look for shows that might prove interesting and rewarding:

guide children to good viewing

— Shows involving exploration or experiments. It was good news when Mr. Wizard, who uses every-day objects to help youngsters understand science, was brought back by Nickelodeon.

exploration and experiments

— Shows that stimulate the imagination. Charlie Brown specials, Jim Henson's Muppet characters and the Disney Channel often do this.

imagination

— Shows in which adults and kids are shown doing things together. A disturbing trend of our times has been the growing isolation of youngsters from adults.

children and adults together

— Shows that promote thought about the special problems of growing up or about conditions in the world. For example, I have been much impressed with "CBS News Sunday Morning." In general, today's news programs give young viewers a better understanding of the world than I ever had at their age.

think about self and world

After reviewing the week's possibilities with my children, I'd help them draw up a viewing schedule. If they were of school age and under 14, I would let them choose up to ten hours of programming from the list—an hour a day Monday to Thursday, two hours a day on Friday, Saturday and Sunday. Preschoolers would be limited to seven hours—one hour a day. If my youngster wanted to watch a two-hour show on a school night, he'd have to skip TV the next night.

make a viewing schedule

At an early age, say by four, my kids would
know that commercials are different from regu-
lar programming. <u>I would explain the purpose</u>   teach them about ads
<u>of ads</u>. We'd talk about any overstatement or
slickness.

Children are tremendously influenced by
the way their own folks behave, so <u>I would try to</u>
<u>be a model for them</u>. If I had young ones today, I   set a good example
wouldn't slouch hour after hour in front of the
tube. I would spend my spare time reading,
helping in some way to make my community
a better place—and most of all, <u>playing with</u>   play with them
<u>my kids</u>.

The final thing you must do at the reading stage is to try to write a short
statement of what the article says. After diagramming the article, we tested
our understanding of it by writing the following short statement without looking back at the article:

> **If I were raising children today, I would worry about
> television's effects on them, and I would try to prevent the ill
> effects of TV.**

Notice that the statement goes a little beyond what the title of the article
suggests. That is, instead of talking just about the hazards of television, the
author also talks about what might be done to prevent those hazards. The
article has two main ideas, and our statement includes both of them.

STEP 2:
State the Controlling Idea

The next step on the way to summarizing is to state the controlling idea of
the article. Remember that the controlling idea should contain the subject of
the article and the author's main point or, as in this article, main points. This
article has only one subject: the hazards of television to children. The author
tells us two things about that subject: what hazards concern him and what he
would do about those hazards if he were raising children today. Our statement of the controlling idea is this:

> **Unsupervised television watching can harm children, but parents can take actions to prevent this harm.**

Having stated the controlling idea, we are ready for the next step.

STEP 3:
Identify Supporting Details

In longer pieces it is, of course, more difficult to identify major details, but turning our statement of the controlling idea into a question and answering it can still help us:

Controlling idea:

> **Unsupervised television watching can harm children, but parents can take actions to prevent this harm.**

Controlling idea question:

> **How can unsupervised television watching harm children, and what actions can parents take to prevent the harm?**

Answers:

> 1. **It can make children materialistic, cynical, and distrustful.**
> 2. **It can limit their activities and their imaginations.**
> 3. **It can make them restless or tired.**
> 4. **Parents can control and limit children's television watching.**
> 5. **Parents can explain advertising to children.**
> 6. **Parents can set a good example.**

Since there are two parts to the controlling idea, we needed to write two parts to the question, each with its own question word. The "how" part asks about harm and the "what" part asks about actions. Answers 1–3 relate to the first part of the question while answers 4-6 relate to the second.

STEP 4:
Write the First Draft

In summarizing single paragraphs, we wrote one-sentence summaries. Most extensive articles, however, require at least a paragraph. There are several important rules to keep in mind as you write your summary paragraph.

1. As you summarize, keep the ideas in about the same proportions and order as those in the original. In the TV article, for example, the author devotes more space to his concerns about the harm of television than to his suggestions for prevention. In our summary, then, we'll discuss the harms more fully than the prevention, and we will discuss the harms first since that is the order of the original article.

2. Identify the author and source in the opening sentence. Note how we do that in our first draft.

3. **Paraphrase**, or put things in your own words. This not only helps you to be sure you understand the piece you are summarizing, but it also reminds you that you're shortening or condensing the ideas, not just choosing a few to quote. Try not to **quote** unless the author has used a word or phrase that is particularly effective. If you do quote, use quotation marks any time you use more than three of the author's exact words. (See Section 24.A of the Handbook for a discussion of quotation marks.)

4. Make every effort to give your readers no more information than they need to understand the author's original message.

5. Include only what the author says. Do not add your own opinions or interpretations.

Here's the first draft of our summary.

First Draft

In his <u>Reader's Digest</u> article, "Warning: TV Can Be Hazardous to Children," Vance Packard says that unsupervised television watching can harm children, but that parents can take actions to prevent this harm. Much TV is good, but children spend as many hours a year watching TV as they spend in school, and many of them watch late-night shows. Children need to have their TV watching supervised. First, television can turn children into materialistic cynics who distrust adults. TV advertising encourages children to nag their parents for advertised products. Young children are especially vulnerable because they believe what they see in the advertisements, but children from seven to ten are bothered by misleading ads. By the time they are eleven or twelve, children are cynical about the ads, and they may be losing the important sense of trust learned from their parents. Second, television watching can make children less active and imaginative. Children who watch a lot of television don't read as well as those who watch little, and they also play less. Play helps children develop their imaginations, improves their verbal skills, and teaches them "how to have arguments and still be friends." Third, because television segments are short, children who watch TV can have short attention spans. They can also become tired from the rapid changing of scenes. To prevent the damage that television can cause, parents can make sure that their children watch shows like Mr. Wizard that involve experiments, shows like the Charlie Brown specials that help the imagination, shows that show children and adults together, and shows that make them think about problems in their lives or the world. Parents can limit children under fourteen to ten hours of TV watching a week and preschoolers to seven hours. They can also talk to their children about advertising. Finally, parents can set a good example for their children and can play with them.

STEP 5:
Revise the Summary

As usual, we didn't attempt a revision until the day after we did our first draft. The time away from it helped us to see some problems with it that we hadn't noticed before. Our first step was to reread the article and then to reread our summary.

We saw that we had included some details from the introduction and some other minor details that are not necessary. Two sentences summarize part of the introduction but do not support the controlling idea of our summary: "Much TV is good, but children spend as many hours a year watching TV as they spend in school, and many of them watch late-night shows. Children need to have their TV watching supervised." Also, our discussion of the kinds of shows children should watch goes into too much detail. The shows which we have named can be lumped together as "educational or imaginative shows," and this technique of lumping or gathering several small ideas into one general term is called *generalizing*. Generalizing is an important way of condensing.

Mainly, our revision leaves out detail that is not necessary in a summary, and it does more paraphrasing—we use more of our own words. Finally, because we want to show the author's scornful attitude toward people who watch too much TV, we include a particularly telling quotation.

Here, then, is our revised summary paragraph.

Final Draft

In his <u>Reader's Digest</u> article, "Warning: TV Can Be Hazardous to Children," Vance Packard says that unsupervised television watching can harm children, but that parents can take actions to prevent this harm. First, TV advertising can make children materialistic and distrustful. Young children believe what they see in the advertisements, but as they get older, children become cynical and may lose the important sense of trust learned from their parents. Second, television watching can make children read less and play less. Third, because television segments are short, children who watch TV can have short attention spans. They can also become tired from the rapid changing of scenes. To prevent the damage that television can cause, parents can do several things. They can make sure that their children watch educational or imaginative shows. They can limit children's TV watching. They can also talk to their children about advertising. Parents can set a good example for their children, rather than "slouch hour after hour in front of the tube." Finally, they can play with their children.

Our revision is more effective because it gives only the information necessary for the reader to understand the author's original message. It paraphrases rather than quotes, and it combines specific ideas into general terms. Finally, it shows the author's attitude toward his subject.

You probably have noticed that our revision is shorter than our first draft, and that's exactly what you need to work for when you revise your summary paragraph.

Now it's time for you to practice summarizing an article. Preview and read the following article, "Battling the Blahs When a Job Seems Routine," by following the checklists on pages 185 and 186. You'll find that the controlling idea is clearly stated and that major details are fairly easy to identify. You might find the last part a bit difficult, though, for instead of directly stating things you can do, it talks about reasons for the blahs and asks some questions. One of your jobs will be to state the suggestions implied in this last part and to decide on how many of the minor details you need to include. You will write a summary in Writing Activity 11.3. This article is from *Family Weekly Magazine.*

Battling The Blahs When a Job Seems Routine

By Peggy Schmidt

Every so often, perhaps during a tedious staff meeting, a trying commute to work, or a seemingly endless afternoon in the office, that feeling of "Why am I doing this?" occurs. It's natural to get down in the dumps about your job from time to time. When the doldrums strike, there are several things you can do to fight them before your ho-hum attitude affects your work.

Boredom is one of the most common causes of feeling blue about your job. "Every job has a lot of repetitive tasks from which you need to take not just a coffee break, but a mental break," says Richard Irish, an executive search expert and author of *Go Hire Yourself an Employer*. He suggests switching gears: if you have a job that involves a lot of paperwork or thinking, consider throwing darts at a board in your office as a diversion, as Irish does himself. For those whose business keeps them on the phone, a crossword puzzle can be refreshing. People whose hands are on a computer keyboard a good part of the day may find a balance in doodling. If your company provides exercise equipment or space (as an increasing number do), use it.

Altering the routine of your job itself is another possibility, says Irish. Rearrange the times when you normally schedule meetings. Or you might initiate a project that is outside of but consistent with your responsibilities. You can also get out of your rut by having lunch with people who work outside your department or company, even people you don't know well, but would enjoy knowing better. Don't feel hesitant about inviting someone new to lunch; most people are flattered that you're interested in learning more about them and what they do.

Another reason for slipping into the job doldrums is not getting positive feedback from your employer. "Each one of us has a recognition quotient that we need filled if we're going to continue turning in good work," says Irish. "Pats on the back are not given out nearly as frequently as they should be."

Rather than feel resentful that you're not appreciated, the next time you turn in an assignment, tell your boss that while you put your best effort into it, you would like to know if there is anything that could be improved upon. If he says yes, you stand to benefit from constructive criticisms. Or you may simply hear what you've been wanting to—that you're doing a great job.

The most serious reason for getting caught in the job doldrums is the frustration that comes with feeling that you're not getting anywhere in your job—or deciding that there is no future for you with your employer. "Plenty of people in that situation slack off because they lose their motivation, but a failure to take positive steps only makes the problem worse," says Irish. Before you take the drastic step of looking for a new job, ask yourself:

— Are you being too impatient? Talk to others with your level of experience and education. If you work for a small company, compare your situation with people who work in other companies.

— What's standing in your way? Often it's the person who has the job you want. Is it worth it to wait for him to retire, move up or on? A personality conflict with a supervisor can also be an impediment. If that's the case, you'll have to win his respect or consider a job move outside his realm of influence. Finally, company policy or precedent may be holding you up, even if you have proven you can handle more responsibility. The challenge is to figure how management can make an exception without risking complaints.

— Do the people in power share your view of your accomplishments? Be aware of what criteria management uses to make judgments. Then ask yourself whether you meet them or want to meet them. Lastly, make sure that management is aware of your desire to take on more responsibility.

If you decide that there isn't much you can do to improve your situation, scouting out new job possibilities will bring renewed enthusiasm. You may even discover that your current position isn't as bad as you had thought.

Writing Activity 11.3

- Write the subject of the article, what the author says about the subject, and your statement of the article's controlling idea.
- Turn your statement into a question and answer the question to form an outline of your summary paragraph.
- Check your work against our suggestions on page 208 and make any revisions you think are necessary.
- Write your rough draft.
- Revise it at least once.

Suggested Responses

Writing Activity 11.1, page 188
Subject: **A difference in birds' eggs**
What the author says: **The eggs differ in size.**

Statement of controlling idea:

> **The eggs of various birds differ greatly in size.**

Writing Activity 11.2, page 192
Subject: **Good preparation for a speech**
What the author says: **There are things you can do to prepare.**

Statement of controlling idea:

> **There are several things you can do to prepare well for a speech.**

Controlling idea question:

What can one do to prepare well for a speech?

Answers:

1. **choose an appropriate topic**
2. **find plenty of good material**
3. **plan the order**
4. **practice**

One-sentence summary:

To prepare for a speech, choose an appropriate topic, find plenty of good material, plan the order of your presentation, and practice.

Writing Activity 11.3, page 207
Subject: **Feeling tired of your job**
What the author says: **There are things you can do if you're tired of your job.**

Statement of controlling idea:

When the doldrums strike, there are several things you can do to fight them before your ho-hum attitude affects your work.

Controlling idea question:

What can you do to fight the doldrums?

Answers:

1. **If you're bored, take a mental break.**
2. **Alter the routine of your job.**
3. **Ask your boss for comments on your work.**
4. **Take positive steps before looking for a new job.**

Our summary:

Peggy Schmidt, author of "Battling the Blahs When a Job Seems Routine," in the <u>Family Weekly Magazine</u>, says

there are several things you can do to fight the blahs. If boredom makes your job seem dull, take a mental break by doing something different for a while. If your routine makes the job dull, change the routine. If you're not getting enough positive feedback, ask your boss for comments on your work. Finally, if you feel that there's no future in your job, take positive steps. Test whether you're being too impatient by comparing your job with those of others. Figure out why you're not advancing, and then find a way to advance. Make sure your accomplishments are noted. If none of these work, looking for a new job might show you that the old one isn't that bad.

Other Suggestions for Writing

1. Turn to Chapter 12 and practice your summary skills on the articles there.

2. Summarize a paragraph, a portion of a chapter, or a whole chapter from one of your other textbooks.

3. Summarize an editorial from your local newspaper.

12 READINGS FOR MORE SUMMARY PRACTICE

> **SKILLS INTRODUCED**
>
> Practicing writing summaries

This chapter offers several readings on which you can practice your skills as a summary writer. Some of these readings are organized quite simply while others are more complex. Regardless of the complexity of the reading, however, your task with each piece remains the same. You must first identify the main idea, then find the major supporting details before you can begin to write your summary. For each article, we identify the author and the source, and we discuss some of the problems you may encounter in finding the controlling idea and major details.

Reading 1: "He Gives the Poor a Voice"

This first reading is a profile, a word picture of a person who is unusual and interesting. Its controlling idea is not directly stated, but the title and the opening and closing paragraphs strongly suggest that idea. The story is told as a narrative of Hugo Morales's life, and the author has selected major events from Morales's life as the major supporting details for the controlling idea. The article is from *Parade Magazine*.

He Gives the Poor a Voice

By Michael Ryan

It was close to 20 years ago that I last saw Hugo Morales. We were both students at Harvard then. I remember him as a genial, outgoing, hardworking young man. He could have used his high-powered education to become a rich man. Many of our classmates have. But Hugo Morales, now 40, has never made more than $17,000 a year—and that doesn't bother him a bit.

We met in a small cafe in a depressed area of Fresno, Calif. There, Morales explained to me why a Mixtec Indian from Mexico, born in poverty, would pass up a gilt-edged opportunity to escape and instead would devote his life to helping his people.

"I grew up in Mixteca, our homeland in Oaxaca," he told me. "I lived with my mother in deep poverty. I never met my father until I was 9. He was in California and was undocumented. Then, when he was legalized, we immigrated to Healdsburg, about 60 miles north of San Francisco. I grew up picking prunes and other crops in what is now the wine country.

"When I was 12 or 13, I ended up in a tuberculosis hospital. When you're poor like that and you're a kid, and they lock you up in a room for nine months, you have a lot of time to think.

"I thought about who I was and my chances of contributing to society. That experience gave me determination. I realized that sometimes there's a perception that people who are poor *deserve* to be poor. But my parents were poor. They sacrificed a lot and got very little, and I saw a lot of rich people who didn't sacrifice at all and got a lot."

After he recovered from tuberculosis, Morales began his impressive career. At Healdsburg High, he was one of a handful of Mexican-Americans in a mostly white, affluent student body. He rode the bus to school while other kids drove their own cars. But his classmates elected him student-body president, and Harvard offered him a scholarship.

For seven years, he studied in Cambridge, Mass., in the winter and picked fruit in Healdsburg in the summer. "My ambition was with the people I grew up with," he said. "I'm not sure they understood why I returned, but I think they appreciated me coming back and not leaving them. What I did then was important—physical labor, working collaboratively—it has its values. There, picking fruit—on your knees on the ground, with your mother and your father and your brother—you realize that's who you are, not some law-school student in Cambridge."

He never even thought of taking a Wall Street job. "I wasn't tempted, and I didn't want to be tempted," he said. Instead, he moved to Fresno, where he thought he could make the biggest impact on the lives of farmworkers. First, he helped start Radio Bilingue, one of the first bilingual public radio stations. It gave farmworkers a source of information about the world around them, telling them about immigration and legal matters, working conditions and cultural opportunities.

Morales was not content to stop there. He organized a chamber of commerce for Fresno's Hispanic small businesses, then helped found Fresno Tomorrow, a coalition that is addressing the problems of the city's young people. "It's a real challenge to work toward opportunity for those children," he told me. "We could conceivably have a society that basically is divided between white people, mostly males with skilled jobs, and masses of almost illiterate people of color working in menial jobs. That would be an ugly society."

As we drove through the San Joaquin Valley in his aging VW Rabbit, we went past acre upon acre of fruit trees and grapevines, cotton plants and olive groves. And everywhere we stopped, the radio was on and the station was Radio Bilingue. For hundreds of miles up and down the valley, people were listening, knowing that they had a community, that they had hope and a future.

Hugo Morales seemed content as he drove back to the city for the second half of his 16-hour workday. "You talk about my sacrifice," he said. "The fact is it's not a sacrifice. I'm very happy."

Then he added with a smile, "I guess I'll be doing this for a while."

Writing Activity 12.1

- Write a summary of "He Gives the Poor a Voice."
- Be sure your first sentence states the controlling idea and includes the author's name and the source information.

• Include only the major supporting details and the necessary explanation.

Reading 2: "Kids Who Beat the Odds"

The second reading contains a clear statement of the controlling idea, but that statement does not appear until after an introduction that is several paragraphs long. Its major supporting details, though, are clearly identified with subheadings. The article was originally published in *Reader's Digest*.

Kids Who Beat the Odds

by Claire Safran

It was a parent's worst nightmare. From a window across the road, a gunman watched as the shouting, happy children poured out of the 49th Street Elementary School in Los Angeles. Suddenly, he began shooting.

The sniper fired round after round at the children. Some youngsters ran screaming across the schoolyard, trying to escape the rifle fire. Others hid behind playground trees or trash cans, or dropped to the ground. Finally, the sniper turned the gun on himself, and the shooting stopped. One young child and a passer-by lay mortally wounded. Eleven other children were injured.

The rest of the children were unhurt, but none escaped the terror of that day in February 1984. More than a year later, youngsters who had crouched close to the dying child were haunted by bad dreams, unable to study or play normally. Many others remained nervous and frightened.

Some children, however, recovered much faster. Dr. Robert S. Pynoos, a psychiatrist at the University of California at Los Angeles, studied 159 of them and found that a few seemed to have an inner strength that sustained them through their terrifying ordeal.

To learn more about such resilient children, researchers have been examining boys and girls to whom the very worst has happened: the survivors of poverty, war or abuse; kids with parents too ill, too drunk or too disturbed to care for them. But instead of looking at sick or troubled children and asking "What went wrong?" they are studying healthy kids who have beaten the odds and asking "What went *right?*"

The answers are important to all children—and their parents. While some children seem to be born resilient, others can become that way. "Luck plays a part," explains Dr. Lyman C. Wynne, psychiatrist at the University of Rochester Medical Center, "but there are things parents can do to make luck more likely." For example:

Begin with love. When Emmy Werner, a University of California psychologist, began studying 700 poor and middle-class children in Hawaii, she found many kids who had the odds stacked against them. One was baby Michael, a premature infant born into poverty, with a 16-year-old disinterested mother and an absent soldier-father. But Michael's paternal grandmother and other family members gave him the loving care and attention that a little child needs.

When Michael was eight years old, his mother abandoned him, but the boy drew strength and confidence from the strong bond he had with his grandmother. This protective shield helped Michael to grow up self-assured, winning a college scholarship and becoming a successful business professional and a happily married father of two.

Michael belonged to the resilient minority. Three out of four high-risk children in Werner's study developed serious learning and behavior problems. The infants who, among other difficulties, did not get enough love and attention are now the adults who are still floundering, some with broken marriages, some in trouble with the law.

Accentuate the positive. Often, the difference between an emotionally strong child and a weak one is how well parental expectations match the child's capabilities. A mismatch can leave a child naked to misfortune.

Psychiatrists Stella Chess and Alexander Thomas studied a group of middle-class children from birth to maturity. One child, Tim, could not do what his father wanted—stick to a task for hours on end. "You have no character," the father raged, "no willpower." Finally, the boy decided his father was right—he had no character, nothing. So he simply gave up, dropping out of school and drifting as an adult.

Another family came close to the same disaster. Their daughter was born with a difficult temperament, intense and explosive. The parents labeled her a "rotten kid," and she played the part by developing behavior problems at school. Then, at age eight, she showed signs of musical and dramatic talent. As teachers praised her, the girl's parents decided her explosiveness was nothing more than an "artistic temperament." Once they began to focus on her strengths, the girl flourished.

Encourage a hobby. When eight-year-old David comes home from school, he often goes to the attic to play. The rafters are hung with model planes, and David can tell his friends about the special features and history of each aircraft.

It's "only a hobby," but for children like David it's a survival secret. In the midst of family turmoil—a mother with mental illness and a depressed father who have recently divorced—David has a refuge. He always knows he has at least one thing he can rely on: his hobby.

For any child, confidence and self-esteem grow with being skilled at something, whether it's model planes or math, baseball or the guitar. In study after study, researchers find that resilient children all had a special interest or activity.

Nurture friendships. "I can't bring anyone home," Alice complains. "My mother scares them." At 13, the daughter of a schizophrenic, Alice manages to keep sane and whole in a troubled, chaotic household by developing friends, including a special grown-up confidante and role model—the school librarian.

Even in a healthy family with loving parents, a child can draw added strength from a favorite aunt, a teacher or coach. Some children find it hard to reach out to others—and that's where parents can help.

"Children learn from the things their parents do," says Dr. Alvin Rosenfeld, director of psychiatric services for the Jewish Child Care Association. "If we bring other adults into the family circle, if we reach out into the community, we teach the child that the world can be a friendly place. If we are open to the world and show good judgment, that helps children find the people who will help enrich their lives."

Share responsibility. Clinical psychologist J. Kirk Felsman of the Dartmouth Medical School analyzed a study of 456 Boston boys. In the study, a youngster named Bill was asked why, unlike many other boys in his neighborhood, he did not steal.

"I don't have to steal," Bill said quietly. "I can earn what I need." At age nine, working after school at such jobs as delivering newspapers and shining shoes, he kept a little for spending money and gave the rest to his mother.

Bill's after-school jobs gave him something money can't buy: a sense of his own power to deal with his life—and a feeling of responsibility. In a dark and crowded walk-up, with the children sleeping four in a bed, Bill and his family shared "a sense of being a family unit," says Felsman, "a strong 'we' feeling."

Children learn cooperation and confidence from chores or a part-time job. In the process, they have to manage their time, solve real-life problems and be more independent. Surveys show that children who have chores at home do better in school.

"A lot of children have so much done for them," says Felsman, "that they miss out on the opportunity to become competent. A child needs to feel he's an important member of the family, with something real to contribute. Then he needs rewards and praise, but only for a job well done."

Instill stick-to-itiveness. As part of a developmental test given in Emmy Werner's study, little children were asked to build towers of wooden blocks. When the tower fell, a few children rebuilt it. When one thing didn't work, they tried a different way. Years later, looking back at those early tests, Werner could see that the persistent children had become the successful adults.

"Like most things, parents teach persistence by example," she says. One day, for example, Sam's father told him to stick with his math problem until he found the solution. As Sam worked, he could hear his father fiddling with an antique radio he was restoring. He had been at it for a week, taking the radio apart, assembling it, taking it apart again. Sam learned from that lesson—and he stuck with his math problem and other challenges he faced right on into adulthood.

Inoculate against stress. To protect children against mumps or measles, we give them little doses of the toxin to build up their immunity. "In a similar way, we may be able to teach children how to deal with stress," suggests Ann Masten, a University of Minnesota psychologist. "A series of small challenges may protect children against the larger crises of life."

Success is the key. "Provide just enough challenge so a child can grow but also can succeed at it and gain confidence," Masten recommends. Good teachers plan their lessons so a child can master one thing before going on to a more difficult challenge. This is also what wise parents do at home, watching, waiting, giving a child the freedom and responsibility he's ready for. They don't teach a youngster to swim by throwing him into the deep end of the pool. They begin at the shallow end.

For an older child, the prospect of going off to college can be stressful. A daughter who's never been away from home for periods of time may need small doses of being on her own. A few weeks at summer camp, a long bike trip or a visit to friends or relatives in another state can help. Each separation becomes the confidence injection she needs for the next challenge.

Provide information. At age two, like many other small children, Joey was afraid of the roar of the vacuum cleaner. When his mother opened the tank and let him look inside, he could see there were no monsters hiding there. Together, they pasted a "smile" face on the tank. The scary machine was now the child's friend.

At any age, information can be a tool against the terror of the unknown. "A child needs to be prepared for a crisis, like going to a hospital to have his tonsils out," explains Dr. Rosenfeld. "If you tell the child the truth about what's going to happen, tell him you'll be there and then give him a chance to ask questions, he will have a better sense of control."

Judith S. Wallerstein is the principal investigator of the California Children of Divorce Project, a study that has followed 131 children from 60 divorcing families for more than ten years. This landmark study showed that children did much better in the immediate aftermath of marital disruption when they knew exactly what to expect—that both parents would continue to love them, and also where everyone would live, where the toys would be and where the children would go to school.

Impart hope. Why does one slum child go to drugs, while another goes to college? Why do some battered children grow up to be batterers themselves, while others become model parents?

In a survey of the many ways in which children successfully deal with disaster, pediatrics specialists Patricia and David Mrazek of the National Jewish Center for Immunology and Respiratory Medicine found one overriding trait: "a basic life view of optimism and hope." For the most part, they say, a youngster acquires this outlook from parents and the family environment they create. So if you are a hoper and planner, chances are your child will be too.

Writing Activity 12.2

- Write your summary of "Kids Who Beat the Odds."
- State the controlling idea and the source information in your first sentence.
- Be sure that you don't overlook any of the major details.

Reading 3: "Are You Drinking Enough Water?"

Our third article is a little deceptive. At first glance, it appears that the controlling idea is the answer to the question asked by the title, but a closer look shows that while the first half of the article is about the amount of water a person should drink, the other half is about something slightly different. Your statement of the controlling idea, then, must contain both of the ideas developed in the article. As you look for the major supporting details, be sure to notice the boldfaced headings. This article is from *Parade Magazine*.

Are You Drinking Enough Water?

by Leroy R. Perry, Jr.

Water is, by far, the most abundant substance on earth and in our bodies. A human embryo is more than 80 percent water, a newborn baby about 74 percent and a normal adult about 60 percent to 70 percent water. Next to air, water is the substance most necessary for our survival. Everything in our bodies occurs in a water medium. We can go without food for two months or more, but without water we can only survive a few days.

Yet most people have no idea how much water they should be drinking. In fact, many Americans live from day to day in a dehydrated state—that is, they don't drink enough water.

The physiology of water. As the late Dr. Albert Szent-Gyorgyi, the discoverer of Vitamin C, said: "There is no life without water . . . water is part and parcel of the living machinery." Without water, we'd be poisoned to death by our own waste products and toxins resulting from metabolism.

When the kidneys remove wastes such as uric acid, urea and lactic acid, those wastes must be dissolved in water. So if there isn't enough water, wastes are not removed as effectively, and it may be damaging to the kidneys. Water also is vital to digestion and metabolism, acting as a medium for various enzymatic and chemical reactions in the body. It carries nutrients and oxygen to the cells through the blood. Water helps to regulate our body temperature through perspiration, which dissipates excess heat and cools the body. Water also lubricates our joints. This is particularly important if you're arthritic, have chronic musculoskeletal problems or are athletically active.

We even need water to *breathe*. Our lungs must be moistened by water to facilitate the intake of oxygen and excretion of carbon dioxide. We lose approximately a pint of liquid each day just exhaling!

So, if you don't drink enough water to be in "fluid balance," as doctors call it, you can impair every aspect of your body's physiological function. And the more you exercise, the more water you need to keep your body in fluid balance. Dr. Howard Flaks is a bariatric physician in Beverly Hills, Calif. (Bariatrics is the branch of medicine dealing with obesity.) He says, "As a result of not drinking enough water, many people encounter such problems as excess body fat, poor muscle tone and size, decreased digestive efficiency and organ function, increased toxicity in the body, joint and muscle soreness (particularly after exercise) and water retention."

Water retention? If you're not drinking enough, your body starts retaining water to compensate for this shortage. So, paradoxical as it may seem, the way to eliminate fluid retention is to drink *more* water, not less.

"Proper water intake is the key to weight loss," says Dr. Donald Robertson, director of the Southwest Bariatric Nutrition Center in Scottsdale, Ariz. "If people who are trying to lose weight don't drink enough water, the body can't metabolize the fat, they retain fluid, which keeps weight up, and the whole procedure that we're trying to set up falls apart."

How much water should you drink? Of course, overweight people are not the only ones who need to drink a lot of water. We all do. Count the glasses if you must to ensure that you get the proper amount.

"I'd say the minimum amount a healthy person should drink is 10 eight-ounce glasses a day," says Dr. Flaks. "And you need to drink more if you're overweight, exercise a lot or live in a hot climate. Overweight people should drink an extra glass for every 25 pounds they exceed their ideal weight."

At the International Sportsmedicine Institute, where we work with Olympic and professional athletes from around the world, we have developed a formula for water intake that accommodates athletes and nonathletes alike. We suggest a daily water intake of 1/2 ounce per pound of body weight if you're a nonactive person (that's 10 eight-ounce glasses a day if your weight is 160 pounds), and 2/3 ounce per pound if you're an active, athletic person (13 to 14 eight-ounce glasses a day if you're 160 pounds). This ISI formula, inspired by East German physicians, has been used with great success for almost two decades.

Your water intake should be spread judiciously throughout the day, including the evening. Dr. Flaks cautions against drinking more than four glasses in any given hour. And you should always check with your physician before embarking on a regimen of increased water intake.

You may be wondering: If I drink this much water, won't I constantly be running to the bathroom? Initially, it has been observed, the bladder is hypersensitive to the increased amount of fluid, and you have to urinate frequently. But after a few weeks, your bladder calms down, and you urinate less frequently but in larger amounts.

Water vs. other beverages. There is a difference between pure water and other beverages that *contain* water. Biochemically, water is water—obviously you can get it consuming such beverages as fruit juice, soft drinks, beer, coffee and tea. Unfortunately, while such drinks contain water, they also may contain substances that are not healthy—and actually contradict some of the positive effects of the added water. As Dr. Jerzy Meduski, a medical doctor and biochemist in Los Angeles, says: "Beer contains water, but it also contains alcohol, which is a toxic substance." And caffeinated beverages like coffee stimulate the adrenal glands, while fruit juices contain a lot of sugar and stimulate the pancreas. Soda contains sodium. Such drinks may tax the body more than they cleanse it.

Another problem with these beverages is that you lose your taste for water.

The way to interpret all this, therefore, is that the recommended daily water intake means just that . . . water!

Tap water or bottled water? It's difficult to speak in generalities about water quality in America, because it varies from location to location—and even from time to time at the same tap!

"Some communities don't even have to treat their water," says Eric Draper, campaigns director of the Clean Water Action Project, a Washington, D.C.-based activist group involved with water issues. "Essentially, the raw water they get from the ground is fine for drinking. In other areas the water source is very polluted, and no matter how sophisticated the treatment and filtration system, some of the chemicals are going to get through."

Utilities are required by law to test the water they provide to consumers. Unfortunately, they're not required to test the water at your tap. And a lot can—and apparently does—happen to water from the time it leaves the treatment facility until it comes out of your tap.

Gene Rosov, president of WaterTest Corp., the nation's largest independent drinking-water testing laboratory, has testified before Congress on water quality. He says, "I believe that the majority of health-related risks that are present in drinking water are a result of contamination added *after* the water leaves the treatment and distribution plant."

The reasons for this, he says, fall largely into three categories: 1) *Contaminants*, such as lead, entering the water as it flows through the pipes to your tap. 2) *Back flow* into the water line, resulting from air-conditioners, stopped-up toilets and sinks. 3) *By-products of chlorination*, the so-called trihalomethanes (which are suspected carcinogens), formed as chlorine acts on debris in the water. An excess of particulate matter in the pipes results in greater trihalomethane levels—especially if the water sits around in the pipes for a while.

Bottled water has become a $2 billion business in this country. And one might ask: Is bottled water the 100 percent-safe alternative to tap water?

Unfortunately, the answer seems to be "no." Both California and New York did studies on bottled water and found many of the same impurities that are present in tap water, although the International Bottled Water Association has charged that both studies were flawed.

"People assume that when they buy bottled water, they're getting a better-quality water than when they turn on their tap," Rosov points out. "It's not always true."

"We did a survey of more than 100 bottled waters. The bottom line of the study was three points: 1) Good-quality bottled water and good-quality municipal water are not that different. 2) The decision to drink bottled water is an aesthetic choice (based on how the water tastes), and that aesthetic choice is usually the compelling reason. 3) You can't shower with bottled water."

That last point is a reference to the fact that many contaminants in water are skin-absorbed (when you're taking a shower, for instance), while others are respirated (we breathe them in). Radon, a carcinogen, is breathed in when we take a shower.

We live in a chemicalized world. The fact is that we can never be 100 percent sure that what we drink or eat is 100 percent safe. But let's not forget that the U.S. probably has one of the safest water supplies in the world. In comparison, millions die each year in Third World countries from water contamination. Our challenge is how to make America's relatively good situation even better.

Our individual responsibility. Concern about the quality of our water has led to a boom in home water-treatment sales. While sales of bottled water are increasing by 10 to 15 percent annually, water-treatment sales are growing at a rate of 20 percent or more a year.

Various types of water treatments are available, including reverse osmosis, activated carbon filters, distillation, ion exchange (water softeners) and ultraviolet treatment. No single technique can remove all contaminants. Each has its own strengths and weaknesses. The type you get should be determined by the type of contamination in your water.

If you're thinking of buying a home-treatment unit, the first step is to have your water tested. A large independent lab like WaterTest can do it, or call your health department for a referral. In fact, testing may be a good idea whether you're thinking of getting a unit or not. How else are you going to determine the quality of your water?

Testing your water for a wide spectrum of chemicals and other pollutants can be quite expensive—$200 or more. You may choose to test simply for radon and lead, "the two worst contaminants," according to WaterTest's Gene Rosov, "because radon, which can cause cancer, kills more people in America than any other water contaminant, and lead affects so many and targets infants and pregnant women [lead impairs the development of brain cells in children]."

In the final analysis, to ensure clean water for our families and the generations to come, we must:

1) Continue to fight for clean-water legislation and support those who are dedicated to environmental preservation.

2) Test our water to make sure it's safe.

3) Use proper filtering systems to remove possible contaminants.

4) Not waste water.

Writing Activity 12.3

- Write a summary of "Are You Drinking Enough Water?"

- Be sure your first sentence includes both sections of the controlling idea.

Article 4: " 'No One's a Born Loser!' "

The controlling idea of this piece is not stated but implied. Its major supporting details, facts about the school and stories about students, lead the reader to a statement about the school itself. That statement is the controlling idea. The story is from *Reader's Digest*.

"No One's a Born Loser!"

by Patricia Skalka

Even as she walked into Enterprise High School in Utica, Mich., Carole wondered why she was bothering. Her drooping shoulders and downcast eyes bespoke despair.

It had been almost two years since the 19-year-old had dropped out of high school midway through her senior year, and Enterprise was her second chance. Still, she was full of doubt about her ability to do the work. *How can this place possibly help me?* she asked herself that September day in 1986, looking around uneasily. *I'm only setting myself up for another fall.*

Art instructor Julie Williams recognized Carole's first-day look. "Hi, I'll be your teacher in this class," she said. "I'm really glad you're here."

Carole shrugged. "I don't much like school," she mumbled.

"This one's different," Julie said, smiling. "You'll get a lot out of it."

"Maybe," Carole said, turning away. "We'll see."

High-school dropouts like Carole pose a growing problem for American education. About one million students—nearly one in every four—now quit before graduation. (In some urban areas the rate reaches 65 percent.) Less than half ever return to school. Dropouts who do find employment tend to work at low-paying, unskilled jobs. Many of the rest are virtually unemployable and frequently turn to crime. (An estimated 60 to 75 percent of prison inmates failed to complete high school.)

The cost to the nation is staggering. The Center for Education Research at Stanford University has calculated the loss to society from the class of 1981. Dropouts from that year alone will cost the nation $228 billion in lost earnings and $68 billion in lost tax revenues over the course of their lives. And the cost in squandered human potential is incalculable.

Enterprise High was Richard R. Benedict's answer to the problem. He developed his program after three years of teaching a course on "life skills" to kids at an inner-city school in Benton Harbor, Mich. Benedict quickly realized that the students who needed the course most weren't around for it. They had already dropped out.

With federal and state funding, the first Enterprise High for dropouts opened its doors six years ago in an abandoned elementary school in Macomb County, north of Detroit. Today, 600 students are enrolled at ten Enterprise Highs throughout Michigan and in Cleveland and Chicago. Prospects hear about the program, which is part of the public-school system, through word-of-mouth and counselors.

For part of every school day, students bone up on English, math, science and other basic subjects. The rest of the day, they work on entrepreneurial projects and share the profits. They run restaurants, repair cars, print wedding invitations, fix computers. One group operates a credit union.

Most of the students have a long history of serious problems. Half are drug users when they come to the program. About one-third have been in trouble with police. Almost one-third are from families on public assistance. "No one is born to be a loser," Benedict tells them. "You're here to realize your potential."

And thanks to Benedict's efforts, most of them do. Nearly 70 percent graduate, and two-thirds of the students get jobs or start their own businesses. For many, Enterprise High is the catalyst for a major life change. "We teach them that work is important, that their lives have merit and that what they do is valuable," says Benedict. "Through enterprise, they get a chance to succeed. If they fail, they understand it's their responsibility and no one else's."

Michael, for example, detoured into drugs and alcohol at 13. He dropped out of high school, and couldn't hold a job. Then a friend told him about Enterprise High and, at 19, Michael enrolled. He didn't expect much. But within a year, he had sworn off drinking and drugs and earned his diploma. Today, at 26, Michael works full time installing home burglar alarms, and he dreams of becoming an engineer. After studying electronics at a technical school at night, he recently graduated.

Sue was 16 when she left school. For the next eight years she lived on the edge, a desperate young mother with a $700-a-day cocaine habit. She and her young daughter were once homeless. At 24, Sue decided she had had enough. She joined a dependency treatment program and enrolled in Enterprise High, earning straight A's. Today, this former welfare mother works as a supervisor at a shelter for battered women.

Carole, the troubled young woman standing in the classroom that September day, also had a sad history. At six, she had been sexually molested. For years, her alcoholic father beat her. Carole grew up lonely in a home short on money and love.

At 15, Carole, argumentative and hostile, started skipping school, then quit. In June 1985, when she should have been graduating, her mother threw her out of the house. A few weeks later, a serious car accident shattered Carole's right leg. Forced to quit her assembly-line plastics job, she lay in the hospital for two weeks, hoping her parents would ask her back. They didn't.

Carole stayed first with a girlfriend's family, then with her unemployed boyfriend. Wary of strangers, withdrawn, she lived behind an emotional wall.

Julie Williams had seen it all before; yet students like Carole, filled with disillusionment and hopelessness at such a young age, still came as a shock to her. She had to work at gaining their confidence and trust. "Here is your second chance at high school—your second chance to do or be anything you want," Julie told this group. "It's up to you. I'll do everything I can to help." Most of the students gave her hard looks. Julie glanced at Carole, who was sitting silent and sullen. Carole, she knew, would be a challenge.

"This school is built around enterprise," Julie continued, "and our enterprise in this class is art. You'll make products and sell them. We have a store right here in school."

Carole frowned. "Nobody's going to buy anything I make."

"There's not one person in this room who can't do something and do it well," Julie said, addressing the class. "I taught myself everything I know about art. And people pay me for what I can make. You can all have the same thing for your future. I can show you how—*if* you'll meet me halfway."

Julie turned back to Carole. "If you could do any art project in the world, what would it be?"

For one brief moment, Carole let her guard down. "Oil painting," she blurted. Then she looked around sheepishly. "But I can't. . . ."

"You *can*," Julie promised.

Many of the kids at Enterprise High had heard from parents, friends and teachers for years that they would never amount to anything. Every day, Julie chipped away at their negative feelings, repeating her message of optimism. But Carole was moody and silent, avoiding contact with other students. She seldom contributed to discussions.

When Carole began her first project—a pen-and-ink drawing of a cluster of grapes—Julie heaped encouragement on her. "That's beautiful work!" Heartened, Carole next made a ceramic doll. "Good detail," Julie said, though she immediately noticed Carole had chosen a dark, somber blue. *Carole's feelings of hopelessness are coming through. But she'll change. . . . I know she will.*

Week by week, Carole's confidence grew. Soon she was making cloth-covered picture frames and tie-dyed T-shirts. To learn to think practically as well as artistically, Carole had to figure the cost of her supplies, her potential profit and the sale price of the finished item. Eventually, Carole switched to crafts for the home. "I can make more money that way," she said.

Every day at noon, Carole left the art room and walked down the hall to her life-management class. Here, she earned a mock paycheck, based on her attendance and classroom performance, and paid simulated bills. In this way, Carole learned to balance a budget, and even figure income tax. She also began learning more about herself. One day she confided to Julie, a trace of surprise in her voice, "You know, I like it here. I think I'm learning something."

But Carole's attendance still was spotty. So Julie asked about it. "My boyfriend drives me to school," Carole explained, "and sometimes we don't have money for gas."

When Julie noticed that Carole had a bad cough in mid-October, she asked if anything was wrong. Carole explained that she and her boyfriend were living in a pickup-truck camper. The couple had to walk more than a half-mile to a gas station just to use the bathroom.

"Where do you eat?" Julie asked.

"We're fine," Carole insisted.

That evening, Julie knocked at the camper door with three bags of groceries. Inside, conditions were even worse than Julie had expected. A single Bunsen burner heated the place. Carole was huddled in a blanket, shivering like a lost child. Julie wrapped both arms around her and pulled her close. "Carole," she said softly, "you can't live like this. We've got to get you back home."

Carole shook her head. "My parents won't have me, and besides, I don't want to go back."

Over the next few weeks, Julie gave Carole groceries and vitamins. She also telephoned Carole's mother, urging her to reconcile with her daughter. In November, just ahead of a harsh Midwestern winter, her mother relented and Carole moved back home.

By now Carole was reaching out in other ways as well—participating in class discussions, sharing her problems and helping other students with theirs. A young woman was living with an abusive boyfriend. Carole persuaded the woman to break up with him and move back with her parents. "It worked for me," Carole said.

Carole began emerging as the class leader. She became manager of the school store and helped run a successful holiday bazaar, which earned the class nearly $700.

During her second semester, Carole finally had the chance to do the oil painting she had longed to try. "I want mountains in my painting," she told Julie, "so I can imagine myself sitting high up where it's beautiful and quiet."

Carole sketched the outlines of peaks and a mountain lake onto the canvas. Every day, she sat for hours in front of her easel, laboring over her creation. Finally, after three months, it was finished. The mountains were hers, captured in bright, rich colors. There were cheers from the class.

In June 1987, Carole and eight other students completed the requirements for a high-school degree. To Julie's delight, the once painfully shy young woman volunteered to give the graduation address. Smiling and full of confidence in her white cap and gown, Carole approached the lectern.

"I told myself I was never going to get a diploma," Carole confessed to the audience. "But at Enterprise High, everyone worked together—like a family." Julie Williams, as proud as any parent, sat teary-eyed in the first row. "This school gave me the opportunity to make something of my life." Head held high, Carole paused. "Now I know I can do anything I set my mind on."

After graduation, Carole landed a job in the accounts-receivable department of a large national trucking firm. She plans to attend college and hopes to become a legal secretary.

Writing Activity 12.4

- Write a summary of "'No One's a Born Loser!'"
- Be sure the controlling idea is stated as a complete sentence.

Article 5: "I Was an Unwed Stepmother"

This fifth article also lacks a stated controlling idea, but for the most part it is divided into sections, each of which illustrates a part of the controlling idea. The article originally appeared in the "My Turn" column of *Newsweek*.

I Was an Unwed Stepmother

by Elizabeth Mehren

Once, while Fox and I were still dating, his son squealed with delight when he learned I was about to interview Bill Cosby. Cosby was a television hero, a big star. This was bound to earn Ethan a lot of mileage among his peers. "Oh boy! Wow!" Ethan said. "Wait'll I tell my friends that my . . . that . . ." Ethan paused. The proper word was eluding him. "Wait till I tell my friends that my Dad's . . . that, um . . ."

I decided to take the pressure off the kid. Ethan was just 11, a roly-poly boy with lots of love and a nonstop sense of humor. I felt lucky that Ethan and his sister Sarah, then 7, had seemed to accept me so rapidly. Their parents were in the throes of a messy divorce, their mother had a live-in boyfriend that neither child particularly cared for—and then I showed up. "Ethan, I'm sort of curious," I asked him. "How do you refer to me when you talk with your friends and teachers?" Ethan looked puzzled, then brightened abruptly. "My mother-in-law!" he announced.

We all laughed, in large part because this morsel of pre-adolescent humor made it easier for us to deal with a potentially sticky situation. Exact figures are impossible to come by, but by some reliable estimates, many thousands of people cohabit without benefit of marriage in homes where there are children by their partner's marriage. Though they may look and act like parents, there's no name for this species. In real terms we are unparents or, as Fox and I took to thinking of it, unwed stepparents.

When Sarah would skin her knee, she came to me, not Fox, to clean and bandage the wound. Both children assumed I would prepare the meals, change the sheets on their beds and supply them with fresh, clean laundry. If there was no toothpaste, I was the one who was expected to magically produce a fresh tube.

But at some deep level, all of us knew that I had no power in this makeshift family structure. I had my own job and my own means of economic support. But Ethan and Sarah knew I had no financial clout in their family. They also knew I had no real authority. If I politely asked them to do something—even if I sternly told them to do something—they could ignore it, and they knew it. Any limits that I attempted to set were meaningless, because they came from a nonempowered person.

I have since learned that social scientists use the term "social parenting" to describe a household where there is a residential adult of the opposite sex who is not married to the parent of the children. But in so many ways it is quite different from stepparenting. For one thing, the kids don't necessarily expect you to stick around. "Stepparent" has at least a semipermanent connotation to it. "Boyfriend" or "girlfriend" does not. The children know that at any moment you may vanish and, in all likelihood, be swiftly replaced. As a result, the children may withhold some level of emotional commitment. On the other hand, they may not. Some children seem to feel that because the unparent is not a certified authority figure, topics that are normally taboo are perfectly acceptable. A friend in San Francisco called me, shaken, after her teenage unstepdaughter calmly asked to see her diaphragm. Not in a million years, my friend knew, would this kid ever pose such a brash question to her real parents or, for that matter, to real stepparents.

As for the "social parent," he or she is likely to bond strongly with the children. They are, after all, living together. If the relationship between the adults does break up, the unwed stepparent often mourns the separation from the children even more than the end of the love affair. With no formalized relationship, the unparent has no "permission" to continue the relationship with the kids.

There are no support groups, as far as I know, for unwed stepparents, no national organizations with T shirts, newsletters or fun picnics. In many circles there's still a stigma to living together unmarried, so the whole situation is tinged with uncertainty. But unwed stepparenting is very seldom taken on casually. It's a rare unwed stepparent who moves into a home with

children on a whim, and it's an unusual real parent who introduces a girlfriend or boyfriend into his or her children's lives
without thinking things through.

Divorces often make people gun-shy about embarking on
subsequent relationships. "Don't get burned again," is often the
feeling. Sometimes, divorces simply take a long time to negoti-
ate, and a new mate enters the picture before the proceedings
are final. And there is the persistent problem of commitment-
phobia, a disease that has by no means vanished with the much-
discussed marriage boom. Joint custody of children is an in-
creasingly prevalent alternative when marriages do split up.
The result is often "trial marriage," an attempt to blend the various elements—children, parent, ex-spouse and new, aspiring
spouse—into some kind of arrangement that works well for all
involved.

Fox and I have now been happily married for several years;
Ethan and Sarah were even attendants at our wedding. We all
seem to have made a comfortable transition from being an unwed stepfamily to being a genuine stepfamily.

But now we have a new problem. We all hate the term "stepmother." It begs for the adjective "wicked," as in Cinderella.
One of the kids' friends calls me their "other mother," a term I
rather like. But I liked it even better when Ethan called me his
mother-in-law.

**Writing
Activity
12.5**

- Write your summary of "I Was an Unwed Stepmother."
- Your summary will be short because the article is
  short, but don't neglect any of the major supporting
  details.

Article 6: "'The Hardest Job on Earth'"

Article six is another profile. Its controlling idea is stated in the introduction, but extracting the major details and expressing their relationship to the
main idea may be a real challenge.

"The Hardest Job on Earth"

by Lou Ann Walker

"It must be the most unmodern doctor's office in the United States," John Eustace Denmark, 90, says of the 125-year-old farmhouse where his wife, the pediatrician Dr. Leila Denmark, 91, has her practice. The floors are bare dark wood (rugs would be too germ-ridden). The equipment is astonishingly simple: a scale for weighing infants, her original 1928 stethoscope, a few basics. On the desk and tacked to a screen are three generations of children's photographs.

I had come to rural Georgia to write a story about one of America's oldest practicing physicians and expected to hear about the early days and how much better the practice of medicine used to be. I was to be constantly surprised.

A handsome woman, her hair gathered in a bun, Dr. Denmark has a spare frame. Her face only slightly weathered, she looks many years younger than her age. Soon after we met, she was freely sharing her opinions on motherhood and child-rearing. She is not the least bit sentimental.

"The hardest job on earth is being a mother," she says. "It should be the best-educated job. I never ask any woman to be a mother if she doesn't want to. A lot of women shouldn't be mothers. Every sorry man was made by a woman—and every good man was made by a woman."

Every weekday but Thursday, Dr. Denmark—who never leaves her house without hat and gloves—sets off to work in her barebones office. By 8 a.m., the rooms are filled with mothers—their babies crying, wriggling, playing. There are no scheduled appointments. A sign-up book rests atop an antique marble-topped table. Some parents drive 90 miles or more to her office, which is 8 miles from the nearest town. There's no nurse. "I don't want somebody saying, 'Hurry up,'" Dr. Denmark explains. She takes as long as an hour getting to know a family. Each day she sees 20 to 30 children.

I watch, fascinated, as she takes a little boy's arm firmly but gently. "This is going to hurt," she warns as she starts to inject him. She never dissembles to children. "They're too honest," she says.

Leila Daughtry was graduated from the Medical College of Georgia in 1928 (she was its third woman graduate), a time when only four or five women were graduating annually from the nation's medical schools. She then became the first intern at Egleston Hospital for Children, now one of the South's largest hospitals. She also began charity work at a clinic in a Presbyterian church, and for the next 56 years she spent every Thursday there, treating maladies from colds to syphilis, often as not giving patients a nickel to get home on the streetcar.

In those days, she made housecalls. "I remember lecturing a mother about sterilizing bottles," she recalls. "But I didn't know how they were living. There was a dirt floor—I couldn't believe they kept a child alive in that dirt."

But Dr. Denmark, who considered herself only a fair student, was always looking for answers in medicine. When a baby found in a trash can didn't respond to treatment, the young woman intern broke the rules by inventing a special formula. The baby lived. In the early 1930s, whooping cough caused seizures and brain hemorrhages in children. After three babies died, Dr. Denmark drew blood from a man with whooping cough who had broken three ribs coughing violently, then she injected the serum in her young patients—a pioneering technique no longer used. They got well. Inoculation against whooping cough is now routine protection worldwide.

"I've been a skeptic about accepting things," Dr. Denmark explains. "I listen carefully and make up my own mind." Many of her treatments—for disorders from milk intolerance to polio—have been innovative.

Although Dr. Denmark calls many of her views "old-fashioned," others are remarkably modern. She's delighted that antibiotics, baby food and immunizations have made parents' and babies' lives easier. Her book, *Every Child Should Have a Chance*, has influenced Georgia mothers for years. In it, she strongly discourages "demand feeding," now in vogue. She also vigorously opposes a mother's drinking or smoking. She tells of one very stiff baby: "It was coming off nicotine addiction. I asked the mother, 'What about when the boy is 5 and he takes a puff?' 'I'll wear it out,' the mother answered [meaning she'd spank him]. 'Well, how can you?' I asked. 'It's just doing exactly what you do.'"

Some of Dr. Denmark's views are controversial: She does not believe mothers should work outside the home. She disapproves of day-care centers because children don't receive enough individual attention—and they snack too much. "Without parents' guidance, children are insecure, immature robots," she says.

"She tells parents to take charge," says Marty Franchot, a mother of three. "Everything she tells you to do works," says Sharon Cannon. "Everything."

As children, Leila and her husband-to-be, John Eustace Denmark (she generally calls him Eustace), lived one farm apart on the rich, black earth of south Georgia. "I remember his blue velvet suit," she says. Leila (pronounced lee-la) was one of 12 children; Eustace had six brothers and a sister. Their first school was a one-room log cabin. "He was always the smartest one," she says. "But I helped with his girlfriends."

As a girl, Leila set her sights on several careers. First, she wanted to be a milliner (she made fancy hats for her mother), then a fashion designer (to this day, she makes her own clothes), then a dietitian (she still loves to cook). In college, when a professor set up a dissecting lab for her, she decided to be a technician; she also worked in a mill town, helping children. Finally, her talents melded. Her goal: to be a missionary doctor.

After college, Leila taught school in poverty-stricken north Georgia. "It was work," she says. Eustace also taught, then headed for Java as a State Department vice consul for two years. Returning in 1926, he attended evening law school, passed the bar, then went into banking.

Eustace and Leila reached an "understanding." She explains wryly: "I went to medical school, and no one would have me. Eustace went around the world, and nobody would have him. And so we joined up." They were married in a chapel in 1928. The day after, Leila got up, fixed breakfast and started her internship. Since that time, Mr. Denmark, now a retired Federal Reserve Bank vice president, has handled the business end of her practice.

"We lived in the best era on earth," Dr. Denmark says in her soft drawl. "People enjoyed things." For 56 years, the Denmarks have sat in the same pew in the Druid Hills Baptist Church. Both are avid hikers, and she especially loves camping in a tent. "I'm as limber as a 16-year-old," she says, touching her toes. Her health habits are simple: She eats heartily but never snacks.

"I'm only addicted to prime rib," she says, laughing. She stopped eating desserts a quarter century ago.

Over the years, the Denmarks have moved farther and farther north of Atlanta. Civilization kept shooting up around them. In 1949, partly because a neighbor complained of babies crying, they packed up again. "In our next house, we built an office across the carport," Dr. Denmark recalls. "A doctor friend said, 'Who in the nation is going to be driving out there?' By 9:30 the day I opened, the parking lot was full up. I was in heaven."

In the early 1970s, the Denmarks agreed to sell that house on a contract: They'd remain 14 years, then a developer would take possession. "We thought we'd be dead and gone when the time came," Eustace Denmark says. They grew to love their home, and suddenly the contract's end loomed. Their solution? They built a virtual duplicate on 81 acres of farmland purchased years before. "Old as we are, you don't want to try and arrange differently," Dr. Denmark says of their spacious home. "We didn't want to have to worry about where pictures and rugs go."

She glances up at a painting of herself tending a child, made from a newspaper photograph. "I don't like my looks as an old person," she says. In the den is a portrait of a younger Dr. Denmark, a glowing brunette, holding her daughter, Mary (who is now married with two grown sons). When Mary was a child, Dr. Denmark recalls, her office was in their breakfast room. A woman cared for Mary all day, with her mother keeping close watch. "I learned more from my own baby than I did in medical school," the pediatrician says.

On her day off, Dr. Denmark's phone rings often. She jumps up to answer. "Give her a tablespoon of milk of magnesia," she says. "There's something in her stomach we have to get out. Don't give her ginger ale." Dr. Denmark is quiet a moment. "Listen to what I'm saying." She repeats her instructions. "If she gets a fever, you call me back."

The phone rings again. "How is the baby today?" Dr. Denmark asks. "Wonderful," she says, hearing good news.

Dr. Denmark has no thought of retiring—perhaps because she doesn't call what she does "work." "Work is something you don't want to do," she says. "Something you want to do—that's play." She adds, "When you see my name in the obituary, that's when you'll know I've retired."

One morning as I watched her walk briskly through the back door of her office at 8 a.m., it was clear that Dr. Denmark was excited about starting the new day. She worked till sundown, not stopping for lunch, brimming with vigor, optimism and a sense of mission.

"There are two classes of people being thrown to the wolves," she told me. "Our little people and our old people. If I can just put one more child on the right track, this life is worthwhile."

I had gone to Georgia to write about an unusual woman at the end of her life, but what I found was a woman *living* an astonishingly rich life. She wasn't just helping young people, she was teaching all people—young, middle-aged and old—to live their lives as fully as they can.

Writing Activity 12.6

- Write a summary of "'The Hardest Job on Earth.'"
- You may wish to pay careful attention to the outlining step as you work.

HANDBOOK

THE MECHANICS OF WRITING

I PARTS OF THE SENTENCE

The sentence is the basic building block of the paragraph, and the sentence is, of course, made up of words. We use a specific vocabulary to talk about the words in sentences, and you need to understand that vocabulary in order to understand what you are doing when you write or revise your work.

SECTION 1:
Some Definitions

First we offer definitions of some common terms. You probably know the terms but do not remember their definitions, but knowing these definitions is not terribly important to your success as a writer. You will probably become familiar with most of these definitions, and you can always refer back to this handbook or to any good college dictionary if you need to have your memory refreshed.

A. Sentence

A **sentence** is a group of words that has a subject and a verb and that expresses a complete thought. It begins with a capital letter and ends with a period, question mark, or exclamation point. In the English language, a sentence can do one of four things.

- The *declarative sentence* makes a statement or a declaration about something:
  The team won the game.

- The *interrogatory sentence* asks a question:
  Did the game last long?

- The *exclamatory sentence* expresses a strong emotion:
  We won!
  An exclamation can be considered a complete sentence even without a
  subject and verb:
  Oh, no!

- The *imperative sentence* gives an order or command:
  Watch the game.
  The subject of an imperative sentence is not written in the sentence.
  Since it tells someone to do something, its subject is understood to
  be "you":
  (You) watch the game.
  We have names for various words and parts of a sentence. Let's look at
  some of those names.

B. Noun

A **noun** is a word that names a person, a place, a thing, or an idea. The
nouns are underlined in the following examples:

> **Franz works in Newport in a garage that's a real antique.**
> **Stacey made the decision that she wouldn't go to school.**

C. Pronoun

A **pronoun** is a word that can take the place of a noun. Pronouns are
underlined in this example:

> **Jeff liked his costume, so he wore it often.**

Every complete sentence has a least one noun or pronoun in it. A noun or
pronoun will be the subject of the sentence, but there may be other nouns and
pronouns in the sentence. We speak of pronouns as being *first, second,* or *third
person* and of being singular or plural.

	Singular	*Plural*
First person:	I	we
Second person:	you	you
Third person:	he, she, it	they

D. Subject

A **subject** is a noun or pronoun that names what the sentence is about. The subject is underlined in these examples:

> <u>Cats</u> scratch.
>
> My <u>cats</u> scratch each other when they fight.
>
> <u>I</u> don't know why I keep cats as pets.
>
> <u>They</u> are a real nuisance.

See Part I, Section 6 (pp. 255–57), for a complete discussion of subjects.

E. Verb

There are two kinds of **verbs**, action verbs and linking verbs. *Action verbs* ("do" words) are underlined twice in the following examples:

> Clarita <u>runs</u>.
>
> Sylvia <u>hit</u> a home run.

Linking verbs are underlined twice in the following sentences.

> The fields <u>look</u> brown and dry.
>
> Winter <u>is</u> on its way.

Every complete sentence has at least one verb in it. The main verb of the sentence tells what the subject does or is. We discuss verbs at length in Part I, Sections 2–5 (pp. 244–55).

F. Adjective

An **adjective** is a word that gives more information about (or modifies) a noun. Adjectives are underlined in this example.

> Wanda's <u>large</u>, <u>yellow</u> Buick was parked on the <u>dead</u> lawn.

Chapter 3 discusses the use of adjectives and nouns in writing descriptions.

G. Adverb

An **adverb** is a word that gives more information about (or modifies) a verb, an adjective, another adverb, or even a whole sentence. Adverbs are underlined in these examples.

> The sun shone <u>brightly</u>. (modifies the verb "shone")
>
> The day became <u>too</u> hot. (modifies the adjective "hot")

We tired <u>very quickly</u>. ("Very" modifies the adverb "quickly," and "quickly" modifies the verb "tired.")

<u>Unfortunately</u>, we had picked the wrong day to hike. (modifies the whole sentence)

Chapter 6 discusses the use of adverbs and verbs in writing about action.

H. Preposition

A **preposition** usually shows how a noun or pronoun relates to another word in the sentence. It usually answers the question where or when and often shows the *position* of something. Prepositions are underlined in this example.

<u>On</u> the table was a picture <u>of</u> my mother sitting <u>under</u> a tree.

Here is a list of prepositions:

about	beyond	outside
above	by	over
across	down	past
after	during	since
against	except	through
along	for	throughout
among	from	to
around	in	toward
at	inside	under
before	into	until
behind	like	up
below	near	upon
beneath	of	with
beside	off	within
between	on	without

I. Article

An **article** is one of three words, "a," "an," or "the," that comes before a noun. Articles are underlined in these examples.

<u>The</u> cow is in <u>the</u> pasture. ("The" is called a *definite article* because it limits the noun to one specific thing. One specific cow is in one specific pasture.)

I

A cow is in a pasture. ("A" is an *indefinite article* because it is less limiting. One cow is in one pasture, but it could be *any* cow, and it could be *any* pasture. "A" is used before nouns that begin with consonant sounds.)

An apple is on the tree. ("An" is also an indefinite article. "An" is used before words that begin with a vowel sound.)

J. Conjunction

A **conjunction** is a word that joins ideas and shows how they are related to each other. Conjunctions are divided into three groups: **coordinating conjunctions, subordinating conjunctions**, and **adverbial conjunctions** (also called conjunctive adverbs). (See Part III, pp. 262–70, for a thorough discussion of how conjunctions are used in sentences.) In the following sentences, conjunctions are underlined:

> **George watches wrestling, but Frank reads books.**
>
> **If the television set is on, Frank goes to the kitchen to read.**
>
> **He likes to read; however, he sometimes prefers to draw.**

SECTION 2:
What Verbs Do

A. Verbs Can Show Action

Some verbs show action. Verbs are underlined twice in these examples.

> **The quarterback passed the ball.**
>
> **Alicia sings Country and Western songs.**
>
> **Darol will plant potatoes.**
>
> **Wilma wept.**
>
> **The policeman shouted at Suleo.**
>
> **Good runners stretch before running.**

B. Verbs Can Link Ideas

Some verbs show a state of being rather than an action. They are said to link ideas, so they are called "linking verbs." Verbs are underlined twice in these examples.

Bernie felt ill.

Debbie is pregnant.

The roses will smell better in the afternoon.

Instead of showing the action of the subject, these verbs link the subject of the sentence with something that tells more about the subject. The most common linking verbs are forms of the verb "be." "Be" has eight forms:

am	were
are	be
is	been
was	being

Other linking verbs are the words:

act	get
appear	grow
become	seem
continue	stay

and the verbs that have to do with the senses:

feel	sound
look	taste
smell	

C. Verbs Show Tense

All verbs change to show time or tense. There are many tenses of English verbs; here are some of the most common. In each example, the verb is underlined twice.

PAST: **I looked.** (The action took place in the past.)

PRESENT: **She looks.** (The action is taking place right now.)

FUTURE: **They will look.** (The action will take place in the future.)

PAST PERFECT: **We had looked.** (The action took place at some specific time in the past.)

PRESENT PERFECT: **You have looked.** (The action took place in the past but is completed now.)

FUTURE PERFECT: **They will have looked.** (The action will be completed at a specific time in the future.)

PAST PROGRESSIVE: **It <u>was looking</u>**. (The action happened in the past, but it was temporary.)

PRESENT PROGRESSIVE: **He <u>is looking</u>**. (The action is happening now, but it is temporary.)

See Part I, Section 4 (pp. 249–51), for an example of verb tenses.

i. Helping Verbs   Some verb tenses require helping verbs. In our examples, the verbs that have more than one word are using helping verbs. The last word is the *main verb*, and the word or words that come before it are the helpers. A helping verb can help either an action verb or a linking verb. In the following examples, "she" is the subject. The main verb and its helping verbs are underlined twice.

She <u>is walking</u>.	She <u>was walking</u>.
She <u>should be walking</u>.	She <u>should have been walking</u>.
She <u>will have been walking</u>.	She <u>could have walked</u>.
She <u>had walked</u>.	She <u>might walk</u>.
She <u>was growing</u> rapidly.	She <u>is being</u> good.

Commonly used helping verbs are:

be	been	should
am	will	could
are	shall	have
is	can	has
was	would	had
were	may	do

Sometimes words are used between the main verb and its helpers:

<u>Have</u> the children <u>eaten</u> yet?

No, they <u>have</u> not <u>eaten</u>.

We <u>may</u> never <u>be</u> entirely <u>finished</u> with this meal.

ii. Regular and Irregular Verbs   Verbs change their tenses in regular and irregular patterns. Regular verbs always form the past and past participle with an "-ed" ending, but irregular verbs do not follow that consistent pattern. The child who says "I digged a hole" is being logical in forming the past tense. He just hasn't learned that "dig" is an irregular verb, with "dug" as its past tense.

	Present	Past	Past Participle	Present Participle
Regular	lift	lifted	lifted	lifting
Irregular	eat	ate	eaten	eating

See Part I, Section 5 (pp. 252–55), for a list of irregular verbs.

D. Verbs Change to Match Singular or Plural Subjects

Verbs sometimes change to match their subjects. That is, when a verb is used with a third person singular subject such as "he," "she," or "it" (see Part V, Section 16A, pp. 283–84), the verb must have an "s" added to it. This happens only in the present tense. Here are some examples:

SINGULAR: **The girl plays**. (The verb adds an "s" so that both the noun and the verb show singular.)

PLURAL: **The girls play**. (The verb drops the "s" when the noun becomes plural.)

SINGULAR: **She cares**. (Verbs add "s" when used with a singular noun or pronoun.)

PLURAL: **They care**. (The "s" is not used when the verb is used with a plural noun or pronoun.)

SINGULAR: **Giff feels happy**. (singular subject and verb)

PLURAL: **Giff and Jeff feel happy**. (plural subject and verb)

Some helping verbs make a similar change, but only with a singular subject (note, also, that these occur in tenses other than the present):

I have played. (present perfect)

You have played.

She has played.

I am playing. (present progressive)

You are playing.

He is playing.

And finally, the verb "be" changes to match a singular subject in the present and past tenses:

Present	Past
I am	I was
You are	You were
She is	He was

I

See Part V, Section 16A (pp. 283–84), for further discussion of subject-verb agreement.

SECTION 3:
How To Find Verbs

A. Look for Tense

An important aid in finding the verb in a sentence is to look for the word you would change in order to change the time (or tense) of the sentence from, say, past to present. The word you change will be either a main verb or a helping verb.

> PAST: **I smelled smoke.**
>
> PRESENT: **I smell smoke.**
>
> PAST: **David was driving too fast.**
>
> PRESENT: **David is driving too fast.**

B. Look for All "Do" or "Be" Words

Sometimes a sentence will have more than one verb. To find all of the verbs, read each sentence carefully, looking at all the words that show what someone or something does or is..

> **We went to the fair and rode the roller coaster.** (We did more than one thing.)
>
> **Dawn is a sailor and will be a pilot soon.** (Dawn is and will be these two things.)

C. Eliminate Verb "Look-Alikes"

Sometimes words are verbs in one sentence but not in another, so look carefully at what the words do.

> **The girl was laughing.** ("Laughing" is the main verb, and "was" is a helping verb. They tell what the girl was doing.)
>
> **The laughing girl sat down.** ("Laughing" is not a verb. It is an adjective that describes which girl sat down.)

D. Look for Helping Verbs with "-ing" Words

A word ending in "-ing" cannot be the verb in a sentence unless it has a helping verb in front of it.

We were swimming and splashing. ("Were" is a helping verb that helps both main verbs, "swimming" and "splashing.")

Swimming and splashing were our favorite activities. ("Swimming" and "splashing" work as nouns in this sentence.)

E. Look for "to" in Front of Verbs

No verb with "to" in front of it will be the main verb unless it has a helping verb in front of "to."

She has to work. ("She" is the subject, "has to" is a helping verb, and "work" is the main verb.)

She is ready to work. ("She" is the subject, "is" is a linking verb. Since "to work" has no helper, we know it is not part of the verb.)

We told them to go. ("We" is the subject, "told" is the verb. Since "to go" has no helping verb, we know it is not a part of the verb.)

We used to be able to do that. ("We" is the subject, "used to be" is the verb. Since "to do" does not have a helping verb in front of it, it cannot be part of the verb of the sentence.)

SECTION 4:
Tenses of Verbs

The following list shows the common tenses of three verbs. We include the verb "be" (the verb that tells what something is) because it changes more than any other verb. We also include an irregular verb, "drink," and a regular verb, "jump." In each example, the verb is underlined twice.

PAST TENSE

singular

I was	I drank	I jumped
You were	You drank	You jumped
She was	It drank	He jumped

plural

We were	We drank	We jumped
You were	You drank	You jumped
They were	They drank	They jumped

I

PRESENT TENSE

singular

I am	I drink	I jump
You are	You drink	You jump
He is	She drinks	It jumps

plural

We are	We drink	We jump
You are	You drink	You jump
They are	They drink	They jump

FUTURE TENSE

singular

I will be	I will drink	I will jump
You will be	You will drink	You will jump
It will be	She will drink	He will jump

plural

We will be	We will drink	We will jump
You will be	You will drink	You will jump
They will be	They will drink	They will jump

PAST PERFECT TENSE

singular

I had been	I had drunk	I had jumped
You had been	You had drunk	You had jumped
She had been	He had drunk	It had jumped

plural

We had been	We had drunk	We had jumped
You had been	You had drunk	You had jumped
They had been	They had drunk	They had jumped

PRESENT PERFECT TENSE

singular

I have been	I have drunk	I have jumped
You have been	You have drunk	You have jumped
He has been	It has drunk	She has jumped

plural

We have been	We have drunk	We have jumped
You have been	You have drunk	You have jumped
They have been	They have drunk	They have jumped

FUTURE PERFECT TENSE

singular

I will have been

You will have
   been

She will have
   been

I will have drunk

You will have
   drunk

He will have
   drunk

I will have
   jumped

You will have
   jumped

It will have
   jumped

plural

We will have
   been

You will have
   been

They will have
   been

We will have
   drunk

You will have
   drunk

They will have
   drunk

We will have
   jumped

You will have
   jumped

They will have
   jumped

PRESENT PROGRESSIVE TENSE

singular

I am being

You are being

It is being

I am drinking

You are drinking

He is drinking

I am jumping

You are jumping

She is jumping

plural

We are being

You are being

They are being

We are drinking

You are drinking

They are
   drinking

We are jumping

You are jumping

They are
   jumping

PAST PROGRESSIVE TENSE

singular

I was being

You were being

She was being

I was drinking

You were
   drinking

It was drinking

I was jumping

You were
   jumping

He was jumping

plural

We were being

You were being

They were being

We were drinking

You were
   drinking

They were
   drinking

We were
   jumping

You were
   jumping

They were
   jumping

I

SECTION 5:
Some Irregular Verbs

As an aid in using verbs and helping verbs correctly, here is a list of commonly used irregular verbs showing each of the four principal parts, or how the verbs change from tense to tense. If you want to use a verb and are not sure of its parts, consult a dictionary. The participle forms of verbs always take helping verbs:

I <u>arise</u> most mornings at 5:00.

I <u>arose</u> yesterday at 7:30.

I <u>have arisen</u> early for ten years.

I <u>am arising</u> early to get to work on time.

IRREGULAR VERBS

Present	Past	Past Participle	Present Participle
arise	arose	arisen	arising
beat	beat	beaten	beating
become	became	become	becoming
begin	began	begun	beginning
blow	blew	blown	blowing
break	broke	broken	breaking
bring	brought	brought	bringing
build	built	built	building
burst	burst	burst	bursting
buy	bought	bought	buying
can	could	been able	being able
catch	caught	caught	catching
choose	chose	chosen	choosing
come	came	come	coming
cut	cut	cut	cutting
deal	dealt	dealt	dealing
dig	dug	dug	digging
dive	dove (dived)	dived	diving
do	did	done	doing

drag	dragged	dragged	dragging
draw	drew	drawn	drawing
drink	drank	drunk	drinking
drive	drove	driven	driving
eat	ate	eaten	eating
fall	fell	fallen	falling
feed	fed	fed	feeding
feel	felt	felt	feeling
fight	fought	fought	fighting
find	found	found	finding
fly	flew	flown	flying
forget	forgot	forgotten	forgetting
forgive	forgave	forgiven	forgiving
freeze	froze	frozen	freezing
get	got	got	getting
give	gave	given	giving
go	went	gone	going
grow	grew	grown	growing
have	had	had	having
hear	heard	heard	hearing
hide	hid	hidden	hiding
hit	hit	hit	hitting
hold	held	held	holding
hurt	hurt	hurt	hurting
keep	kept	kept	keeping
know	knew	known	knowing
lay	laid	laid	laying
lead	led	led	leading
leave	left	left	leaving
let	let	let	letting
lie	lay	lain	lying
lose	lost	lost	losing
make	made	made	making

Present	Past	Past Participle	Present Participle
meet	met	met	meeting
pay	paid	paid	paying
put	put	put	putting
quit	quit	quit	quitting
read	read	read	reading
ride	rode	ridden	riding
ring	rang	rung	ringing
rise	rose	risen	rising
run	ran	run	running
say	said	said	saying
see	saw	seen	seeing
seek	sought	sought	seeking
sell	sold	sold	selling
send	sent	sent	sending
set	set	set	setting
shake	shook	shaken	shaking
shine	shone	shone	shining
show	showed	shown	showing
shut	shut	shut	shutting
sing	sang	sung	singing
shrink	shrank	shrunk	shrinking
sink	sank	sunk	sinking
sit	sat	sat	sitting
sleep	slept	slept	sleeping
speak	spoke	spoken	speaking
spend	spent	spent	spending
spring	sprang	sprung	springing
stand	stood	stood	standing
steal	stole	stolen	stealing
swim	swam	swum	swimming
take	took	taken	taking
teach	taught	taught	teaching

tear	tore	torn	tearing
tell	told	told	telling
think	thought	thought	thinking
throw	threw	thrown	throwing
understand	understood	understood	understanding
wake	woke (waked)	woken (waked)	waking
wear	wore	worn	wearing
win	won	won	winning
write	wrote	written	writing

SECTION 6:
How to Find Subjects

A. Find the Main Noun or Pronoun

Find the noun or pronoun that names what the sentence is about. Not every noun in a sentence will be the subject, but every subject will have a noun or pronoun in it. In the following examples the subjects are underlined once.

> **A snoring <u>dog</u> lay in the room.** ("Dog" and "room" are both nouns, but "dog" is the subject. The sentence says something about the dog, not about the room.)

B. Find the Noun That Goes with the Verb

Find the verb and ask "Who or what does the action of the verb?" The answer will be the subject of the sentence.

> **<u>Veronica</u> skis.** (Who skis? Veronica does, so "Veronica" is the subject.)
>
> **<u>Veronica</u>, my friend from Vermont, skis.** (Who skis? Again, Veronica does, and "Veronica" is the subject of the second sentence also.)

C. Look at the Entire Sentence

Often the subject is found at the beginning of the sentence. Sometimes, though, you must look at the middle or end of a sentence for the subject.

> **There is the black <u>dress</u> I've always wanted.**
>
> **There was a <u>thief</u> in the parlor.**

I

Here is a <u>picture</u> of a fountain.

Here is Myrnalee's new <u>computer</u>.

Many students want to call "there" and "here" the subjects of the samples above, but "there" and "here" are not nouns or pronouns, so they cannot be subjects. The sentences say that something (the subject) was or is there or here.

D. Look for Plural Subjects

Some sentences have a plural subject, that is, more than one subject. In cases like that, the subject is every noun that names what the sentence is talking about.

> **<u>Daisy</u> and <u>Laurel</u> spent the afternoon talking.** (Who spent the afternoon talking? Daisy and Laurel did.)

> **<u>Champagne</u>, <u>cheese</u>, and <u>pears</u> make a wonderful appetizer combination.** (What makes a wonderful appetizer combination? Champagne, cheese, and pears do.)

> **My <u>sister</u> and <u>I</u> are good friends.** (Who are good friends? My sister and I are.)

E. Eliminate Prepositional Phrases

Remember that the subject is *never in a prepositional phrase*. A prepositional phrase is a phrase that begins with a preposition (see Part I, Section 1H, p. 243) and ends with a noun. The following are all prepositional phrases:

> **on the table**

> **on the dining room table**

> **on the large, round, oak dining room table**

In each of these examples, "on" is the preposition that begins the phrase, and "table" is the noun that ends it. In

> **across the wide, bumpy street**

"across" is the preposition that begins the phrase, and "street" is the noun that ends it. A prepositional phrase always begins with a preposition and ends with a noun, but that noun is *never* the subject of the sentence.

In the examples that follow, the subject of each sentence is underlined once, the verb is underlined twice, and the prepositional phrases are in parentheses. Identifying and eliminating prepositional phrases is an easy way to reduce a sentence to its essentials. Then you can more easily spot the subject.

Either (of these lawn mowers) **is** a good buy. ("Of" is the preposition that starts the prepositional phrase, and "lawn mowers" is the noun that ends it.)

A **box** (of apples), four **erasers**, and two **bags** (of brownies) **cluttered** the back seat (during our trip).

(In the red house) (on the hill), three **people live** (with seven dogs) but (without running water).

I

II BUILDING SENTENCES

Sentences are made up of clauses and phrases. Some clauses can form sentences by themselves, but other clauses cannot. Those that can stand on their own as sentences are called *independent clauses*, while those that cannot are called *dependent clauses*. A phrase can never stand on its own as a sentence. Clauses and phrases can be combined in many ways to express ideas.

SECTION 7:
Clauses

A clause is a group of related words that has a subject and a verb. A clause can be either independent or dependent.

A. Independent Clauses

An independent clause can stand (independently) on its own as a sentence. It does not depend on another clause to make it a complete thought. An independent clause always expresses a complete thought. The subjects are underlined once and the verbs are underlined twice in the following examples of independent clauses.

> **The hills across the valley of the Ebro were long and white.** Ernest Hemingway

> **One fly deposits hundreds of eggs.** Charles Darwin

> **There is a simple difference between government and society.** Jacob Bronowski

> Outside the ring of dancing warriors with spears and axes <u>stood</u> the <u>wolves</u> at a respectful distance, watching and waiting. J. R. R. Tolkien

Each example has a subject and a verb, and each expresses a complete thought and can thus stand independently on its own.

Independent clauses are also called main clauses, for they express the main or most important ideas of sentences. A sentence may have more than one independent clause, but every sentence has at least one independent clause. Here are examples of sentences with more than one independent clause. The independent clauses are underlined.

> <u>The cold passed reluctantly from the earth,</u> and <u>the retiring fogs revealed an army stretched out on the hills, resting.</u> Stephen Crane

> <u>Mrs. Hale scarcely finished her reply,</u> for <u>they had gone up a little hill and could see the Wright place now,</u> and <u>seeing it did not make her feel like talking.</u> Susan Glaspell

---

Remember this: Every complete sentence needs at least one independent clause.

B. Dependent Clauses

A dependent clause cannot stand on its own. It has a subject and a verb, but it does not express a complete thought. It needs (or depends on) another clause to finish its thought.

> Which <u>Lil</u> <u>bought</u> to go roller skating

> Since <u>I</u> <u>gave</u> my geraniums to Shirley

Each example has a subject and a verb but does not express a complete thought. Neither can stand alone as a sentence. A dependent clause must be combined with at least one independent clause to make a sentence. The dependent clause is underlined in this example:

> <u>Before love struck and roiled his vision like a stirred pool,</u> Ed had a fine and appraising eye for a woman. John Steinbeck

> Their kiss was lingering, prolonged, <u>as if they had not met for years.</u> Anton Chekhov

A sentence can have more than one dependent clause. Here are examples of sentences with more than one dependent clause. The dependent clauses are underlined.

> Some years earlier a wolf bitch <u>who was raising her family only a mile or two from the camp</u> <u>where Ootek was then living</u> was shot and killed by a white man <u>who was passing through the country by canoe</u>. Farley Mowat

> Then there was a black bonnet <u>which had to be adjusted carefully</u>, and an umbrella <u>which was mislaid</u>, and a bag full of necessaries <u>which had to be collected from here and there</u>—the man being nearly crazy with anxiety in the meantime. Upton Sinclair.

Remember this: A dependent clause written by itself is not a complete sentence. It is a sentence fragment.

SECTION 8:
Phrases

A phrase is a group of related words that does not have both a subject and a verb. A phrase does not express a complete thought; it is only a part of a complete sentence. A phrase looks like this:

> with the aid of a cane

> ransacking the drawers of the dresser

> to row Uncle George

Phrases are used in sentences to add information to, or modify, the sentence or some part of it. Phrases are underlined in these examples.

> Manischevitz hobbled along <u>with the aid of a cane</u>. . . . Bernard Malamud

> <u>Ransacking the drawers of the dresser</u> he came upon a discarded, tiny, ragged handkerchief. O. Henry

> The young Indian shoved the camp boat off and got in <u>to row Uncle George</u>. Ernest Hemingway

Remember that phrases are different from clauses. A clause is a group of related words with both a subject and a verb. A clause may express a complete thought and be able to stand alone as a complete sentence. A phrase *does not* have both a subject and a verb, and it can *never* stand alone as a complete sentence. It can, however, work as an important part of a sentence, adding information that helps both the reader and the writer to understand more clearly what is being discussed. See Part I, Section 6E (pp. 256–67), and Part III, Section 10 (pp. 270–71), for discussions of particular kinds of phrases, the prepositional phrase and the participial phrase.

II

III JOINING IDEAS

We write to communicate ideas, and how we join those ideas together has a great deal to do with how well they are communicated. Let's consider some of the basic principles and techniques of joining words, phrases and clauses to make sentences that communicate effectively.

SECTION 9:
Ideas in Clauses

A. Coordinating Conjunctions

Two or more independent clauses can be joined together by a comma and a coordinating conjunction. When a coordinating conjunction is used to join two independent clauses, it is almost always preceded by a comma.

> **Western Montana has severe winters, but its summers can be warm and pleasant.**

Here is a block diagram of this punctuation pattern.

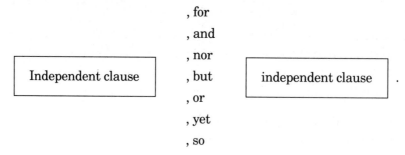

Coordinating conjunctions are used to join ideas that are of equal or coordinate importance, and the coordinating conjunctions are *"for," "and," "nor," "but," "or," "yet,"* and *"so."* (You can remember them by recalling that their first letters spell "FAN BOYS.") A coordinating conjunction is a word that shows a logical relationship between ideas. It is important to understand the relationships shown by these words.

- "For" and "so" show a cause and effect relationship between the two ideas expressed in a sentence. They show what happened and why it happened.

  Howe looked at the class with a sternness he could not really feel, for there was indeed something ridiculous about this boy. Lionel Trilling

  I didn't want my father to have to keep on being funny about it, so I got up and went to bed. Floyd Dell

- "And" is like a plus sign. It adds information.

  He is our national idol, and everybody else is our national fink. William Zinsser

  It was a thin little oar, and it seemed often ready to snap. Stephen Crane

- "Nor" and "or" offer choices. "Nor" offers a negative choice while "or" offers a positive choice.

  I'm not a schizophrenic, nor do I take hallucinogens. . . . Joan Didion

  Galileo may have seen that the warts on a peasant's face formed a perfect isosceles triangle, or he may have noticed that just as the officiating priest was uttering the solemn words, *ecce agnus Dei* [behold the lamb of God], **a fly lit on the end of his nose.** James Harvey Robinson

- "But" and "yet" show contrasts. They join ideas that seem opposite to each other.

  She was, to be sure, a girl who excited the emotion, but I was not one to let my heart rule my head. Max Shulman

  His writing filled his mornings, and should perhaps have filled his life, yet it did not. Lionel Trilling

When a coordinating conjunction joins two independent clauses, it is usually preceded by a comma, but be aware that a coordinating conjunction isn't always preceded by a comma. In the sentence above, the comma precedes the "and" because that word introduces an interrupting clause. In the sentence,

> **His writing should have filled his mornings and evenings, yet it did not.**

"and" is not preceded by a comma because its only function is to join two nouns; "yet" is preceded by a comma because it joins two independent clauses. (See Part VII, Section 21A, pp. 297–98.)

B. Semicolons

Independent clauses can also be joined together with a semicolon (;). The semicolon is used when the ideas are closely related and when the relationship is clear. Here are examples:

> **The snow had fallen thick over everything; in the pale starlight the line of bluffs across the wide, white meadows south of town made soft, smoke-colored curves against the clear sky.** Willa Cather
>
> **She had no more vicarious tears; the hot drops she shed were for herself.** Dorothy Parker
>
> **Evening wrapped about me the quickening moisture of its twilight sheets; evening laid a mother's hand upon my burning forehead.** Isaac Babel

The semicolon works just like a period except that we do not capitalize the first word of the second independent clause when we use a semicolon.

C. Adverbial Conjunctions

In addition to using just a semicolon to join independent clauses, you may use a semicolon and an adverbial conjunction (also called a conjunctive adverb). When the relationship between two ideas is obvious, use the semicolon by itself. When you want to call your readers' attention to the relationship, use an adverbial conjunction. Such conjunctions show relationships so clearly that writers often write the second clause as a complete sentence, introducing it with the adverbial conjunction. Here is a list of adverbial conjunctions:

accordingly	consequently	however
also	furthermore	indeed
besides	hence	instead

likewise	nonetheless	then
moreover	otherwise	therefore
namely	similarly	thus
nevertheless	still	

- Use "also," "besides," "furthermore," and "moreover" to show the addition of ideas.

  Even [life's] troubles, indeed, can be amusing. Moreover, they tend to foster the human qualities that I admire most—courage and its analogues. H. L. Mencken

  I don't have time to do it; besides, I don't really want to.

- Use "however," "instead," "nevertheless," "nonetheless," "otherwise," and "still" to show contrast or opposition.

  Man only truly lives by knowing; otherwise, he simply performs. . . . Alice Walker

  We Americans tend to scoff at political oratory; nevertheless, we have seen a presidential election influenced materially, perhaps crucially, by a series of television debates. John E. Jordan

- Use "accordingly," "consequently," "hence," "therefore," and "thus" to show cause and effect.

  The plane's engine caught fire shortly after takeoff; consequently, the pilot turned back.

  Since the deer's natural predators were wiped out by the first settlers, the only control over their numbers now is starvation or hunting. Thus, so many deer must be killed in a deer management area. Arthur C. Tennies

- Use "likewise" or "similarly" to show comparison.

  The wedding was spectacular; likewise, the reception was superb.

- Use "then" to show a time relationship.

  She flopped on her back and grinned at him as he tickled her chest and belly; then she jumped to her feet and danced around his legs as he walked into the kitchen to get something to eat. Patricia Curtis

- Use "namely" or "indeed" to introduce a specific example or other specific information.

  There was a lot of work to do; namely, there were pipes to repair, brush to cut, and a garage to rebuild.

If we learn more about the brain, can we learn more about ourselves? Indeed, are we anything *other* than brain? Richard Restak, MD

Punctuation note: When one of these joining words joins two independent clauses, it *must* be preceded by a period or a semicolon and is *usually* followed by a comma. Since most of these words can also be interrupters in a sentence (see Part VII, Section 21E, pp. 301–02), be sure that there is an independent clause on each side of the word before you use a semicolon or a period in front of it.

Write,
Fran wanted to walk; however, Almut chose to drive.

| Independent clause | ; however, | independent clause | . |

But write,
Fran wanted to walk; Almut, however, chose to drive.

| Independent clause | ; | independent, (interrupter), clause | . |

Write,
The brakes failed; therefore, the car rolled swiftly down the hill.

| Independent clause | ; therefore, | independent clause | . |

But write,
The brakes failed. The car, therefore, rolled swiftly down the hill.

| Independent clause | . | Independent, (interrupter), clause | . |

D. Subordinating Conjunctions

Of course every sentence must have an independent clause, but sentences can also contain dependent clauses. Ideas that are coordinate are equal to each other in importance and are usually written as independent clauses, but an idea that is subordinate to another is of lesser importance and is usually placed in a dependent clause. We use *subordinating conjunctions* to begin such clauses; like coordinating conjunctions, subordinating conjunctions show relationships between ideas. Here is a list of subordinating conjunctions:

after	if	until
although	in order that	whatever
as	provided	when
as if	since	whenever
because	so that	where
before	supposing	whereas
even if	though	wherever
even though	till	whether
ever since	unless	while

A clause that begins with one of these words is a kind of dependent clause called a *subordinate clause*. Here are some examples with the subjects underlined once and verbs underlined twice.

Although the <u>son</u> <u>was</u> but twenty-one

If the <u>nation</u> <u>returns</u> to business as usual

"The son was but twenty-one" is a complete sentence—an independent clause—but the word "although" makes it dependent. "Although" shows a contrasting relationship between two ideas, and we need to know the second idea before the thought is complete. This second idea must be an independent clause. Here's one way to make the thought complete. The dependent clause is in parentheses, and the subject and verb are underlined in both the dependent and the independent clause.

(Although the son was but twenty-one,) <u>he</u> <u>had</u> already <u>served</u> a term in jail. Sherwood Anderson

The sentence is now complete.

The dependent clause "if the nation returns to business as usual" gives us the same problem. What will happen "if the nation returns to business as usual"? Again, we need an independent clause to make the thought complete:

Those who hope that the Negro needed to blow off steam and will now be content **will have** a rude awakening (if the **nation returns** to business as usual). Martin Luther King, Jr.

In addition to indicating the relative importance of the ideas, subordinating conjunctions show logical relationships.

(Although I had invited her), Yoko didn't come to the party.

(Although Yoko didn't come to the party), I had invited her.

The first sentence calls attention to the fact that Yoko didn't attend the party because that information is placed in the independent clause. The second sentence places information about the *invitation* in the independent clause, so it stresses the fact that Yoko had been invited. The word "although" shows a contrast or opposition between the two ideas. Other subordinating conjunctions show different relationships.

- Use "as," "because," "since," or "whereas" to show cause and effect.

    Thin people turn surly, mean and hard at a young age (because they never learn the value of a hot-fudge sundae for easing tension). Suzanne Britt Jordan

- Use "as" or "as if" to show a comparison.

    (As I would not be a *slave*), so I would not be a *master*. Abraham Lincoln

- Use "after," "as," "before," "ever since," "till," "until," "when," "whenever," "where," "wherever," and "while" to show time or place relationships.

    (When in the course of human events, it becomes necessary for one people to dissolve the political bands which have connected them with another, and to assume among the powers of the earth, the separate and equal station to which the Laws of Nature and of Nature's God entitle them), a decent respect to the opinions of mankind requires that they should declare the causes which impel them to the separation. Thomas Jefferson

    The whirlwinds of revolt will continue to shake the foundations of our nation (until the bright day of justice emerges). Martin Luther King, Jr.

- Use "even if," "even though," "if," "provided," "supposing," "though," "unless," "whatever," and "whether" to show a condition or a possibility.

    (But even if we should succeed in stopping production), (and even if we should succeed in bringing about significant reductions), there will still be thousands of nuclear weapons. Roger Fisher

• Use "in order that" or "so that" to show a purpose.

(So that we can finish more quickly), we'll each do a different part of the experiment.

Remember that while the subordinate clause may begin or end the sentence, the idea you want to emphasize must go in the independent clause; the ideas in the dependent clauses are subordinate to the idea of the main or independent clause.

E. Relative Clauses

Sometimes we join ideas simply to add information to the main point we want to make. The addition of information is the purpose of the *relative clause*, a dependent clause that has a relative adjective, adverb or pronoun as its subject. Relative adjectives are words like "what," "whatever," "whichever," "whose," and "whosever." Relative adverbs are "where," "when," "why," and "how." Relative pronouns are words like "who," "whose," "whom," "which," "what," "that," "whoever," "whomever," and "whatever." In the examples that follow, the relative clauses are in parentheses, and the subjects are underlined once and the verbs are underlined twice in both the dependent and independent clauses.

The old woman (who lives next door to me) will be 93 tomorrow.

"Who lives next door to me" has a subject (who) and a verb (lives), but it cannot stand alone as a complete thought. It is a dependent clause. The independent clause, "The old woman will be 93 tomorrow," is a complete thought, but the dependent (relative) clause gives more information about the woman.

The thing (that was written on the paper) might be a threat, a summons, an order to commit suicide, a trap of some description. George Orwell

"That" is the subject of the dependent clause and "was written" is the verb, but "that was written on the paper" is not a complete thought. The independent clause, "The thing might be a threat, a summons, an order to commit suicide, a trap of some description," is a complete thought, but the dependent clause adds information that clarifies or explains the thought.

Dependent clauses that begin with relative pronouns are not quite as easy to pick out as are dependent clauses that begin with subordinating conjunctions, but if you memorize the five relative pronouns, "who," "which," "whose," "whom," and "that," you will be able to identify most relative clauses. Check for a subject and a verb, and let your ear and your sense of the language guide you in distinguishing between dependent and independent clauses:

Whose hat is this? (This is a question and a complete sentence.)

Whose hat is on the chair (Unless this is asked as a question, it does not express a complete thought and thus is not an independent clause.)

Whose hat this is (Clearly, this does not express a complete thought.)

Here are more sentences with one independent clause and one relative clause. The relative clause is in parentheses in each.

On the thirteenth of January of this present year, 1865, at half-past twelve in the day, Elena Ivanovna, the wife of my cultured friend Ivan Matveitch, (who is a colleague in the same department, and may be said to be a distant relative of mine, too), expressed the desire to see the crocodile now on display at a fixed charge in the Arcade. Fyodor Dostoyevski (trans. Constance Garnett)

At the end of the fourth night it woke just before dawn and took wing in a strange blackness (which did not lift with the coming of the sun). Neil Bell

We wondered (why the mistake had been so costly).

I suppose I looked like a man (who had escaped a den of wild beasts, and barely escaped them). Frederick Douglass

The few patches (that remained) were small and sparse, like the patches of snow lingering on in sunless spots in New England in March and April. William Humphrey

---

Punctuation note: When a relative clause has commas around it, it is not necessary to the meaning of the sentence. That is why it is set off by commas. When the clause is necessary to the meaning of the sentence, it is not set off by commas.

Section 10:
Ideas in Phrases

Independent clauses can also be combined with phrases, and among the most common and useful phrases is the *participial phrase*. This is a phrase like "running down the street" or "wishing he were famous." These phrases are sometimes called "-ing modifiers" because they begin with a word ending in "-ing" (a participle) and because they modify (or add information to) the independent clause.

Using participial phrases can help you pack information into a sentence without undue repetition. For example, Edith Wharton writes,

> **Having lowered the shade, Lydia sat down, leaving the length of the carriage between herself and Gannett.**

The independent clause is "Lydia sat down," and the two phrases let you know what she did before she sat down and where she sat down. The writer could have written,

> **Lydia lowered the shade.**
>
> **Then she sat down.**
>
> **She left the length of the carriage between herself and Gannett.**

But note how much more interesting is Wharton's original sentence.

While participial phrases can enhance a sentence, they can also muddy its meaning if they are not correctly placed. Notice, for example, the difference in meaning between these two sentences.

> **Running down the street, Roger saw the rabbit.**
>
> **Roger saw the rabbit running down the street.**

In the first sentence the participial phrase says that Roger was running, but in the second it says that the rabbit was running. The placement of the phrase so that it clearly modifies what you intend it to, then, is crucial.

Here are some examples of how professional writers have used these phrases. The participles and participial phrases are underlined.

> **Miss Kate and Miss Julia were there, <u>gossiping and laughing and fussing</u>, <u>walking after each other to the head of the stairs</u>, <u>peering down over the banisters</u> and <u>calling down to Lily to ask who had come</u>.** James Joyce
>
> **<u>Throwing off his sack of food</u>, Rainsford took his knife from its sheath and began to work with all his energy.** Richard Connell
>
> **It was Harold, twenty-three years old, wifeless, jobless, <u>sacrificing nothing even in the act of death</u>, <u>leaving the world with his life not started</u>.** Stanley Elkin
>
> **They moved toward the front hall, <u>wading through a blur of dancing, yelping dog</u>.** Anne Tyler
>
> **Uncle Ebeneezer trudged in the ditch, <u>jogging from side to side like an old ploughman coming home from work</u>.** Robert Louis Stevenson

IV FOUR SENTENCE TYPES

     Clauses and phrases can be combined into four different types of sentences that offer writers an almost endless variety of ways to combine and present ideas to a reading audience. Read through this section to become familiar with the four sentence types. As you write, experiment with them. As you read, watch how other writers use them.

SECTION 11:
The Simple Sentence

A *simple sentence* has one independent clause:

> **It may have been that mother was responsible.** Sherwood Anderson
>
> **Flakes of warm sunlight fall on the congealed fields.** Henry David Thoreau

A block diagram of the simple sentence looks like this:

> | Independent clause | .

The simple sentence focuses the reader's attention on just the one idea expressed by the independent clause:

> **Emily Dickinson wrote more than 1,000 poems.**

The simple sentence might contain a great deal of information in addition to the independent clause, but its center of interest and information will be in the single, independent clause that forms its heart.

<u>Emily Dickinson</u>, Amherst's reclusive but now famous poet, <u>wrote</u> <u>more than 1,000</u> short, untitled <u>poems</u> in her 56-year lifetime.

The words and phrases that are added to the independent clause may clarify the sentence and make it more interesting, but they are not of primary importance.

Section 12:
The Compound Sentence

A *compound sentence* has more than one independent clause. It focuses the reader's attention on two or more ideas that are closely related and of equal importance:

> **The horses were standing in the corral, and there was a beef carcass hanging on the shady side of a big pine in front of the house.** Leslie Silko

| Independent clause | , and | independent clause | . |

> **His skin emptied and drooped; his very skull seemed to collapse and settle like a kicked tent.** Annie Dillard

| Independent clause | ; | independent clause | . |

> **In a minute he had crossed the pasture and climbed the fence; however, the difficult part still lay before him.**

| Independent clause | ; however, | independent clause | . |

Section 13:
The Complex Sentence

A *complex sentence* has one independent clause and one or more dependent clauses. The dependent clauses are in parentheses in the following examples:

(When dusk had fallen), I should experience the double delight of being able to see by artificial light. . . . Helen Keller

> (Dependent clause), independent clause .

He seemed to know the presence of objects (before he touched them). D. H. Lawrence

> Independent clause (dependent clause) .

The tricks (that he has to master) are the tricks most useful to a corn doctor at a county fair. H. L. Mencken

> Independent (dependent clause) clause .

While a compound sentence shows relationship between two ideas of equal (or coordinate) importance, a complex sentence shows one main idea and one or more other ideas that are subordinate to, or less important than, the main idea.

Section 14:
The Compound-Complex Sentence

A *compound-complex sentence* has two or more independent clauses and one or more dependent clauses. The dependent clauses are in parentheses in the following examples:

> The horizon narrowed and widened, and dipped and rose, and at all times its edge was jagged with waves (that seemed thrust up in points like rocks). Stephen Crane

> Independent clause , and independent clause (dependent clause) .

The punctuation rules remain the same as those for compound and complex sentences. Here's another example:

> **Denny often visits the whitewater streams of the Northwest (because he thinks kayaking is the king of sports), but he also likes sailing, so he spends a lot of time on Cape Cod (where he has a cottage).**

This sentence has three independent clauses: "Denny often visits the whitewater streams of the Northwest," "he also likes sailing," and "he spends a lot of time on Cape Cod." It has two dependent clauses: "because he thinks kayaking is the king of sports," and "where he has a cottage." The pattern here is

| Independent clause (dependent clause) | , but |

| independent clause | , so | independent clause (dependent clause) | . |

Here's a final example:

> **My cousin Doris, (who lives on a ranch in Wyoming), is a joy to visit, for she's interested in everything, reads anything she can get her hands on, and loves to talk.**

Here we have an independent clause interrupted by a dependent clause and joined to a second independent clause with a comma and a coordinating conjunction. The pattern is

| Independent, (dependent clause), clause | , for | independent clause | . |

V FIXING SENTENCE PROBLEMS

When you have learned to combine phrases and clauses into sentences, you are ready to take a closer look at your sentences. This part discusses some of the more common sentence problems that interfere with meaning. These are problems that you should find and correct as you proofread your work.

SECTION 15:
Whole-Sentence Problems

Whole-sentence problems can often be corrected with punctuation. Sometimes incomplete sentences are punctuated as if they were complete, and sometimes independent clauses are not joined with proper punctuation. Either problem can needlessly confuse a reader.

A. Sentence Fragments

A fragment is a part of something, and a *sentence fragment* is only a part of a sentence. It is a phrase or a dependent clause written as if it were a sentence. It does not express a complete thought. Remember that a complete sentence must have a subject and a verb and must express a complete thought. A sentence fragment may or may not have a subject and verb, but it never expresses a complete thought.

i. Finding Fragments   We usually write fragments because our minds are paying attention to the flow of ideas, not the punctuation, as we write. And that's as it should be. However, there comes a time when we must proofread to find and correct the errors we make. There are two effective ways to proofread.

First, read your work aloud (or have someone read it to you), pausing a little longer at punctuation marks than you ordinarily would. This allows you to hear the flow of the ideas and hear how the ideas connect to each other, but it also allows you to listen to the sentences as individual units. Thus if you have written a sentence fragment, you will probably hear that the idea expressed is not complete.

The other effective way to proofread is to start with your last sentence, read it carefully, and then read the sentence in front of it and so on. Here's a short example to illustrate the technique.

> **The tiny pygmy owl tootled quietly from the top of the fir tree. Which was the tallest in the small grove. The birdwatchers below gazed in fascination, for it was the first pygmy owl many of them had seen.**

Reading the sentences from last to first isolates each one and lets you look at it as a unit.

> **The birdwatchers below gazed in fascination, for it was the first pygmy owl many of them had seen.**
>
> **Which was the tallest in the small grove.**
>
> **The tiny pygmy owl tootled quietly from the top of the fir tree.**

Your eye and ear will tell you that the middle sentence is a fragment. The real advantage of this backward reading is that your mind cannot get caught up in the flow of ideas, so you can more easily look at the mechanics of what you have written. Now let's look at ways in which you can correct fragments once you have found them.

ii. Correcting Fragments   To correct a fragment, combine it with other material in the paragraph or rewrite it to make it into a complete sentence. In the following examples, fragments are underlined. The corrections show one or two of several possible ways to eliminate the fragment.

> FRAGMENT: **We walked through the rain and mud all that day. Because we had no choice. The drill instructor wouldn't let us stop.**
>
> CORRECTION: **We walked through the rain and mud all that day because we had no choice. The drill instructor wouldn't let us stop.**
>
> FRAGMENT: **We finally arrived in Denver. After we had driven for sixteen hours.**
>
> CORRECTION: **We finally arrived in Denver after we had driven for sixteen hours.**

CORRECTION: **After we had driven for sixteen hours, we finally arrived in Denver.**

FRAGMENT: **Most of the time, the best way to learn is through experience. Although that can be painful.**

CORRECTION: **Most of the time, the best way to learn is through experience. Those experiences can be painful.** (Rewriting the dependent clause to make it independent helps to emphasize the idea it expresses.)

FRAGMENT: **If I could just talk to him for ten minutes.**

CORRECTION: **I wish I could just talk to him for ten minutes.** (In conversation, we use "if" to mean "I wish," and our voice tones make the meaning clear. In writing, however, meaning must come from the words on the page, not voice tones. "If" fragments should often be rewritten as complete sentences.)

FRAGMENT: **A room in my house that looks like a second-hand store.** (The subject is "room," but the only verb, "looks," is the verb of the dependent clause. "That" is the subject of the dependent clause. There is no independent clause because there is no verb that goes with "room.")

CORRECTION: **I have a room in my house that looks like a second-hand store.** (The independent clause "I have a room in my house" combines with the dependent clause to make a complete sentence.)

CORRECTION: **A room in my house looks like a second-hand store.** (The relative pronoun "that" is dropped. "Room" becomes the subject of the independent clause and "looks" is the verb.)

FRAGMENT: **Felicia has been looking for work for more than a month. Yesterday, she finally made an appointment with a job counselor. Who says he can help her find a job.**

CORRECTION: **Felicia has been looking for work for more than a month. Yesterday, she finally made an appointment with a job counselor who says he can help her find a job.** (The dependent clause is combined with the previous sentence.)

CORRECTION: **Felicia has been looking for work for more than a month. Yesterday, she finally made an appointment with a job counselor. He says he can help her find a job.** (The dependent clause is rewritten to make it an independent clause.)

FRAGMENT: **We finally saw the lost dog. Running along the street.**

CORRECTION: **We finally saw the lost dog running along the street.**

FRAGMENT: **The four of us spent the afternoon fishing. <u>Crammed into a rubber boat built for two people.</u>**

CORRECTION: **The four of us spent the afternoon fishing. Unfortunately, we were crammed into a rubber boat built for two people.**

B. Run-On Sentences

Read the following sentence. Does it cause you some confusion?

I left without my coat on the bus I tripped and fell.

The sentence is confusing because it needs punctuation to clarify the ideas it expresses. A sentence written this way is called a *run-on sentence*. There are two independent clauses (see Part II, Section 7A, pp. 258–59), so there are actually two sentences here. Each is made up of one independent clause and one phrase (see Part II, Section 8, pp. 260–61, and Part IV, Section 13, pp. 273–74). The independent clauses are underlined, and the phrases are in parentheses.

<u>I left</u> (without my coat). (On the bus) <u>I tripped and fell.</u>

i. Definition   A *run-on sentence* is two independent clauses written together with no punctuation or with just a comma between them. (Another name for two independent clauses written together with just a comma is "comma splice.")

RUN-ON: **Tomorrow is a holiday let's go to the beach.**

RUN-ON: **Tomorrow is a holiday, let's go to the beach.**

Run-on sentences are incorrect because they can confuse a reader, so let's look at four ways of correcting them.

ii. Correcting Run-On Sentences

RUN-ON: **We decided to fix up the old Chevrolet it had been in the family for years.**

a. Use a period between the two independent clauses.

CORRECTION: **We decided to fix up the old Chevrolet. It had been in the family for years.**

When you add a period to correct a run-on sentence, you must capitalize the first word that follows it since that word begins a new sentence.

b. Use a semicolon between the two independent clauses.

> CORRECTION: **We decided to fix up the old Chevrolet; it had been in the family for years.**

When you use a semicolon to correct a run-on sentence, you do not need to capitalize the word that follows it. Use a semicolon only when the ideas are closely related.

c. Use a comma and a coordinating conjunction ("for," "and," "nor," "but," "or," "yet," "so") between the independent clauses.

> CORRECTION: **We decided to fix up the old Chevrolet, for it had been in the family for years.**

d. Use a subordinating conjunction ("since," "although," "because," "when," "if," "before," and so on) to make one of the independent clauses into a dependent clause (see Part II, Section 7B, pp. 259–60, and Part III, Section 9D, pp. 267–69).

> CORRECTION: <u>Since</u> **it had been in the family for years, we decided to fix up the old Chevrolet.**

> CORRECTION: **We decided to fix up the old Chevrolet since it had been in the family for years.**

iii. More Examples

> RUN-ON: **I watched small shadows creep from the rocks and saw birds in black flocks homeward bound to the scattered bush I began to consider my own home and a hot bath and food.**

> RUN-ON: **I watched small shadows creep from the rocks and saw birds in black flocks homeward bound to the scattered bush, I began to consider my own home and a hot bath and food.**

> CORRECTION: **I watched small shadows creep from the rocks and saw birds in black flocks homeward bound to the scattered bush. I began to consider my own home and a hot bath and food.**

> CORRECTION: **I watched small shadows creep from the rocks and saw birds in black flocks homeward bound to the scattered bush, and I began to consider my own home and a hot bath and food.** Beryl Markham

> CORRECTION: **I watched small shadows creep from the rocks and saw birds in black flocks homeward bound to the scattered bush; I began to consider my own home and a hot bath and food.**

> CORRECTION: **As I watched small shadows creep from the rocks and saw birds in black flocks homeward bound to the scat-**

tered bush, I began to consider my own home and a hot bath and food.

All of the corrected examples are properly punctuated, but some are more effective than others. When you separate or combine your sentences, think about how you can best show what you really want to say.

RUN-ON: **Jim and Linda have a large family they can easily form two teams for a baseball game.**

CORRECTION: **Jim and Linda have a large family; they can easily form two teams for a baseball game.**

BETTER: **Jim and Linda have a large family, so they can easily form two teams for a baseball game.**

RUN-ON: **Walking around a shopping mall usually bores me, I have fun at one when I'm with you.**

CORRECTION: **Walking around a shopping mall usually bores me, but I have fun at one when I'm with you.**

BETTER: **Although walking around a shopping mall usually bores me, I have fun at one when I'm with you.**

SECTION 16:
Internal Problems

This section deals with three kinds of internal sentence problems: agreement, shifts, and modifiers.

A. Agreement

Nouns and pronouns must agree in person, and subjects and verbs must agree in number. Thus, if you use a third person singular noun such as "John," any pronoun you use to refer to John must also be third person singular ("he," for example). Likewise, if you use a singular subject, your verb must also be singular.

i. Noun-Pronoun Agreement   Nouns and the pronouns that refer back to them must always agree with each other. For example, we write,

Justin left Roseburg because he couldn't stand the rain. (We use the singular pronoun "he" to refer to the singular noun "Justin.")

Gabe and Justin left Roseburg because they wanted freedom. (We use the plural pronoun "they" to refer to our plural subject, "Gabe and Justin.")

We speak of pronouns as being *first, second,* or *third person* and of being singular or plural.

	Singular	*Plural*
First person:	I	we
Second person:	you	you
Third person:	he, she, it	they

In making sure that pronouns agree with their nouns, remember that the subject is never found in a prepositional phrase (see Part I, Section 6E, pp. 256–57).

> **Each of the women owns her own home.** (This sentence is correct because the subject "each" is singular and therefore the verb "owns" and the pronoun "her" must also be singular.)

> **All of the women own their own homes.** (This is correct because the subject "all" is plural and therefore the verb "own" and the pronoun "their" must be plural.)

ii. A Note on Pronouns   You'll hear and see a great deal of variation in the use of pronouns because of a problem with the English language. We do not have a third person singular pronoun that we can use to refer to people without identifying them as male or female.

For many years, people wrote, "In his work, a doctor must always be sure that he advises his patients carefully," or, "A good first grade teacher will always be sure her students are quiet at rest time." This use of our language contributed to sex stereotyping: we thought of doctors as men and of first grade teachers as women. Here are some commonly used solutions to the problem.

• Use plural nouns and pronouns.

Good first grade teachers will be sure their students are quiet at rest time.

• Leave out the pronoun.

A good first grade teacher will be sure students (or the students) are quiet at rest time.

• Alternate male and female examples.

One teacher might ask her students to sing, while another may have his students dance.

Some solutions are awkward and should be avoided in writing.

• Don't use "he or she," "s/he," and similar forms.

AVOID: **In his or her work, a doctor must always be sure that he or she advises his or her patients carefully.** (You can see that this form can become awkward and annoying.)

USE: **In their work, doctors must always be sure that they advise their patients carefully.**

USE: **In her work, a doctor must always be sure she advises her patients carefully.**

• Don't use a plural pronoun to refer to a singular noun.

AVOID: **When you see the judge, tell them you're sorry and won't do it again.**

USE: **When you see the judge, say that you're sorry and that you won't do it again.**

USE: **When you see the judge, tell him you're sorry and that you won't do it again.**

Of course if you're writing about a male, use masculine pronouns, and if you're writing about a female, use feminine pronouns. The rule is to avoid sex stereotyping and to recognize the equality of women and men in your writing.

iii. Subject-Verb Agreement   The subject of each sentence must agree with its verb. If the subject is plural, the verb must be plural; if the subject is singular, the verb must be singular (see Part I, Section 2D, p. 247, for a discussion of plural and singular verbs). If you're a native speaker of English, your ear will tell you that you should write "Mark is going," not "Mark are going," or to write "Mark and Doug are going," not "Mark and Doug is going." The singular form of the verb "is" agrees with the singular subject "Mark." The plural form "are" agrees with the plural subject "Mark and Doug." In the following examples the subject is underlined once and the verb is underlined twice.

SINGULAR: **There was a box of apples on the back seat.**

PLURAL: **There were a box of apples and a French horn on the back seat.**

In the first example, there was only one thing on the back seat, a box, so our verb is the singular form "was." In the second example, there were two things on the back seat, a box and a horn. The verb, then, is the plural "were."

Here's another pair of sentences to illustrate number agreement.

Here are two wrenches and a hammer.

Here are a hammer and two wrenches.

The first sentence sounds just fine because a plural noun follows a plural verb. The second, though, sounds a little odd because the plural verb is followed by a singular noun. Nevertheless, the plural verb must be used in both cases because the subject of each sentence—"two wrenches and a hammer," and "a hammer and two wrenches"—is plural.

Several pronouns are always singular and therefore require singular verbs. These pronouns are always singular:

anybody	neither
anyone	no one
each	nobody
either	one
everybody	somebody
everyone	someone

When one of these pronouns is the subject of your sentence, use a singular form of the verb. For example,

> **Neither** of them **anticipates** a problem.
>
> **Everyone** at the party **is having** a good time.
>
> Because of illness, **each** of the boys **has to stay** at home.

B. Shifts

A shift is a change that causes confusion for a reader. Just as you become confused when you are talking with someone and that person suddenly shifts from one idea to another without warning, your reader can be confused by shifts in your writing.

i. Shifts in Tense   One writing problem that can cause a reader to become confused is a shift in tense or time within a sentence or paragraph. Note how the following sentence shifts from present to past:

> **Jean and Richard went to Florida last winter because Minnesota was too cold. Later, they wish they'd gone to Arizona.**

The verb "went" is in the past tense, and it is clear that the second sentence is also about something that happened in the past. The verb "wish," however, is in the present tense, and so there is a shift in tense or time. If you start writing in the past tense, stay in the past tense. Don't shift from past to present or from present to past. Here's how we would correct our example:

> **Jean and Richard went to Florida last winter because Minnesota was too cold. Later, they wished they'd gone to Arizona.**

Here's another example:

> WRONG: **He gives her pearl earrings to match her pearl neck-lace, and she smiled with delight.**

> RIGHT: **He gives her pearl earrings to match her pearl necklace, and she smiles with delight.**

ii. Shifts in Person   A shift in person often causes problems in writing and can confuse your reader.

> **If a student is writing a paper, you might find a word processor helpful.**

Here the shift is from the third person "a student" to the second person "you." (See Part V, Section 16A, pp. 281–82, for a discussion of first, second, and third person pronouns.) Here are three ways to correct the sentence:

> WRONG: **If a student is writing a paper, you might find a word processor helpful.**

> RIGHT: **If a student is writing a paper, he might find a word processor helpful.**

> RIGHT: **If students are writing papers, they might find word processors helpful.**

> RIGHT: **If you are writing a paper, you might find a word processor helpful.**

Use the second person "you" only if you are addressing your reader directly. To make a general statement about people, use the third person.

iii. An Example   We have underlined verbs twice and pronouns once in the following paragraph. Before you read the corrected version, see if you can spot and correct the shifts in tense and person on your own.

> **Last winter we had a record snowfall, and that makes for the best sledding ever. One weekend in particular had perfect weather, so I get on the phone and invite all my friends. Soon the house was full of kids, adults, dogs, and coats, but not for long. Everyone has toboggans, inner tubes, sleds, and flying saucers, so you all go out to the pasture to slide. After an hour or two of flying down hills, narrowly missing fences and trees, crashing into each other, and generally having a grand time, you all end up by the fire. Outside, the snow had begun to fall again.**

Here is our corrected version. We've kept everything in the past tense because it's about an event that happened in the past. We've also eliminated the shift from first to second person.

Last winter <u>we</u> <u>had</u> a record snowfall, and <u>that</u> <u>made</u> for the best sledding ever. One weekend in particular <u>had</u> perfect weather, so <u>I</u> <u>got</u> on the phone and <u>invited</u> all my friends. Soon the house <u>was</u> full of kids, adults, dogs, and coats, but not for long. <u>Everyone</u> <u>had</u> toboggans, inner tubes, sleds, and flying saucers, so <u>we</u> all <u>went</u> out to the pasture to slide. After an hour or two of flying down hills, narrowly missing fences and trees, crashing into each other, and generally having a grand time, <u>we</u> all <u>ended</u> up by the fire. Outside, the snow <u>had</u> <u>begun</u> to fall again.

C. Modifiers

To modify something is to change it. A *modifier* is a word or group of words that changes an idea by giving additional information about it.

i. One-Word Modifiers We have already seen how adjectives (Chapter 3) and adverbs (Chapter 6) can work as modifiers, but let's take another look at how these one-word modifiers can help a sentence.

The car stopped.

This sentence simply states an action. It gives no visual image. See how much more effective this sentence becomes with the addition of just one adjective to modify "car" and one adverb to modify "stopped."

The battered car stopped jerkily.

Modifiers can help explain or clarify ideas, and where we place modifiers can change the meaning of a sentence. Compare the following two sentences:

We almost spent all our money.

We spent almost all our money.

The placement of the modifier "almost" changes the meaning of the sentence. If we came close to spending the money and then changed our minds, the first sentence would be accurate, but if we had actually spent the money and had spent nearly all of it, the second would be our choice.

Where we put a modifier can make a large difference in meaning. As an illustration, try placing the word "only" at different places in the following sentence:

I kissed him on the ear yesterday.

ii. Longer Modifiers We often use one-word modifiers to help the reader visualize a scene or understand an idea, but we also use clauses and phrases to do the same thing.

Running onto the field, I frantically waved my arms.

The first group of words, "Running onto the field," modifies the second, for it gives additional information about what the speaker did. "Running onto the field" modifies the subject of the independent clause that follows it. It modifies "I."

iii. Correcting Misplaced Modifiers   If they're used improperly, modifiers can confuse or amuse the reader. Modifiers become confusing in a sentence when they are misplaced, that is, not placed close enough to the word they modify. For example:

Soaring above Nantucket Harbor, Bob watched the great blue heron.

That says that Bob—not the heron—was actually doing the soaring. The sentence should read like this:

Bob watched the great blue heron soaring above Nantucket Harbor.

Here are more examples.

MISPLACED MODIFIER: **The North Cascades attract climbers with challenging peaks.** (This says climbers have challenging peaks.)

CORRECTED: **With their challenging peaks, the North Cascades attract climbers.** (Now this says the North Cascades have challenging peaks.)

MISPLACED MODIFIER: **A diamond earring hung from her earlobe that shone brilliantly.** (This says her earlobe shone brilliantly.)

CORRECTED: **A diamond earring that shone brilliantly hung from her earlobe.** (Now this says the earring shone brilliantly.)

CORRECTED: **Shining brilliantly, a diamond earring hung from her earlobe.** (This also says the earring shone brilliantly.)

MISPLACED MODIFIER: **The dress hung on the hanger torn to shreds by the cat's claws.** (This says the hanger was torn to shreds.)

CORRECTED: **Torn to shreds by the cat's claws, the dress hung on the hanger.** (Now this says the dress was torn to shreds.)

CORRECTED: **The dress, torn to shreds by the cat's claws, hung on the hanger.** (This also says the dress was torn to shreds.)

One way to analyze a sentence you're having trouble with is to break it down into its simplest parts. In the last example above, there are four main ideas:

1. **The dress was hanging.**
2. **It was on a hanger.**
3. **It was torn to shreds.**
4. **The cat's claws had torn it.**

Seeing the ideas separately can help you decide how to arrange them clearly. How the ideas are arranged in a sentence is up to the writer, but the writer's aim must always be to communicate ideas clearly.

iv. Correcting Dangling Modifiers   Modifiers are called dangling when there is no word in the sentence for them to modify.

> DANGLING MODIFIER: **Cheering wildly, the team won the game with a last-second touchdown.**

A modifier in the position of "Cheering wildly" will modify the subject of the independent clause that follows it. The subject of the independent clause is "the team." Was the team cheering wildly? Probably not, at least not while the play was going on. It was probably the crowd that was cheering, but the sentence doesn't say so. "Cheering wildly" is called a dangling modifier because it modifies the incorrect noun "team"; the sentence has no word that "cheering wildly" correctly modifies. We need to say who was doing the cheering to eliminate any confusion. We can change either the modifier or the main sentence to make the meaning clear.

> MODIFIER CHANGED: **While the crowd cheered wildly, the team won the game with a last-second touchdown.**

> MAIN SENTENCE CHANGED: **Cheering wildly, the crowd watched the team win the game with a last-second touchdown.**

Here are more examples:

> DANGLING MODIFIER: **Angry about the delay, the reservations were cancelled.** (This says the reservations were angry.)

> MODIFIER CHANGED: **Because we were angry about the delay, the reservations were cancelled.** (Now this says we were angry.)

> MAIN SENTENCE CHANGED: **Angry about the delay, we cancelled the reservations.** (This also says we were angry.)

DANGLING MODIFIER: **Never having done any surfing before, the waves looked threatening.** (This says the waves had never done any surfing before.)

MODIFIER CHANGED: **Since I had never done any surfing before, the waves looked threatening.** (Now this says I had never done any surfing before.)

MAIN SENTENCE CHANGED: **Never having done any surfing before, I thought the waves looked threatening.** (This also says I had never done any surfing before.)

Again, breaking the sentence into its parts can help:

1. **I had never done any surfing before.**

2. **The waves looked threatening.**

Breaking the sentence into its parts shows that there are two subjects, "I" and "waves." The example with the dangling modifier leaves out "I," but the two corrected versions include both subjects.

V

VI IMPROVING SENTENCE STYLE

Your aim in writing is to communicate effectively and well. Your first goal, of course, is to express your ideas clearly so that you can examine them and be sure you want to share them with others. Once you make the decision to share, you must concern yourself with expressing your ideas gracefully so that your readers not only will follow the ideas accurately but also will enjoy doing so. Our aim in this section is to give you tools that will help improve your clarity and grace as a writer.

SECTION 17:
Parallel Structure

One writing technique that helps make the relationships of ideas clear to a reader is the use of parallel structure. This means constructing your sentences so that the various parts follow a common pattern. Here's an example of a sentence without parallel structure:

> **Gracie enjoys hiking in Nepal, elephant riding in India, and to backpack in New Zealand.**

Once you have set up a pattern in a sentence, stick with that pattern, for you have led your readers to expect it to continue. Once the readers see "Gracie enjoys hiking," they expect to see that pattern again:

> **Gracie enjoys hiking.**
>
> **Gracie enjoys elephant riding.**
>
> **Gracie enjoys to backpack.**

See the problem with the last part of the sentence? It's easily corrected by making the last part parallel with the first two parts:

Gracie enjoys hiking in Nepal, elephant riding in India, and backpacking in New Zealand.

The sentence now has parallel structure because each of its elements repeats the "-ing" form: hiking, riding, backpacking. Here's another example:

I'd like to be a lawyer, an engineer, or go into banking.

The pattern here is "I'd like to be . . . ."

I'd like to be a lawyer.

I'd like to be an engineer.

I'd like to be go into banking.

Again, there's a problem with the last part. Here's the sentence rewritten to give it parallel structure:

I'd like to be a lawyer, an engineer, or a banker.

This sentence now has parallel structure because each of its elements repeats the noun form: lawyer, engineer, banker. Here are a few more examples:

NOT PARALLEL: **She wanted to know whether I could type and my ability to take shorthand.**

PARALLEL: **She wanted to know whether I could type and take shorthand.**

NOT PARALLEL: **We looked for a car with power steering, air conditioning, good tires, and it had to have a good stereo.**

PARALLEL: **We looked for a car with power steering, air conditioning, good tires, and a good stereo.**

NOT PARALLEL: **Alexis is witty, charming, tells jokes, and polite.**

PARALLEL: **Alexis is witty, charming, funny, and polite.**

One of the most common techniques that professional writers use to make their writing powerful, smooth, and elegant is parallel structure. Here are some examples for your enjoyment.

She wanted to go back to the farmhouse, take a good cold bath, dust herself with plenty of Maria's violet talcum powder—provided Maria was not present to object, of course—put on the

thinnest, most becoming dress she owned, with a big sash, and sit in a wicker chair under the trees. Katherine Anne Porter

The week that followed was the worst of his life. He did not eat and lost weight. His beard darkened and grew ragged. He stopped attending seminars and almost never opened a book. Bernard Malamud

These people—the very prototypes of the bores you took me away from, with the same fenced-in view of life, the same keep-off-the-grass-morality, the same little cautious virtues and the same little frightened vices—well, I've clung to them, I've delighted in them, I've done my best to please them. Edith Wharton

It occurred to him—as he oiled a hinge, as he tightened a doorknob—that the house reflected amazingly little of Muriel. Anne Tyler

SECTION 18:
Using Appositives

An appositive renames or restates a word or phrase. The appositive is underlined in the following example:

My great-grandfather, <u>a Civil War veteran</u>, wrote a fascinating history of his life.

Appositives can be used as an effective and economical way to include information in a sentence. For example, compare the following:

He was my grandfather. He was a musician, and he had managed to hold on to his violin, but he had lost his land.

He was my grandfather, a musician who managed to hold on to his violin but not his land. Toni Morrison

The appositive makes the sentence much more effective. Here are two more examples of sentences with appositives:

My father, a fat, funny man with beautiful eyes and a subversive wit, is trying to decide which of his eight children he will take with him to the county fair. Alice Walker

A novel that Abraham Lincoln called "the book that made this great war," *Uncle Tom's Cabin* was extremely popular.

SECTION 19:
Sentence Variety

A writer's style is marked, at least in part, by the ways in which he varies his sentence structures. A writer can also use sentence structures to highlight important information or to show action. Notice in the following paragraph how William Faulkner varies his sentence structures, and notice especially the last two sentences. "Then the buck was there," a five word sentence set off by itself, shows the suddenness with which the buck appears. The last sentence is much longer, expressing the manner in which the sight stands out in the boy's memory and the rhythm of the running deer.

> At first there was nothing. There was the faint, cold, steady rain, the gray and constant light of the late November dawn, with the voices of the hounds converging somewhere in it and toward them. Then Sam Fathers, standing just behind the boy as he had been standing when the boy shot his first running rabbit with his first gun and almost with the first load it ever carried, touched his shoulder and he began to shake, not with any cold. Then the buck was there. He did not come into sight; he was just there, looking not like a ghost but as if all of light were condensed in him and he were the source of it, not only moving in it but disseminating it, already running, seen first as you always see the deer, in that split second after he has already seen you, already slanting away in that first soaring bound, the antlers even in that dim light looking like a small rocking-chair balanced on his head.

In your writing, strive to vary your sentences both to make the material more interesting for your audience to read and to give your ideas the emphasis and form that they need.

SECTION 20:
Constructions to Avoid

Some commonly used sentence structures are ineffective because they delay or hide the important information that the sentence has to offer. This section discusses several of these structures and shows how to change them to make them more effective.

A. "There Is" and "There Are" Constructions

Notice the difference between these two sentences:

There was a shark swimming toward the life raft.

A shark swam toward the life raft.

The second is more effective than the first because it brings the reader's attention immediately to the subject ("shark"), and it changes the verb ("was swimming") to a more active form ("swam"). Something similar happens in the next example.

There are trees along the boulevard.

Trees line the boulevard.

Here the second version again puts the subject "trees" first, but the most important change is the change in the verb. The picture in the reader's mind becomes much clearer, and the clarity has been achieved with fewer words. In the following examples, we have rewritten some sentences by professional writers; our rewrites appear first and are followed by the more effective original versions.

There was a kind of brass band in Yellow Sky, which played painfully, to the delight of the populace.

Yellow Sky had a kind of a brass band, which played painfully, to the delight of the populace. Stephen Crane

There were some people holding an old-fashioned revival meeting on the sidewalk across from me, near the entrance to a barbecue joint.

On the sidewalk across from me, near the entrance to a barbecue joint, were some people holding an old-fashioned revival meeting. James Baldwin

There was a sudden hush that fell on the crowd as Mr. Summers cleared his throat and looked at the list.

A sudden hush fell on the crowd as Mr. Summers cleared his throat and looked at the list. Shirley Jackson

B. Passive Voice

Passive is the opposite of active. In a sentence written in the *passive voice*, the subject receives the action of the verb rather than doing the action of the verb. Here's an example:

The prunes were picked by the crew.

In a sentence written in active voice, the subject does the action:

The crew picked the prunes.

In the passive sentence, the focus is on the prunes which are being acted upon; we don't actually see any action. In the active sentence, though, the focus is on the actors (the crew) and their action (picked). On occasion you may want to use the passive voice, but most of the time you'll find that the active voice communicates more effectively.

Writing sentences in the active voice makes them more direct and more alive. Here are some examples:

PASSIVE: **Clues were found in the basement by the police.**

ACTIVE: **The police found clues in the basement.**

PASSIVE: **A mistake was made by the administration.**

ACTIVE: **The administration made a mistake.**

In these examples, you can easily see what needs to be the subject of the revised sentence, but frequently you will see (and maybe write) passive sentences where the actor isn't identified:

PASSIVE: **A need exists for more study of the problem.**

ACTIVE: **We must study the problem more carefully.**

PASSIVE: **It is hoped that this winter's snowfall will not damage the city's budget.**

ACTIVE: **City officials hope that this winter's snowfall will not damage their budget.**

This use of the passive voice is common when people do not want to take responsibility for their own ideas or actions. What parent, for example, has not heard something like "We were playing and the lamp got knocked over"? In his famous essay "Politics and the English Language," George Orwell says, "Never use the passive where you can use the active," and we agree.

C. Easy Word Choices

Sometimes the first word or phrase that comes to mind is exactly the wrong one, for it is the one that everyone else uses. Here are some examples:

i. A Lot   It's easy to write,

A lot of people were in the room.

but such wording has almost no power to create an image in a reader's mind. You might say,

> **Fifty people crowded into the room.**

or

> **A standing-room-only crowd was on hand.**

Instead of "a lot," use an exact number or a word or phrase that will give your reader a mental image of what you are discussing.

ii. Very   Often, when students want to emphasize a word, usually an adjective or an adverb, they add "very" in front of it rather than seek a more effective word. The difference between

> **The football game was very exciting.**

and

> **The football game was electrifying.**

or

> **The football game was a thrilling display of strategy and strength.**

is readily apparent. Rather than using "very," use a word or a phrase that will convey the intensity of feeling to your reader.

iii. Worn Out Comparisons   You have all heard "hot as an oven" or "light as a feather," but these phrases have been used so often they have lost their power to create an image in a reader's mind. Look, instead, at these examples from professional writers:

> **The warmth inside the door felt heavy, like a steamed towel laid against his face.** John Updike
>
> **The child's light, faint breath was a mere shadowy moth of sound in the silver air.** Katherine Anne Porter
>
> **Fishbein, his long yellow face a dying light bulb, looked from here to there, craning forward to catch sight of the faces down the row.** Philip Roth
>
> **Poplars are standing there still as death.** Arna Bontemps
>
> **His coat floated to the surface and surrounded him like a strange gay lily pad and he stood grinning in the sun.** Flannery O'Connor

Some of these comparisons use comparative words ("like" and "as") but some do not. Still, the writer makes a comparison in language that evokes a vivid image in the reader's mind.

VII Punctuating Sentences

When people read what you write, they cannot see your facial expressions and gestures, and they cannot hear the tones of your voice. These expressions and tones are the signals—the punctuation, if you will—that we use when we speak. When we write, then, we must use a different set of signals to tell the reader when a thought is changing, and the signals we use are punctuation marks. Part VII shows you how to use punctuation for effective communication.

In your reading, you will see that writers and editors differ from each other in their uses of punctuation, and you will also see that punctuation changes over time. Writers of English two hundred years ago punctuated quite differently from writers of today, yet we can still read and understand what they wrote. What we offer you here is a description of some of the most common conventions of punctuation in use today. If you follow our recommendations, you will have little difficulty communicating in written English.

SECTION 21:
The Comma

Student writers tend to use too many commas rather than too few, so our usual advice is that you should not use a comma unless you can state a reason for doing so. Here are some of the most common uses:

A. With Independent Clauses

Put a comma before *for, and, nor, but, or, yet*, or *so* when one of these words joins two independent clauses.

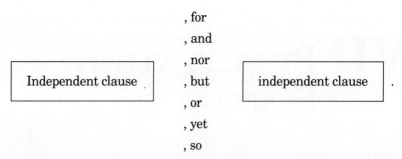

This rule is a little easier to remember than it looks. The first letters of the seven words that need a comma in front of them—For, And, Nor, But, Or, Yet, So—spell FAN BOYS. If you use one of the FAN BOYS to join two independent clauses, put a comma in front of it like this:

> **He left, for she had hurt him.**
>
> **She had hurt him, and she was glad.**
>
> **He didn't want to leave, nor did she want him to go.**

Always check to be sure you do, in fact, have two independent clauses. The sentence "She had hurt him and was glad" for example, wouldn't take a comma before "and" because "was glad" is not an independent clause. The easiest way to check is to put parentheses around all the words on each side of the connecting word, like this:

> **(She had hurt him) and (she was glad).**

If the words within each set of parentheses form an independent clause, you need a comma before the connecting word.

If the clauses are short and the relationship clear, you can sometimes omit the comma:

> **The moors are around us and the stars are above our heads.** Virginia Woolf
>
> **The dust rolled away over the fields and the departing sun set it ablaze with colors.** Sherwood Anderson

If you have any doubts whatever, though, include the comma:

> **Life is indeed a strange gift, and its privileges are most mysterious.** William Hazlitt

B. With Items in a Series

Put commas between items in a series. A series is usually three or more words, phrases, or clauses. Here are some examples:

COMMAS: **I have lived in Duluth, Laramie, Wallace, and Butte.**

Every day we arrived at work, ate doughnuts, laughed in meetings, and otherwise enjoyed ourselves.

Bill cooked the chicken, Jan made the salad, and Jim fixed the lemonade.

Sometimes a connecting word ("and," "but," "or") is repeated before each item of a series. When it is, no comma is used to separate the items:

NO COMMAS: **Bill cooked the chicken and Jan made the salad and Jim fixed the lemonade.**

Be sure to stop using commas when you've stopped listing.

INCORRECT: **Snow, sleet, ice, and rain, caused our plane to turn back.** (The four items in the series form the subject of the sentence, and placing a comma after "rain" puts a comma between the subject and the verb of the sentence. Be careful not to do this.)

CORRECT: **Snow, sleet, ice, and rain caused our plane to turn back.** (Only the items in the series are separated by commas.)

C. With Introductory Elements

Put a comma after a dependent clause that introduces an independent clause and after other introductory words and phrases that do not flow smoothly into the sentence. Here are some examples of introductions that need to be set off by commas:

COMMAS: **When the thermometer in our laundry reached one hundred and eleven degrees on summer afternoons, either my mother or my father would say that it was time to tell another ghost story so that we could get some good chills up our backs.** Maxine Hong Kingston

In the dark shadows of the skyscrapers, a cold wind howled.

Meanwhile, J. R. waited at the office.

Satisfied, Bobby walked in with Sue Ellen.

For several good reasons, we decided not to run the marathon.

To mention just one, our knees protested violently with every step we took.

Walking up the stairs, we became convinced we had made the right decision.

When a sentence contains both a dependent clause and an independent clause, use a comma only when the dependent clause introduces the independent clause:

| Independent clause | dependent clause | . |

| Dependent clause | , | independent clause | . |

COMMA: **Because I felt sorry for him, I gave him twenty dollars.**

NO COMMA: **I gave him twenty dollars because I felt sorry for him.**

COMMA: **When I was turned away in this manner, the silence gathered and struck me.** Annie Dillard

NO COMMA: **The silence gathered and struck me when I was turned away in this manner.**

COMMA: **Even though it was snowing heavily, we had a picnic near the river.**

NO COMMA: **We had a picnic near the river even though it was snowing heavily.**

D. With Unnecessary Material

Put commas before and after material that is not necessary to the meaning of the sentence.

My youngest brother, who is an accountant, really enjoys fishing.

Note that the dependent clause "who is an accountant" is not necessary to the meaning of the sentence. It is simply added information, and we set it off with two commas. In another sentence, the same clause might be necessary to the meaning:

My brother who is an accountant really enjoys fishing.

Here the clause is necessary to identify the brother. It distinguishes him from my brother who is a teacher and my brother who is a truck driver.

Unnecessary information needs commas both before *and* after it. Many students want to put a comma after "accountant" in the last example because there is a tendency to pause there. That single comma, however, separates the subject and the verb. *Do not use a single comma between the subject and the verb.*

> WRONG: **Riding the ferries that travel Puget Sound, is exciting.**

> RIGHT: **Riding the ferries that travel Puget Sound is exciting.**

Remember, commas are used in pairs when you set off unnecessary material in the middle of a sentence.

Here are more examples:

> COMMAS: **In this society, where athletes are important, baseball players earn high salaries.**

> **People, who usually live in houses, are a common life form.**

> **Betty Jean, a girl I dislike, finally left town.**

> NO COMMAS: **Baseball players earn high salaries in a society where athletes are important.**

> **People who live in houses outnumber those who live in caves.**

> **The girl I dislike finally left town.**

Phrases and clauses like those in these examples are sometimes referred to as "restrictive" or "non-restrictive" modifiers. A modifier gives additional information about part of a sentence; a restrictive modifier restricts, or limits, the noun it modifies. In the sentence,

> **All students who do their homework are sure to pass.**

the modifier "who do their homework" is restrictive; it limits the group of students who are sure to pass. However, in the sentence,

> **Jennifer and Katie, who do their homework, are sure to pass.**

the modifier "who do their homework" is non-restrictive. The subject tells us which people are sure to pass. The modifier gives us additional but unnecessary information about why those people are sure to pass. Again, commas go before and after material that is not necessary to the sentence.

E. With Interrupters and Direct Address

Put commas before and after words or phrases that interrupt the sentence, and put commas before and after names of people being directly addressed.

> COMMAS: **I'm sure, Jinny, that the cold won't bother you. Dress warmly, however.**

> **We find, therefore, that the defendant is guilty.**

I suggest, my dear child, that you come home before midnight.

In two hundred years it is, as we have found, easy to lose the thread. Lewis Thomas

Listen carefully, my fine friend.

He wants, most of all, understanding. Sherwood Anderson

NO COMMAS: My dear child is always home before midnight.

Jinny won't be bothered by the cold.

F. In Dates and Addresses

Use commas to separate the parts of most dates and addresses.

COMMAS: June 27, 1983, is a day I will never forget.

I'd just as soon forget December 2, 1985.

Milford, New Hampshire, is a pleasant town.

The address is 4121 Qualchan Drive, Santa Fe, New Mexico 87501. (There is no comma between the state and the ZIP code.)

London, England, is a huge city.

NO COMMAS: I joined the Army on 16 April 1981.

May 1968 was a cold month.

G. Misuses of the Comma

The best general rule for commas is this: *Do not use a comma or any other punctuation mark unless you can state a definite reason for doing so.* There are some more specific cautions to keep in mind, though.

i. Do not separate the subject from the verb with one comma.

WRONG: Some <u>people</u> who go to school, <u>enjoy</u> the social life.

RIGHT: Some <u>people</u> who go to school <u>enjoy</u> the social life.

Be particularly careful when using one of the FAN BOYS ("for," "and," "nor," "but," "or," "yet," "so") to join two verbs rather than two independent clauses.

WRONG: He studied all night, but worked all the next day.

RIGHT: He studied all night but worked all the next day.

RIGHT: He studied all night, but he worked all the next day.

ii. Do not use just a comma between two independent clauses. This use is called a *comma splice*. Avoid comma splices.

WRONG: **He was late for dinner, we decided to eat without him.**

RIGHT: **He was late for dinner. We decided to eat without him.**

RIGHT: **He was late for dinner; we decided to eat without him.**

RIGHT: **He was late for dinner, so we decided to eat without him.**

RIGHT: **Because he was late for dinner, we decided to eat without him.**

iii. Do not use a comma between an independent clause and a dependent clause when the independent clause starts the sentence.

WRONG: **We were glad to see him, because he had brought gifts.**

RIGHT: **We were glad to see him because he had brought gifts.**

iv. Do not use a comma before the first word or after the last word in a series.

WRONG: **He brought, tuna, eggs, milk, and honey, from the store.**

RIGHT: **He brought tuna, eggs, milk, and honey from the store.**

Section 22:
The Semicolon

There are only two common uses of the semicolon (;).

A. Use a semicolon to join two independent clauses.

A semicolon is like a period in that it separates two independent clauses. It is used to show a closer relationship between ideas than that suggested by a period. It is not followed by a capital letter:

| Independent clause | ; | independent clause | . |

Here are examples:

We must not squander our powers, helplessly and ignorantly, squirting half the house in order to water a single rose-bush; we must train them, exactly and powerfully here on the very spot.
Virginia Woolf

A leader stood alone in the centre of the ring and began the chant; he struck the spark of their song and it caught on the tinder of their youth and ran around the ring like a flame. Beryl Markham

Everything around me was darkling fast and quieting down; the quail alone were calling out at infrequent intervals. Ivan Turgenev (trans. Bernard Guilbert Guerney)

Words like "however," "therefore," "finally," "nevertheless," "likewise," and "furthermore" are sometimes used to join independent clauses. When they are, they must be preceded by a semicolon or a period. These joining words are called adverbial conjunctions (see Part III, Section 9C, pp. 264–66) and are usually followed by a comma:

Independent clause	; therefore, ; however, etc.	independent clause	.

We had forgotten to eat breakfast; consequently, we collapsed in the afternoon.

Lifting weights is good exercise; therefore, most coaches prescribe it.

I used plenty of yeast in the bread dough; however, it didn't rise.

Think of the joining word as simply the first word of the second independent clause.

When you use the semicolon to join independent clauses, check to see that you do, indeed, have two independent clauses. Words like "however" and "therefore" are often used as interrupters in sentences, and in such cases they are set off with commas.

AS INTERRUPTER: **We left early, however, to avoid the rush.**

AS JOINER: **We left early; however, we didn't avoid the rush.**

AS INTERRUPTER: **The project, therefore, was stalled by a computer breakdown.**

AS JOINER: **The computer broke down; therefore, the project was stalled.**

AS INTERRUPTER: **We will, instead, have dinner at the Space Needle.**

AS JOINER: **We planned to eat at the wharf; instead, we will have dinner at the Space Needle.**

VII

B. Use a semicolon to separate items in a series when the items themselves contain commas. That sounds more complicated than it actually is. Here are some examples:

> **I have lived in Duluth, Minnesota; Laramie, Wyoming; Wallace, Idaho; and Butte, Montana.**

> **Marcia heated, reheated, and reheated the pizza; Glen and Ed had it for breakfast, lunch, and dinner; and Stacey and Jeff ignored it all.**

This use of the semicolon can keep a reader from getting confused in complicated lists.

SECTION 23:
The Colon

Use a colon (:) after a complete thought to introduce a word, list, quotation, or explanation that follows.

> **Then I saw Mamma herself: I threw myself upon her.** Marcel Proust (trans. C. K. Scott Moncrieff)

> **I can look on it as a picture: stiff column in a shock of light, or splash of green shot with the delicate blue and silver of the background.** Martin Buber

> **My mother had a gentle way of forgiving people: "I'm sure he wanted to do the right thing."**

> **From this arises the following question: whether it is better to be loved than feared, or the reverse.** Niccolo Machiavelli (trans. George Bull)

> **Trust thyself: every heart vibrates to that iron string.** Ralph Waldo Emerson

Do not use a colon if the list follows a verb.

> WRONG: **My favorite activities are: skiing, bowling, reading, and tennis.**

> RIGHT: **My favorite activities are skiing, bowling, reading, and tennis.**

> WRONG: **You should bring: warm coats, warm boots, and mittens.**

> RIGHT: **You should bring warm coats, warm boots, and mittens.**

WRONG: **My brothers are: Sloan, Darol, and David.**

RIGHT: **My brothers are Sloan, Darol, and David.**

RIGHT: **I have three brothers: Sloan, Darol, and David.**

SECTION 24:
Quotation Marks and Underlining

A. Word-for-Word Quotations

We use quotation marks (" ") to show word-for-word quotations from written or spoken sources. Here are examples:

> **"You ought to see the look in your eyes," Frances said, "as you casually inspect the universe on Fifth Avenue."** Irwin Shaw

> **"It's exam time and I'm down with this horrible cold," croaks the sufferer coughing dramatically. "Can you rush me that prescription of Dr. Murphy's?"** Phyllis McGinley

> **Mom shouted, "No more piano for today!"**

> **Columnist Dave Barry writes about Christmas, "A favorite tradition in our family is to try to find a parking space at the mall."**

Do not put quotation marks around paraphrases and indirect quotations. To distinguish between a direct and an indirect quote, ask yourself whether you are stating the exact words another writer or speaker used:

> INDIRECT: **Cynthia said that artichokes are a marvelous addition to a salad.** (The sentence reports what Cynthia said, but not necessarily in the exact words she used.)

> DIRECT: **Cynthia said, "Artichokes are a marvelous addition to a salad."** (The sentence reports Cynthia's exact words.)

> INDIRECT: **Marty promised he would get his shopping done early this year.**

> DIRECT: **Marty promised, "I'll get my shopping done early this year."**

Think about what people actually say when they talk to you. Would Marty walk up to you and say, "He would get his shopping done early this year"? Of course not; it is therefore an indirect quotation.

Use a comma between the identification of the speaker or writer and the quotation itself, but do not use commas with indirect quotations.

INDIRECT: **William Butler Yeats said that only God could love a certain woman for herself alone and not her yellow hair.**

DIRECT: **William Butler Yeats said, "Only God, my dear, could love you for yourself alone and not your yellow hair."**

Commas and periods always go inside the final quotation marks.

"It's twenty degrees," she shivered.

George complained, "I hate weather like this."

"If you don't like it," Bill said, "move to Arizona. That's what I plan to do."

This is known as "justice."

Colons and semicolons always go outside final quotation marks:

Jeremiah said, "You really ought to do it"; therefore, we did.

Too late I remembered my mother saying, "A fool and his money are soon parted": my wallet was empty, and my checkbook showed a balance of $1.26.

Question marks and exclamation points go inside or outside the ending quote, depending on whether they punctuate the quotation itself or the whole sentence in which the quotation appears:

Andy yelled, "Get out of the water! There are alligators in there!"

I can't believe Elton said, "I've never been to California"!

Did he really say, "I'd like to visit Paris next year"?

Janet murmured, "Would you mind if I go with you?"

B. Use in Titles

Use quotation marks around the titles of poems, songs, short stories, magazine articles, newspaper articles, or other works that appear in longer publications. Underline the names of the longer publications. Here are examples:

"To the Head of the Class" in the December 9 <u>Sports Illustrated</u> talks about Michigan's win over Georgia Tech.

Of all the poems in Ann Darr's <u>Cleared for Landing</u>, I like "Relative Matter" best.

Two stories in James Joyce's <u>Dubliners</u> are "Araby" and "Counterparts."

Section 25:
The Dash and Parentheses

Use dashes (—) or parentheses ( ) to show an abrupt interruption or change of thought. (On a typewriter or word processor, make a dash by typing two hyphens.)

> **Keen, calculating, perspicacious, acute, and astute—I was all of these.** Max Shulman

> **What was galling was the suspicion that they would forgive all sorts of antisocial behavior—shoplifting, say, flagrant adultery, embezzlement, and, of course, mugging—provided some acceptable frailty of the psyche or pocketbook could be dredged up to excuse it.** Timothy Foote

> **Lying is universal—We *all* do it; we all *must* do it.** Mark Twain

> **At that instant (the instant is essential to my drama) the train did halt. . . .** Alexander Black

> **If you think living longer is rough now, wait until the 1990s when today's Me Generation potheads and coke sniffers begin taking care of the elderly (today's middle-aged joggers).** Mike Royko

> **But, for all that, everyone knows that it is a rare thing to find a boy of the middle or upper classes who can read aloud decently, or who can put his thoughts on paper in clear and grammatical (to say nothing of good or elegant) language.** T. H. Huxley

Parentheses are always used in pairs, while the dash may be used singly at the end of a sentence. Use dashes if you want an interruption to stand out strongly; parentheses make the interrupter less forceful. If a sentence needs punctuation without parentheses, it still needs punctuation with the parentheses.

> **Tired of driving (she'd been at it all day), Anna pulled into a truck stop.**

> **The truck stop was crowded (though she couldn't see why); she had to share a booth with three strangers.**

If you put a complete sentence within parentheses, punctuate it as you would any other sentence.

> **Driving a car with a stick shift is hard for some people. (That says less about their intelligence than about their coordination.) My dearest friend is one such person.**

SECTION 26:
The Apostrophe

The apostrophe (') is a punctuation mark with only two uses. It shows contraction and it shows possession. A contraction is a shorter version of something, and we use contractions all the time. Only in a very formal situation would we say "I do not like her." We're much more more likely to say, "I don't like her."

A. In Contractions

In contractions, put an apostrophe where a letter or letters are left out. Often a contraction is a joining of two words, with the first letter or so of the second word left off, like this:

we have	**we've**
they are	**they're**
he will	**he'll**
it is	**it's**

Sometimes, though, the letters are left out of another part of the word, like this:

would not	**wouldn't**

And one word changes quite a bit:

will not	**won't**

Regardless of how the contraction is made, though, the apostrophe shows where letters have been left out.

B. In Possessive Nouns

In possessive nouns, use an apostrophe and an "s" to show possession or ownership. Possessives are a little bit tricky, but they're not really hard to master. You need to follow only two steps. First, decide whether there is possession. Second, decide whether the apostrophe must go before or after the final "s" in the possessive noun. Let's look at some examples of the possessive apostrophe, and then we'll explore the two steps:

> **John's house is the nicest on the block.** (The house belongs to John.)

> **It is much nicer than the Smiths' house.** (The house belongs to the Smiths.)

Frank Jones' house is nearly as nice, though. (The house belongs to Frank Jones.)

All the yards are littered with children's toys. (The toys belong to the children.)

The girls' clubhouse stands in the vacant lot. (The clubhouse belongs to the girls.)

Note that in each example, the possessive noun is followed by another noun: John's house, the Smiths' house, Frank Jones' house, children's toys, girls' clubhouse. If a noun ending in "s" is closely followed by another noun, the first noun is probably possessive. Put another way, the second noun is probably the name of something that belongs to the first noun. There may be words between the two nouns, usually adjectives but sometimes adverbs as well, but the two nouns will be closely related. Here are two more examples.

Carolyn's ancient, brown Volkswagen sat in the driveway. ("Ancient" and "brown" are adjectives that modify "Volkswagen," and the Volkswagen belongs to Carolyn.)

Ralph's carefully maintained tractor is a familiar sight in the neighboring fields. ("Carefully" is an adverb that modifies "maintained," and "maintained" is an adjective that modifies "tractor." The tractor belongs to Ralph.)

Once you have determined that your sentence does have a possessive noun, you must decide whether to put the apostrophe before or after the final "s," and there's a foolproof way to do this. Teresa Ferster Glazier, in her book *The Least You Should Know About English*, says that you should ask "Who (or what) does it belong to?" If your answer ends in "s," put the apostrophe after the "s." If your answer doesn't end in "s," put the apostrophe before the "s."

The children's toys are on the rug. (Who do the toys belong to? They belong to the children. Our answer does not end in "s," so we add an "s" and put the apostrophe before the "s.")

The boy's trike is in the corner. (Who does the trike belong to? It belongs to the boy. Our answer does not end in "s" so we add an "s" and insert the apostrophe before the "s.")

My mother's house is burning down. (Who does the house belong to? It belongs to my mother. Our answer does not end in "s," so we add an "s" and place the apostrophe before the "s.")

The boys' championship soccer team lost its game. (Who does the team belong to? It belongs to the boys. Our answer ends in "s," so the apostrophe goes after the existing "s."

The parents' party was ruined. (Who does the party belong to? It belongs to the parents. Our answer ends in "s," so the apostrophe goes after the existing "s.")

James' new clothes were a mess. (Who do the clothes belong to? They belong to James. Our answer ends in "s," so the apostrophe goes after the existing "s.")

Be very careful to ask the question exactly. If you ask "Whose house is it," for example, your answer won't be in a form that will help you decide where the apostrophe goes. Ask "Who does it belong to?"

There are instances when the question sounds a little odd, but it still works.

He worked for a day's wages. (Who do the wages belong to? They belong to one day. Our answer does not end in "s," so we add an "s" and put the apostrophe before the "s.")

She received two weeks' wages. (Who do the wages belong to? They belong to two weeks. Our answer ends in "s," so the apostrophe goes after the existing "s.")

They didn't complete last Wednesday's assignment. (Who does the assignment belong to? It belongs to last Wednesday. Our answer does not end in "s," so we add an "s" and place the apostrophe before the "s.")

Note that the possessive apostrophe is used only in nouns. Never use the apostrophe in these possessive pronouns:

yours	**ours**
his	**theirs**
hers	**whose**
its	

Joe's car runs well.	BUT **His car runs well.**
The building is Mary's.	BUT **The building is hers.**
The dog is Ada's and Sam's.	BUT **The dog is theirs.**
The cat drank the cat's milk	BUT **The cat drank its milk.**

Use "it's" only for a contraction of "it is" or "it has." If you can't substitute "it is" or "it has" in your sentence, don't use an apostrophe in "its."

It's raining again today. ("It is" raining again today.)

It's been raining for weeks. ("It has" been raining for weeks.)

I like the coast, but I don't like its weather. (We can't substitute "it is" or "it has.")

Again, watch how writers use the apostrophe as you read, and practice its use in your own writing.

Section 27:
Capitalization

A. In Sentences

Alway capitalize the first word in a sentence.

Sailing around the islands is Kristi's favorite sport.

B. Proper Names

Always capitalize names of people, nationalities, races, languages, and religions.

My friend Jim Pollard used to be a policeman.

My Laotian friend Pao is very talented.

My sister is Protestant, but her husband is Jewish.

I never know whether to speak French or English when I'm with Jean.

C. Names of Places

Capitalize specific names of states, streets, cities, buildings, bodies of water, and so on.

I attend Kansas State University.

She lives on Riverside Avenue.

We visited New York City last year.

His office is in the Paulsen Building.

I've never seen the Atlantic Ocean.

Don't capitalize names that are not specific.

I attend a state university.

She lives on the avenue that runs between here and the railroad.

We visited several cities last year.

We saw many interesting buildings.

Next year we'll go to the ocean.

D. Names of Times

Always capitalize names of months, days, and holidays.

We usually have good weather in June.

Last Monday and Saturday were busy days.

On the Fourth of July we swam in Ely Lake.

E. Names of Seasons

Never capitalize names of seasons.

Next fall we're going to Michigan.

Our winter activities vary from year to year.

F. Family Names

Capitalize *mother, grandfather, uncle* and so on if you use them as part of a name, but do not capitalize them otherwise.

I wish, Mother, that you'd stay home next week.

BUT

My mother loves to travel.

My dad's brother, Uncle Harry, was a real cowboy.

BUT

My uncle was a real cowboy.

G. Titles

Capitalize people's titles when they are used as part of a name, but do not capitalize them otherwise.

Good morning, Dr. Jones.

BUT

I said good morning to my doctor.

I accidentally tripped Professor Hollowell in the hall.

BUT

The professor seemed a little startled.

H. Courses and Subjects

Capitalize names of specific courses, but not of academic subjects.

I'm not sure I can pass Physics 232.

BUT

I'm taking history this quarter.

I. Book Titles

Capitalize important words in titles. That is, capitalize all words except articles, prepositions, coordinating conjunctions, and "to" unless they're the first or last words of the title or unless they occur after a colon.

Even Cowgirls Get the Blues is a funny book.

Elton John sings "I Guess That's Why They Call It the Blues."

Dylan Thomas wrote "A Process in the Weather of the Heart."

J. Directions

Capitalize names of directions when they indicate a specific area but not when they merely show direction.

Let's spend next winter in the South.

BUT

Let's go south next winter.

VIII Ways to Improve Spelling

Section 28:
What You Can Do

Spelling is a problem for many people, and if it's a problem for you, there are several things you can do about it.

A. Use a Dictionary

Develop the habit of using a dictionary regularly. The more you know about a word and its definitions and origins, the more likely you are to spell it correctly.

B. Use a Spelling Dictionary

These are little books with titles such as *The Word Book II* or *Webster's New World 33,000 Word Book*, and they are available in most bookstores. They give you spelling, show you how the words are broken into syllables, and distinguish between words that look or sound alike. They are small and easy to carry, and they show nearly 100 words per page so that you can usually find the word just by guessing fairly close to the correct spelling.

C. Use an Electronic Spelling Checker

Most good word processor software includes a spelling checker that compares the words you type on the screen with the words that it has in its dictionary. When the spelling checker "sees" a word that is not in its dictionary, it highlights the word, usually offers you several words that might be correct, and offers you an opportunity to change the word, to skip the word, or to enter the word into the dictionary. Some students view the use of the spelling checker as "cheating," but we view it as simply another aid. In our experience, students tend to become better spellers as they use the spelling checker, perhaps because they get tired of the computer's stopping at the same words all the time.

Do not view the spelling checker as a substitute for proofreading, though. It will not find a mistake like an accidental typing of "or" for "our," and most will not find the substitution of "there" for "they're."

Several companies also make independent spelling checkers. These are hand-held devices on which you type the word you want to check and the machine offers you several choices of words correctly spelled. Your job is to pick out which of the correctly spelled words you want to use.

D. Keep a List

Since you probably consistently misspell the same words, keep a list of the words that give you trouble. (Chances are, you have fewer than fifty words that give you trouble.) Any time your instructor marks a spelling error, or any time you find one on your own, write the correct spelling of that word on your list. Don't just jot the spellings on envelopes or scraps of paper; make a formal list in a part of your notebook that you look at often. Review the list regularly.

E. Use Index Cards

A variation on keeping a list is using a stack of index cards. Write each word you need to learn on the blank side of a 3×5 card, and write the pronunciation and definition on the lined side. Carry the cards with you and review them regularly. Have a friend quiz you on the spellings.

F. Use the Visual Motor Method

In this method, you look carefully at the word, perhaps tracing over its letters with your finger or pencil. Cover the word and see if you can write it correctly; check *carefully* to see that you've got it right. When you can spell it right three times in a row, you probably have it. Practice to be sure.

G. Develop Memory Tricks

Develop a set of tricks to help you remember spellings. To remember the difference between "advice" and "advise," for example, you might remember the phrase "advice about ice." "Loose as a goose" might help you remember the difference between "loose" and "lose." "There's iron in the environment" can help you remember how to spell "env<u>iron</u>ment."

SECTION 29:
Problem Word Pairs

Some words look or sound alike, and it's easy to become confused about which one to use. Here is a list of the most common of these confusing word pairs.

accept, except	"Accept" means to approve of or to receive willingly.
	"Except" means "but" or "excluding."
	This sentence might help you remember the difference (the capitalized letters show similarities in spelling):
	I'll Accept Advice from anybody EXcept my EX-wife.
advice, advise	The "s" in "advise" is pronounced like "z."
	"advise" is always a verb.
	I'd advise you not to go.
	"Advice" is never a verb.
	I took his advICE about the thin ice.
affect, effect	"Affect" is almost always a verb. It means to have an influence on.
	Spring pollen always affects my sinuses.
	"Effect" is almost always a noun. If you can put "a," "an," or "the" in front of it, spell it "effect."
	The effect of spring pollen is often severe.
all ready, already	"All" means "completely." If you can say "completely ready" or just "ready," use "all ready."
	I'm all ready for bed. ("I'm completely ready for bed," or "I'm ready for bed" say the same thing.)
	Use "already" if you can't leave off the "all" or say "completely" and have it make sense.
	I've already told you five times.
all right	"All right" is the only form that is acceptable. Always spell it "all right."
a lot	"A lot" is the only form that is acceptable. Always spell it as two words: "a lot."
are, our	"Are" is always a verb.
	We are having fun.

"Our" means something belongs to us.

We like our new car.

brake, break

The "brake" is what you push to slow your car or what you do when you push that pedal.

Put on your brakes; there's a stop sign ahead.

Don't brake hard on icy roads.

"Break" tells what happens to the glass that you drop. It means to shatter or to end. "Break" also means a pause.

The glass will break on that concrete floor.

You'll break her heart if you break your engagement.

Isn't it time for our coffee break?

choose, chose

"Choose" is present tense, "chose" is past.

You must choose one of these gifts right now.

Yesterday I chose not to go to school.

clothes, cloths

You wear "clothes," but you use "cloths."

She always wears nice clothes.

Use only soft cloths on your camera lens.

coarse, course

Something that is "coarse" is rough or not fine.

Burlap is a very coarse cloth.

Use coarse sandpaper on that rough board.

That ground pepper is a little too coarse for my taste.

Use "course" for all other meanings.

Did the river change its course?

Of course it did.

I learned that in my geology course.

complement, compliment

"Complement" with an "e" means to complete something (as an outfit) or to make it perfect (as in a perfect combination).

That hat is the perfect complement to my new suit.

"Compliment" with an "i" means to say nice things or to praise.

Be sure to compliment him on his hat.

That's the nicest compliment I've ever received.

Remember that a complEment compleEtes something and that I lIke a complIment.

conscience, conscious

Your "conscience" is that little inner voice that tells you when you're doing wrong.

My conscience wouldn't let me lie to you.

If you are "conscious," you are awake and aware.

The boxer was no longer conscious.

She was suddenly conscious of someone else's presence.

If you are cOnsciOus, both your eyes are probably open, and the two "o"'s can remind you of two open eyes. If your coNscieNce says something to you, it's probably "No, No," and the two "n"'s can help you remember that spelling.

desert, dessert

A "dessert" is what you eat after dinner. It is So Sweet that you want a second helping.

I'm gaining weight, so I shouldn't eat dessert.

"Desert" is used for all other meanings.

The desert is a hot, dry place.

He hated the army and wanted to desert.

do, due

To "do" is to act.

I do many things during the day.

If you do that again, you'll be in trouble.

What did he do to the car to make it run?

"Due" means owed or expected.

The rent is due on the fifth.

The paper is due tomorrow.

have, of

"Have" is a main verb or part of a helping verb.

I have time to do it now.

You should have been here last week.

We could have gone to the party.

When we say, "You should've been here," or "We could've gone," that *sounds* like "should of" or "could of."

It is *never* correct to use "of" as part of a helping verb.

"Of" is used only as the first word of a prepositional phrase (see Part I, Section 6E, pp. 256–57).

> **This is a picture of my father.**
>
> **Today is the fifth of December.**

hear, here

"Hear" tells what you do with your ear. You hEAR with your EAR.

> **I can't hear the music.**

"Here" identifies a place. HERE tells wHERE something is. If it's HERE, it's not over tHERE.

> **I like living here.**
>
> **Here is your new coat.**

it's, its

"It's" has only two possible meanings. It means "it is" or "it has."

> **It's time to go.**
>
> **It's been a long time since I saw you.**

"Its" is a possessive pronoun. It does not take an apostrophe (see Part VI, Section 26B, pp. 309–12).

> **The cat drank its milk.**

knew, new

"Knew" is the past tense of "know," and both words deal with knowledge.

> **I knew the answer to that question.**
>
> **I knew her when she was a child.**

"New" means unused or not old.

> **She bought a new car, not a used one.**
>
> **Isn't that a new shirt?**

know, no

"Know" is the present tense of the verb that shows knowledge. (See "knew" above).

> **He doesn't know how to do that.**

"No" means refusal or "not any."

> **No, I don't plan to see her.**
>
> **I have no way to get to her house.**

loose, lose

"Loose" is the opposite of "tight." It also means "free."

> **That knot is too loose to hold.**
>
> **My horse was tied, but he got loose last night.**

VIII

We speak of someone being "loose as a goose," and re-membering that phrase can help you remember that the word takes two "o"'s.

"Lose" is the opposite of "win." Remember that if you get 0 points you'll probably lOse the game.

I didn't think we could lose that game.

passed, past

"Passed" is always a verb.

The car passed me on a curve.

We always ran when we passed the graveyard.

"Past" is never a verb.

Let's forget about the past.

We always ran past the graveyard.

peace, piece

"Peace" is the opposite of war. We have peAce in the Absence of wAr.

During the war, we prayed for peace.

A "piece" is a part of something. We ask for a PIEce of PIE when it's time for dessert. The two words share the letters "pie."

This puzzle is missing a piece.

principal, principle

Something that is principAl is very important. It comes first, just as the letter "A" comes first in the alphabet.

The principal called us to his office.

Our principal problem is a lack of money.

How much interest you earn depends on how much principal you invest.

A principLE is a ruLE.

He lived by one principle: be honest.

I know how to work the problem, but I can't explain the principle.

quiet, quite, quit

"Quiet" means silent, and both words have two sylla-bles, quI-Et and sI-lEnt.

We spent a quiet evening together.

"Quite" means completely or very. It has only one sylla-ble, QuIte rhymes with bIte.

I'm not quite done.

It's quite cold outside.

VII

"Quit" means to stop.

> **I wasn't finished, but I quit anyway.**

real, really   "Real" means genuine.

> **We got a real deal on this house!**

> **Is that a real diamond, or is it a fake?**

"Really" means very.

> **My grandfather is really old.**

> **It was really hot yesterday.**

Don't use "real" when you mean "really."

right, write   Something that is "right" is correct.

> **I don't think that's the right answer.**

"Write" means to record on paper. You <u>WRITE</u> with a pen or type<u>WRITE</u>r.

> **You should write to your mother more often.**

sense, since   Use "sense" when you talk about sensations such as feeling, tasting, hearing, and so on, or when you talk about intelligence.

> **She has a good sense of smell.**

> **I sensed there was something near me.**

> **He doesn't have good sense.**

Use "since" to talk about t<u>I</u>me or cause.

> **It's been years since I was there.**

> **Since the party was over, we left.**

than, then   "Th<u>A</u>n" is a word that comp<u>A</u>res things.

> **My car is much older than theirs.**

"Th<u>E</u>n" always tells wh<u>E</u>n.

> **I started my homework; then my brother came by.**

> **We'll do the dishes first, and then we'll go to the movies.**

their, there, they're   "Their" is always a possessive pronoun.

> **They watched their daughter win the race.**

"<u>THERE</u>" tells w<u>HERE</u> something is, or it points something out.

If it's not here or there, I don't know where it is.

There were six vultures circling overhead.

"They're" is always a contraction of "they are."

They're sure to win if they practice.

threw, through | "Threw" is the past tense of "throw." It is always a verb.

I threw the rock.

Use "through" for any other meaning.

Are you through with your breakfast?

Don't walk through that door.

to, too, two | "Two" has only one meaning. It is a number.

There are two lions on the hood of the car.

"Too" has two "o"'s and two meanings. It means also, and it means more than enough.

Heather brought mustard, and Sara did, too.

That meant we had too much mustard.

Both meanings of "too" show that something is added. Remembering that can remind you to add the extra "o."

Use "to" for any meaning other than the three shown above.

I'd like to escape from here.

I think I'll go to China.

weather, whether | "Weather" is what happens outdoors. One form of we<u>A</u>ther is r<u>A</u>in.

The weather today is terrible.

"Whether" refers to a choice. It means "if."

I don't know whether to sleep or exercise.

Whether you do it is up to you.

were, where | "Were" is always a verb.

They were looking for their dog.

"Where" talks about a place. If you ask w<u>HERE</u> something is, you'll be told it's either <u>HERE</u> or t<u>HERE</u>.

Where have all the flowers gone?

who's, whose | "Who's" is always a contraction of "who is" or "who has."

Who's been sleeping in my bed?

Who's been sitting in my chair?

"Whose" is a possessive pronoun.

I know whose woods these are.
She's the one whose sister is a surgeon.

you're, your   "You're" is always a contraction of "you are."

You're the one who broke it.

"Your" is a possessive pronoun.

Your brother is the one who broke it.

VIII

INDEX